T0384392

The Crisis of Marxist Ideology in Eastern Europe

First published in 1988, *The Crisis of Marxist Ideology in Eastern Europe* states that since de-Stalinisation began in Eastern Europe, the 'dead hand' of institutional Marxism has been eroded by revisionist Marxism, with the turn to young Marx and the philosophy of human emancipation to undermine prevailing orthodoxies. But this revisionism clung to the old socialist dogmas and refused a total break with the system, and the effort eventually failed. The result was the emergence of a dissident counterculture rejecting the system entirely. Independent social movements (such as unofficial peace groups and trade unions like Solidarity) have given this counterculture a major role in Eastern Europe, whilst the ruling elites have responded with confusion. Tismaneanu concludes that the only hope for the anti-totalitarian intellectuals of Eastern Europe is to oppose the regimes with non-Marxist ideas – otherwise they will be permanently reduced to the status of a hopeless, albeit heroic minority. This book will be of interest to students of economics, political science and international relations.

The Crisis of Marxist Ideology in Eastern Europe

The Poverty of Utopia

Vladimir Tismaneanu

First published in 1988
By Routledge

This edition first published in 2022 by Routledge
4 Park Square, Milton Park, Abingdon, Oxon, OX14 4RN
and by Routledge
605 Third Avenue, New York, NY 10017

Routledge is an imprint of the Taylor & Francis Group, an informa business

© 1988 V. Tismaneanu

All rights reserved. No part of this book may be reprinted or reproduced or utilised in
any form or by any electronic, mechanical, or other means, now known or hereafter
invented, including photocopying and recording, or in any information storage or
retrieval system, without permission in writing from the publishers.

Publisher's Note
The publisher has gone to great lengths to ensure the quality of this reprint but points
out that some imperfections in the original copies may be apparent.

Disclaimer
The publisher has made every effort to trace copyright holders and welcomes
correspondence from those they have been unable to contact.

A Library of Congress record exists under ISBN: 0415004942

ISBN: 978-1-032-45859-5 (hbk)
ISBN: 978-1-003-37902-7 (ebk)
ISBN: 978-1-032-45862-5 (pbk)

Book DOI 10.4324/9781003379027

The
Crisis of
Marxist
Ideology in
Eastern Europe

The Poverty of Utopia

VLADIMIR TISMANEANU

London and New York

First published 1988
by Routledge
11 New Fetter Lane, London EC4P 4EE

Simultaneously published in the USA and Canada
by Routledge
a division of Routledge, Chapman and Hall, Inc.
29 West 35th Street, New York, NY 10001

Reprinted 1990

© 1988 V. Tismaneanu

Printed in Great Britain by Antony Rowe Ltd
Typeset by Pat and Anne Murphy, Highcliffe-on-Sea, Dorset

All rights reserved. No part of this book may be reprinted or
reproduced or utilized in any form or by any electronic,
mechanical, or other means, now known or hereafter invented,
including photocopying and recording, or in any information
storage or retrieval system, without permission in writing from
the publishers.

British Library Cataloguing in Publication Data

Tismaneanu, Vladimir

The crisis of Marxist ideology in Eastern
Europe: the poverty of Utopia
1. Eastern Europe. Marxism, to 1987
I. Title
335.4′0947

ISBN 0-415-00494-2

Library of Congress Cataloging-in-Publication Data

ISBN 0-415-00494-2

Contents

Acknowledgements

Introduction   1

1   An Autopsy of Stalinism   8

2   Soviet Ideology and Eastern Europe   42

3   The Decay of Stalinism   61

4   The Search for Renewal   77

5   Poverty of Utopia   91

6   Reconstruction or Disintegration?   108

7   From Criticism to Apostasy   121

8   Peace, Human Rights, Dissent   160

9   Neo-Stalinism and Reform Communism   183

Epilogue   216

Index   226

Acknowledgements

This book was completed during my stay as a Hooper Fellow in International Security Affairs at the Foreign Policy Research Institute in Philadelphia, where I found encouragement for innovative ideas, open-mindedness, and a constant interest in the dynamics of contemporary communism. Daniel Pipes, the director of FPRI and editor of *Orbis*, the institute's quarterly journal of world affairs, was particularly supportive in what looked like an interminable, labyrinthine project. My colleagues on the research staff were helpful with fresh insights about radical ideologies and their metamorphoses at the end of the 20th century. Parts of the manuscript were masterfully typed by Thelma Prosser. Eraj Shervani, my research assistant, accompanied me in countless bibliographical adventures. Bronwen Ewens and Mary Sladex patiently indexed this daunting onomastic encyclopaedia.

Portions of this book initially appeared in *Orbis* and *Problems of Communism*, and the author is deeply indebted to the editors of these journals — John H. Maurer and JoAnn Tomazinis from *Orbis*, Wayne Hall and Sonia Sluzar from *Problems of Communism* — for their suggestions and the welcome improvement of my somewhat esoteric language. I must also mention fruitful discussions on Marxism and its fate in East–Central Europe with Andrew Arato (New School for Social Research, New York), Richard J. Bernstein (Haverford College), György Márkus (University of Sydney, Australia), Ivan Volgyes (University of Nebraska), as well as the long dialogues in New York and Paris with the Hungarian dissident philosopher Gaspar Miklós Támás. Dorin Tudoran, the Romanian dissident writer, enlightened my understanding of the situation of the intelligentisa in the country where we were both born and, for better or worse, educated. Ferenc Fehér and Agnes Heller (New School for Social Research) patiently reviewed the manuscript and helped me with most valuable suggestions. This study originated with my first Western contribution in *Praxis International* (October 1983), a journal which was then edited by Richard J. Bernstein and Mihailo Marković. As always in these cases, the author assumes full responsibility for all the statements contained in his book. Last but not least, a special word of gratitude for David Croom, who generously

Acknowledgements

offered me the possibility of publishing my manuscript with
Croom Helm — which in the meantime has become Routledge —
and for my editor, Andrew Lockett, who consistently stimulated
my work on this essay.

V.T.
Philadelphia, September 1987

Introduction

It is a strange and sad story that remains to be told and remembered.
                            Hannah Arendt — *On Revolution*

Hannah Arendt's melancholy phrase evokes the whole capital of
illusions, dreams, nostalgias and chimeras that has been the
emotional background of modern social upheavals we have come
to describe under the generic name of revolution. It calls to mind
that never fulfilled, perhaps impossible, blueprint of revolutionary
councils, the exhilarating, uplifting expectation of a mundane
redemption through genuine human solidarity. It is also a
memento of the lost illusions of successive revolutionary generations, the tragic story of the 'God that failed', the momentous
collapse of grandiose projections into the utopia of an earthly paradise. This essay wants to explore the multiple, sometimes arcane,
ways this dream was exploited, disfigured, turned into a nightmare. In other words it is a research into the palpable body of contemporary forms of alienation, and particularly into the most
elusive, misleading variant of estrangement: the ideological one. I
tried to evince and explain the metamorphosis of Marxism from a
theory of alleged total human emancipation into a doctrine of
universal bondage. It is important therefore to illuminate the
mechanisms of self-deception that have facilitated this debasement
and to discover the grounds for this devolution in the very structure of the Marxist doctrine. My premise is that no social theory
can aspire to the privilege of innocence at the moment its ideas
have resulted in the opposite of what its founders have proclaimed
as their chief goal. Dozens of volumes have been written on
Friedrich Nietzsche's or Martin Heidegger's responsibility for the
'destruction of reason' (Lukács) and the triumph of National
Socialism. Possibly because it is the ideology of the victors,
Marxism is still widely regarded as a form of humanism, and
Leninism, or Stalinism, as regrettable deviations from the
originally altruistic project.

Because of its polemical thrust, this book is destined to challenge
many conventional views. It is bound to irritate those who, out-
spokenly or subliminally, decently or indecently, still pay tribute
to a dogma conspicuously contradicted by reality. Years ago,

1

French political philosopher Kostas Papaioannou wrote a path-breaking essay on the cold ideology (*l'idéologie froide*). Even now, with all we have learned regarding the vicissitudes of Marxism in its Soviet, Polish, Chinese, East-German, Yugoslav, North-Korean, or Kampuchean hypostases, we witness attempts to treat this philosophy as a living — and enlivening — reflexive exertion. For obstinate votaries of Marxism as the philosophy of opposition, the unsurpassable incarnation of the philosophical figure of negativity, all tragic occurrences in the field of real history would be irrelevant. They may bemoan the excesses of Leninism, or the crimes of Stalinism, but they stick to their beliefs in the possibility and necessity of humanistic socialism.

The Leninist version of Marxism, the only one that has proved successful in terms of political praxis, has failed to offer a vindication for all the hopes invested in its promises of emancipation. The Marxist pledge to suppress all human misery and alienation sounds nowadays, in the light of the enduring concentrationary achievements of Stalinism, more utopian than ever. Open terror may have disappeared in traditional Soviet-type societies, but the uniformisation and conditioning of human life is still there. The individual is still a negligible quantity, forced to obey the dictates of an overwhelming, Kafkaesque bureaucracy. Texts by Soviet and East European dissidents highlight the transformation of hard censorship into a 'soft' one, more perfidious and no less watchful of any potential heresy. Harnessing the intelligentsia is still the major task of the Agitprop departments. The discourse of the *nomenklatura* has become more sophisticated than in Zhdanov's times, but the jealous preservation of its spiritual power remains unaltered.

Compared to Lenin's or Stalin's times, ideology is less powerful and binding. It has lost a great deal of its supercilious pretence and functions only as an appendage to an increasingly routinised system of bureaucratic manipulation. The era of adamant, unquestionable beliefs is a matter of the past. What remains is a conglomerate of naïve philosophical assumptions, demagogic promises of happiness, monotonous exhortations, and hidebound slogans. This book aims to document the stages of this decline, the objective factors that have led to this bastardisation of Marxism. It is therefore both an exercise in the history of ideas and an attempt to link political and cultural history.

This author has himself experienced some of the intellectual adventures described in this essay: too young to have shared the obsessions of the 'revisionist' generation, he was nevertheless attracted to the obscure pages of various 'negative dialectics'. Against the triumphalist jargon of bureaucracy, young Marx's philosophy of alienation seemed an extraordinary protective shield. The same was true for the works of unorthodox Marxist writers like Georg Lukács, Karl Korsch, Walter Benjamin, and Antonio Gramsci. Later, readings from such diverse authors as Thomas Mann, Max Weber, Raymond Aron, Hannah Arendt, George Lichtheim, Claude Lefort, Cornelius Castoriadis, Sidney Hook, Karl Jaspers, Maurice Merleau-Ponty, and many others, convinced me that the problem with Marxism is not Leninism, or Stalinism, but Marxism itself. I tend now to regard Marxism as a climactic moment — together with *Lebensphilosophie*, the German philosophy of life — in the long romantic tradition. It seems to me that there is a voluntaristic, almost irrational undercurrent in Marxism that could account for many of the perversions this doctrine was bound to undergo. Together with the romantics, Marxism emphasises the ontological superiority of the community over the individual. It was precisely because of this hidden romanticism that young Lukács's conversion to Marxism was less tormenting an experience than the adoption of a really rationalistic and matter-of-fact worldview. The same may be true with regard to the intellectual paths of other Marxist thinkers: we should only remember Antonio Gramsci's perennial interest in Croce and Sorel, or Henri Lefebvre's unrepentant fascination with Nietzsche.

Marxism is a scientism, to be sure, but a very peculiar one. The positivistic dogma is in this case ammended by an unavowed wager placed on the omnipotence of social willingness. Universal reason, world history, the collective wisdom of the proletariat serve as the main terms to define the Marxist lack of concern for ultimate moral values. I regard Marxism as a most elaborated form of ethical relativism and I consider therefore that both Leninism and Stalinism are not alien to the ideological intentions of the founding father. This is not to say that all developments were foreordained, and that Lenin or Stalin, as historical personalities, did not make any difference. This would be an utterly absurd conclusion and no one would try to make such a ludicrous point. The crux of the matter is to indicate the logical links between various embodiments of the same ideology, since Leninism may be palpably distinct from original Marxism as a philosophy, but less so in terms of ideological practice. In his polemics with Proudhon, Bakunin, and

Lassalle, Marx was not more tolerant than his Bolshevik disciples. His oracular wisdom could not be challenged with impunity. In Marx's view, those who held different conceptions about socialism were either incurable utopians, or 'objective' enemies of the working class. In all fairness, however, it should be noted that Marx himself partook with his rivals a respect for theory that was to evaporate in the Bolshevik cult for *Realpolitik*.

Seven decades after the October Revolution, revolutionary messianism has lost momentum in Western industrial democracies. It is still influential in the Third World, but this is already a different story. Ironically, it was precisely its triumph in Russia that has led to this disintegration of the pristine faith. Later, the dismal performances of the 'people's democracies', the tortuous road of the Chinese revolution, and the blatant ineptitude of Marxist-Leninist elites to handle serious economic issues, have further diminished the appeal of the Marxist message. 'Eurocommunism' was the result of this paradoxical situation: parties created to meet Lenin's criteria of revolutionary militantism in the aftermath of the October Revolution, openly rebelled against the Leninist legacy.[1]

This essay is therefore intent upon telling the story of the decomposition of the Marxist myth in those societies where communist parties came to power. Nothing can be considered more deleterious to the survival of the Marxist-Leninist credo than the experience of 'really existing socialism'. Soviet dissident Boris Weil gave a most perceptive description of the extinction of the Marxist faith in the USSR:

> Do you remember Lenin's observation that 'Russia *vystradala* Marxism', or groped towards it through suffering? It is easy to understand why no philosophy is more unpopular than Marxism in the Soviet Union today. For monstrous deeds have been perpetrated under cover of a Marxist terminology that no longer excites anything but indifference, or even disgust, among the majority of the population. Who indeed would not feel utterly disgusted by something imposed on him by violence? Even the most beautiful of things arouses nothing but aversion if imposed by force.[2]

At the same time, I want to stress the persistence of hopes for change and renewal in those countries. It might well be that one day oppositional groups will rediscover the value of Marxist dissatisfaction with the *status quo*. A new theoretical synthesis might then emerge, one that will take into account the Marxist critique of bureaucratic estrangement as a part of the Western anti-totalitarian legacy. I do not think here of the obsolete 'revisionist' investigations into Marxian humanism, but rather of the coagulation of a counter-ideology of opposition, particularly articulate in the writings of Polish and Hungarian dissident intellectuals. To take only the example of Adam Michnik, one of the founders of the Polish Workers' Defence Committee: his essays bear witness about the excruciating strifes, passions, political diseases, and moral hopes of this century. Nothing is more important from Michnik's point of view than the salvation of the human soul in a political order established on ideological terror.[3] The same is true with regard to other distinguished East European writers like Leszek Kolakowkski, Jacek Kuron, Milovan Djilas, Danilo Kiš, Václav Havel, Ivan Svitak, Milan Kundera, Paul Goma, Dorin Tudoran, Agnes Heller, Ferenc Fehér, Miklós Haraszti, George Konrád, Aleksandr Zinoviev, Andrey Siniavskiy, Lev Kopelev, and the list could easily continue. All other differences notwithstanding, they share with Aleksandr Solzhenitsyn the visceral disgust with the omnivorous state ideology, the conviction that truth should become the guiding value for those who refuse to succumb to the mystique of conformity. Living in truth, as Václav Havel put it, is the only solution for the survival of the reflexive ego in the age of totalitarian rule.[4] In his most recent book, Milovan Djilas points precisely to this everlasting clash between ideas and ideologies: the former lead to the strengthening of human freedom, whereas the latter tend to be dogmatised, congealed, turned into instruments of manipulation and domination.[5] Fanatic revolutionaries are prisoners of ideology. Genuine rebels relish the spontaneity of ideas.

We know it from Hannah Arendt — totalitarian order could not exist without the sacralisation of ideology:

> The trouble with totalitarian regimes is not that they play power politics in an especially ruthless way, but that behind their politics is hidden an entirely new and unprecedented concept of power, just as behind their *Realpolitik* lies an entirely new and unprecedented concept of reality. Supreme disregard for immediate consequences rather than ruthlessness; rootlessness and neglect of national interests rather than nationalism; contempt for utilitarian motives rather than unconsidered pursuit of self interest; 'idealism', i.e., their

5

unwavering faith in an ideological fictitious world, rather than lust for power — these all have introduced into international politics, a new and more disturbing factor than mere aggressiveness would have been able to do.[6]

Marxism-Leninism, proclaimed to be the *alpha* and *omega* of human knowledge, has thus become the main device employed by the hegemonic bureaucracies in their effort to asphyxiate consciousness. Now, when the erosion of the Marxist paradigm can hardly be denied, it seems that Soviet-type regimes have lost their main intellectual underpinning. The withering away of utopia can bring about unpredictable spiritual phenomena: commitment to mercantile values, widespread cynicism, increasing interest in drugs and exotic sects, all sorts of vicarious ways to find out individual solutions to escape the ideological constraints imposed by authorities. Transgression of old taboos is a consequence of this disenchantment with the hollow nature of official Marxism. The return of the repressed past (*le retour du refoulé*) cannot be forever procrastinated. Following two decades of deafening silence over the crimes of the Stalin era, the new Soviet leadership under Mikhail Gorbachev is forced to resume the Khrushchevite experiment in party-controlled liberalisation. Calls for moral transparence, once the privilege of the beleaguered dissident counter-culture, are now uttered by party doctrinaires. Gorbachev himself acknowledged that the absence of any criticism has led into a political blind alley. This is not to say that the communist parties will indulge in democratisation, but rather that it has become obvious, even for ideological watchdogs, that old tenets have lost all credibility and that a revamping of the prevailing ideoogy is urgent. They will not hesitate to assimilate topics developed by dissidents and stimulate commitment to pluralist values. As Miklós Haraszti has shown, the ideological dictatorship has created the most ingenious mechanisms of self-defence:

> An era of greater generosity is about to dawn. Just as in ancient, long-enduring empires, renegade mandarins might establish Taoist monasteries. Similarly, the modern socialist state regards its die-hard dissidents as members of a monstrous, weird, misanthropic sect, disenchanted with educating the people . . . but nonetheless essentially innocent and, indeed, not without their uses.[7]

Introduction

Some passages in this book may sound too gloomy. The author would like to warn his readers that he does not despair over the possibility of a rational society. He is however deeply distrustful of all promises of revolutionary re-shaping of human nature. In this respect, Karl Popper's conclusions about the pitfalls of historicism have not lost anything of their relevance.[8] As for the risk of being labelled a pessimist, I take pride in recalling Walter Benjamin's paradoxical aphorism: *Nur um der Hoffnungslosen willen, ist uns die Hoffnung gegeben* (It is only because of those who are hopeless that hope is given to us).

Notes

1. See Joan Barth Urban, *Moscow and the Italian Communist Party* (Ithaca and London: Cornell University Press, 1986); Vernon V. Aspaturian, Jiri Valenta, David P. Burke, *Eurocommunism between East and West* (Blooming-ton, Ind.: Indiana University Press, 1980).
2. See Boris Weil, 'Marx and Lenin read in the camps' in El Manifesto (ed.), *Power and opposition in post-revolutionary societies*, a conference organised by the Italian leftist formation *Il Manifesto* in November 1977 (London: Ink Links, 1979), p. 91; Vladimir Voinovich, *The anti-Soviet Soviet Union* (New York: Harcourt Brace Jovanovich, 1986).
3. See Adam Michnik, *Letters from prison and other essays* (Berkeley: University of California Press, 1986).
4. See Jan Vadislav (ed.), *Václav Havel or living in truth* (London and Boston: Faber and Faber, 1987).
5. See Milovan Djilas, *Of prisons and ideas* (New York: Harcourt Brace Jovanovich, 1986).
6. See Hannah Arendt, *The origins of totalitarianism* (New York: Harcourt Brace Jovanovich, 1973), pp. 417–18.
7. See Miklós Haraszti, *The velvet prison: artists under state socialism* (New York: A New Republic Book/Basic Books, 1987).
8. See Karl R. Popper, *The poverty of historicism* (London: Routledge & Kegan Paul, 1961).

1

An Autopsy of Stalinism

We might find it appalling that free societies of the Western type are based on greed as the main human motivation, but it is still better than compulsory love, for that can only end in a society of prisoners and prison warders.

Leszek Kolakowski

Marxism, in this century, evolved as a historical tragedy, with heroes and martyrs, sacrificial rituals and an endless longing for collective salvation. Stalin himself, Lenin's self-appointed heir, performed the role of grand priest of this decayed philosophy.

Writing about the fate of Polish communism, Isaac Deutscher offered a convincing explanation of the enormous emotional appeal of Stalinism:

> What was decisive . . . was the Party's psychological attitude — its misguided conception of solidarity with the Russian Revolution, its belief that any conflict with Moscow must be avoided, no matter at what cost. The moral authority of the Soviet Party, the only one which had led a proletarian revolution to victory, was so great that the Polish communists accepted Moscow's decisions even when Moscow abused its revolutionary authority. Stalinism was indeed a continuous succession of abuses of this kind, a systematic exploitation of the moral credit of the revolution for purposes that often had nothing to do with the interests of communism but served only to consolidate the bureaucratic regime of the USSR.[1]

A symbol and an embodiment of the party apparatus, Stalin

engineered the rise of an unparalleled cult of personality. Not only Soviet communists, but all 'proletarian detachments', all segments of 'progressive mankind' were supposed to partake in that orgy of irrational veneration. Stalin needed that tremendous 'cult of personality' to consolidate and perpetuate the legend of the exceptional nature of the Soviet regime. 'Socialism in one country', Stalin's only theoretical contribution, required as symbolic counterpart the exaltation of the charismatic leader, the sole guarantor of the established order. Furthermore, he needed the mysticism surrounding his person to rule out whatever doubts may have occurred in the minds of his subjects. Adam Ulam, a most perceptive analyst of the Stalin myth, points precisely to this psychological dimension:

> . . . why did Stalin need so much slavish adulation? He had all the power any man could desire; he was master of life and death; he had beaten all his rivals — why demand worship? My answer is that Stalin's need for the chorus of adulation to grow louder the deeper he waded in blood was due to his own inability to believe the whole monstrous web of lies which he had loosed on the country. It was . . . a constant and much needed reassurance that it was not one man's irrational whim and suspiciousness but the interests of Russia and of the new social order that were exacting these apalling sacrifices . . .[2]

The 'oceanic feeling', the ecstasy of solidarity, aptly described by Arthur Koestler[3] was the emotional ground for revolutionary commitment. Community, defined in terms of class, was the antipode of the execrated egotism of the bourgeois individual. The self had to be denied in order to achieve real fraternity. Generations of Marxist intellectuals hastened to cremate their dignity in this apocalyptical race for ultimate certitudes. The whole heritage of Western sceptical rationalism was easily dismissed in the name of the revealed light emanating from the Kremlin. The age of reason was thus to culminate in the frozen universe of rational terror. Orthodoxy was monolithic and exclusive: Lenin was the only God and Stalin his sole prophet. Determinism was surreptitiously transposed into an unbridled voluntarism. The subject, the human being — totally ignored at the level of the philosophical discourse — was eventually abolished as a physical entity in the vortex of the 'great purge'. These images are more than metaphors, since metaphor usually suggests an ineffable face of reality, whereas what happened under Stalin was awfully visible and immediate.

The practice of Stalinism can and should be conceptualised if we want to go beyond outbursts of moralistic incantations. On the other hand, totalitarianism cannot be dealt with in a cold, detached manner. It could hardly be denied that Stalinism is the antithesis of Western humanist legacy and should be described as such. Naturally, it would be preposterous to restrict ourselves to mere ethical condemnation. But it would not be, by any means, commendable to gloss over the moral implications of Stalinism. Louis Althusser's structuralist school, quite influential in the French intellectual climate of the late 1960s and early 1970s, has excelled in this objectivistic treatment of the development of historical materialism. Althusser's ultra-deterministic outlook, based on a 'derogation of the lay actor' as it was rightly said, postulates the absolute primacy of objective conditions and discards the role and the potentialities of subjective will. There is no exaggeration therefore in charging this school with functionalism, i.e., the conception that regards human agents 'as no more than "supports" for modes of production'.[4]

It is important, when pondering the fate of Marxism in this century, to grasp the split of personalities, the clash between lofty ideals and abject practices, the methods of the Stalinist terrorist pedagogy in its endeavour to produce a new type of human being whose loyalties and behaviour would be decreed by the party.[5] Among other roles, the Communist party is administrator of happiness, guardian of virtue, and arbiter of truth.

A poor theorist as he certainly was, Stalin was nonetheless a master of successful vulgarisation and deft mystification. The notorious *Short course of the history of the Communist Party of the Soviet Union (the Bolsheviks)*, published in 1938, irrevocably put an end to any form of ideological pluralism. It was indeed the codification of Stalin's simplistic views on the history of the Russian revolutionary movement as well as a perplexingly primitive description of the Marxist dialectic. Once the *Short course* was institutionalised as the ideology *par excellence*, there was no room for the slightest deviation from the sacrosanct norm. Doubting its validity was a mortal sin. And this was not the case only with non-Marxist conceptions, long since banned, but also with attempts to formulate less rigid Marxist-Leninist opinions. This situation was to outlive Stalin, as members of the Budapest School have shown in their pathbreaking examination of collectivistic-authoritarian regimes:

In the Soviet system of domination all ideological types of Marxism are outlawed for the simple reason that they embody pluralism by their very ideological nature. They were, however, always present in all Soviet states even during the period of terroristic totalitarianism.[6]

It is certain that garrison uniformity cannot allow the development of parallel ideological trends, but it is still debatable whether such currents would be correctly depicted as alternative forms of thought. It is not obvious, on the other hand, that even such a modicum of 'pluralism' could have been detected in the Soviet intellectual life after the publication of the *Short course*. What happened indeed was that the whole articulation of Leninism was turned upside down in order to meet Stalin's ideological requirements.[7] A demonology was devised, with Trotsky-Satan as the eternal conspirator, the arch-scoundrel — Emmanuel Goldstein of Orwell's *1984* — whose ideas cannot be but poisonous and should be inclemently uprooted.

A degraded philosophy for all intents and purposes, Marxism-Leninism in its Stalinist version borrowed the fatalistic dimension from Nikolay Bukharin's rigid determinism. Its driving force was the strange and self-assuring belief that historical forces are 'on our side'.[8] The *Short course* was meant to provide a basis for perpetual ideological purification. Mechanical repetition of its tenets became the unique content of Soviet social sciences under Stalin.

Unflinching belief in the superior wisdom of the founding fathers of the doctrine, a characteristic of the Bolshevik intellectual tradition, was superseded by unlimited loyalty to the person of the general secretary. Marxism was thus reduced to a canonical system of unquestionable and unverifiable statements formulated by the providential *vozhd* (guide). As for those who clung to their original faith, unembarrassed by pragmatic considerations, their fate had been announced in those lines of the *German ideology* where communism was described as a fundamentally negative activity: a real movement that suppresses the existing order.[9] In other words, this movement is not a hospitable place for those enamoured with universal principles of equity and freedom. Justice and ethics, as Lenin said, are determined by class criteria. One man's Good is another man's Evil or, in Marxist parlance, proletariat and bourgeoisie have opposed moral outlooks and commitments. Eventually. party mindedness, the political principle revered by all Leninists, resulted in the infallible image bestowed on the general secretary.

11

The fetishism of the official doctrine is not eternal; when the ensnaring force of ideology is extinct, communist intellectuals start to harbour legitimate feelings of distress. What usually follows is the already too well-known history of dissent and apostasy, with the party functioning as the repository of historical justice and the oppositionists condemned to engage in disgraceful self-flagellation. As Leszek Kolakowski put it:

> All forms of revolt against the ruling party, all 'deviations' and 'revisionism', fractions, cliques, rebellions — all alike had appealed to the ideology of which the party was the custodian. Consequently, that ideology had to be revised so as to make it clear to all that they were not entitled to appeal to it independently — just as in the Middle Ages unauthorized persons were not allowed to comment on the Scriptures and the Bible itself was at all times *liber haereticorum* (book of the heretics).[10]

The germs of resistance had to be eradicated by all means, at all cost, for Marxism to remain a sacred value, or better said a cult object, like one of those enigmatic things worshipped by primitive tribes. The archaeology of belief is of no interest to mystical thought. The revealed dogma is taken for granted. Faith in the thaumaturgic qualities of the revered object supersedes critical intelligence. New prophets are usually banished, slandered and, if need be, assassinated. The grand inquisitor knows better than God himself what it is all about: that history is not a morality play, that politics and happiness are more often than not incompatible, that there is an ethics of the means and another one, which he regards as irretrievably quixotic, of the ends.

Mortification of the imagination, Stalin anointed *princeps scholasticorum* (prince of the philosophers), universal acceptance of the dreary climate of blind obedience, compliance with a boundless opportunism: *homo sovieticus* was thus born. Aleksandr Zinoviev, the exiled Soviet logician, political sociologist, and novelist summed up this anthropological revolution and highlighed the psychological infrastructure of Stalinism. His books are an uninterrupted meditation on the astounding paradoxes of Soviet reality under Stalin. In a highly controversial interview with George Urban, Zinoviev voiced his doubts about conventional Western interpretations of Stalin's era:

> Well, life was extraordinarily fascinating, even if it was hard.

An Autopsy of Stalinism

I knew many people who realised that they were about to be shot — yet they praised Stalin. Stalin was a symbol of hope and vigour. A relative of mine, who knew that he was due to start a long prison sentence in a year's time, was (as people often were under Stalin) suddenly appointed to run a large factory. He grabbed the opportunity because, for him, the challenge of that single glorious year was worth more than a thousand years spent in uneventful living. 'I know they will kill me — but this year is going to be *my* year', he said. He was filled with the consciousness of making history.[11]

Zinoviev's point is that Stalin's times were more ambiguous than current moralistic theories assume. Good and evil were intertwined in post-revolutionary agonies. According to Zinoviev, not all those who gave countenance to Stalinism were abject scoundrels. To be sure, some did it for opportunistic reasons, whereas others were lured by revolutionary propaganda.

In Zinoviev's picture, *homo sovieticus* ignores compassion and remorse: 'no mercy for the enemies of the people', the slogan chanted frantically during the Moscow show trials suggests this psychic transfiguration. Cruelty against the class enemy is the ultimate virtue. Himmler professed not too much different a faith urging his SS underlings to make allowance for the greatness of their 'historical deed' in having perpetrated the 'final solution'. Stalin manifested no compunction in unleashing the war against the peasantry in the name of an ill-defined, though compulsive utopia. The same may be said about the politically induced famine in the Ukraine in the 1930s and the systematic persecution of the peasantry in that country.[12]

Finality and totality, expiation and salvation, mystical teleology and objective rationality, all were thus reconciled in the figure of the 'besieged fortress'. Unbounded nationalism supplanted the original cosmopolitan impetus of Marxism. The denouement of this drama was the irresistible impoverishment of socialist thought, the elimination of the Hegelian-Marxist dialectic from the official discourse, the solidification of an inedible corpus of pseudo-scientific commonplaces and its promulgation as a *summum* of human sagacity. This insurrection against original Marxism was certainly cloaked in Marxist jargon. To add insult to injury, it took Stalin no great pains to have distinguished philosophers (Georg Lukács and Ernst Bloch included) ready to endorse his hilarious exercises and extoll them as the apogee of historical materialism. In the

13

meantime, Antonio Gramsci perished almost forgotten in Mussolini's Italy, the few surviving Western Hegelian Marxists were fighting to defend at least the promise of truth, whereas a flabbergasted Trotsky witnessed the decay of a regime he had pertinaciously considered as sociologically superior to the capitalist inferno. Revenge of history on its worshippers — thus could be depicted the terrorist psychosis of the Stalinist massacres. To quote Alvin W. Gouldner's illuminating interpretation:

> The central strategy of the Marxist project, its concern with seeking a remedy to *unnecessary* suffering, was thus in the end susceptible to a misuse that betrayed its own highest avowals. The root of the trouble was that this conception of its own project redefined pity . . . The human condition was rejected on behalf of the historical condition.[13]

Power and ideology

Power and ideology are inextricably linked in the totalitarian universe. Without the immense force of ideology, without its enthralling effects, the domination exerted by the ruling apparatus would not have reached the perfection of Stalin's times. In Zbigniew Brzezinski's view, it is the ideological factor that makes for the essential difference between totalitarian and other forms of authoritarian regimes. Ideology has many functions in such systems, but the primordial one is to abolish traditional moral norms. It is important to understand that in single-party regimes, the absolutist character of their ideology 'frees the movements of any moral or traditional-legal restraints on their power, and they consider themselves justified in undertaking even the most ruthless steps to consolidate their power and execute their ideology'.[14]

The magic impact of power in classical Stalinism would have been unthinkable in the absence of ideology. They breed and feed each other; power derives its mesmerising force from the seductive potential of ideology. Man is proclaimed omnipotent, and ideology supervises the identification of abstract man with concrete power. Veneration of power is rooted in contempt for traditional values, including those associated with the survival of reason. It is important therefore to repress the temptation of critical thought, since reason is the enemy of total regimentation. In one of his late aphorisms, Max Horkheimer hinted at the philosophical revolution provoked by Marxism. The point of view of the individual was replaced by the collective subject-object of history. Defending the dignity of the individual subject becomes a seditious undertaking, a challenge to the prevailing myth of homogeneity:

> However socially conditioned the individual's thinking may be, however necessarily it may relate to social questions, to political action, it remains the thought of the individual which is not just the effect of collective processes but can also take them as its object.[15]

Political shamanism, practised by alleged adversaries of any mysticism, thwarts the attempts to resist the continual assault on the mind. Marxism-Leninism, which is the code name for the ideology of the *nomenklatura*, aims to dominate both the public and the private spheres of social life. Man, both as an individual and as a *citoyen*, has to be massified.

The atomisation of public life and the dissolution of civil society are preconditions for effective totalitarian domination. Totalisation involves ceaseless control over the whole body politic, and mobilisational rituals are the favourite means employed by those regimes to achieve this goal. Members of the Budapest School refer to this process as the opposite of enlightenment:

> If, according to Kant, enlightenment is humankind's release from its self-incurred tutelage, de-enlightenment means the relapse into that same tutelage. . . . de-enlightenment requires that one should never use it (the intellect) but should rely upon the collective intellect of the Party which does the thinking, instead of the person's own intellect.[16]

The same themes were accentuated by Yugoslav critics of political alienation in Marxist-Leninist regimes. Formulating the programme for a philosophy of genuine emancipation, Mihailo Marković offered a synthesis of anti-authoritarian objectives: '. . . the most important means are *truth*, bold *demystification* of existing social relationships, *dethronement* of deified persons and institutions, and above all a *great moral strength* . . .'[17]

Human needs are determined by party leaders who act as ideological oracles: the Central Committee is the repository of all knowledge, and those who question this postulate are bound to

15

come to grief. The Politburo decides over matters of life and death and its resolutions cannot be discussed. Experts are consulted only on the means to achieve the politically defined objectives.

A climate of fear is needed to preserve monolithism. To cement this frail cohesion, the Stalinist conspiratorial mind contrives the diabolical figure of the traitor. Who are the enemies? Where do they come from? What are their purposes? Providing answers to these questions was the main function of the show trials. Maintaining vigilance and preserving the psychology of universal anguish, those were the tasks Stalin had assigned to the masterminders of successive purges. No fissures are admitted in the Bolshevik shield, no doubts can arise that do not conceal some mischievous stratagems aimed at undermining the system. Time and again the refrain was harangued by restless sycophants: we are surrounded by sworn enemies, we are invincible only inasmuch as we keep united. Expressing dissenting views necessarily means weakening the revolutionary avant-garde. Breaking ranks is considered the mortal sin, and suspiciousness is the ultimate revolutionary virtue.

Dialectical imagination ended in the morass of ideological prostration. Minds and souls had to be purged in order to have them prepared for Stalinist *operationes spirituales*, those tantalising efforts to comprehend successive changes of the party line. Karl Korsch, who had once been anathematised by the Comintern chairman Grigoriy Zinoviev for heretical propensities, alluded to this situation when, in his late works, he described Marxism as an intellectual dead end.[18]

With Lenin and Stalin, utopian single-mindedness triumphed over the original scepticism expressed in Marx's favourite dictum, an invitation to creative doubt: *De omnibus dubitandum* . . . Marxism itself was stripped of its original significance: from an instrument of liberation, it became a means to justify violence and oppression. Revolutionary pathos gave in to submission and cynical calculus. The past was periodically rewritten to suit the needs of the present; had not Marx and Engels foreseen this situation when they wrote in the *Manifesto of the Communist Party* that 'in Communist society, the present dominates the past'?[19] In this universe of fear and cynicism, willingness, a basic faculty required to maintain one's psychological identity, was systematically calcined. Union, united, unification — all these catchwords symbolise the reduction of man to the condition of cog in the all-embracing social mechanism.

16

Defiance of the Stalinist logic was possible, but it was utterly dangerous and, therefore, it represented rather the exception than the rule. Heroism is understandably rare under totalitarian conditions. Saying this is not to deny it but, on the contrary, to emphasise the moral grandeur of those who refuse to comply with the system. When acquiescence is the golden rule, it takes great moral courage to assume the status of the rebel. In the homogeneous space of totalitarian domination, opposition amounts to crime and opponents are treated as mere criminals. They incarnate the figure of difference and are therefore seen as outcasts. Ostracisation leads ultimately to the mental emancipation, the autonomy of the mind acquired by Solzhenitsyn's *zeks*, the population of Stalin's *gulag*. The barbed wire is thus the symbol of a new kind of boundary: that between absolute victims and relative accomplices of the evil.

Ideology helps the system to preserve and perpetuate itself. Its ultimate outcome is to create willing participants in the consolidation of the dictator's total power. André Glucksmann, the French philosopher, refers precisely to this phenomenon of ideological numbness:

> The ideas that pass within the head of the dictator are less important than the absence of ideas of those who dare not oppose him. In order to mobilize and kill, an ideology must make itself accepted and tolerated thanks to a pre-ideological anchorage.[20]

Initiated as a philosophy of history, developed as a sociology of total revolutionary change, a 'methodology of historical action' (Gramsci), turned by Stalin into a compendium of trite statolatric statements, Marxism could not hope for resurrection without an ethical criticism of its own foundations. Such an operation would lead, in the last analysis, to distressing conclusions about the relationship between means and ends in the Marxist praxis. The paradox of the dirty hands formulated by Jean-Paul Sartre, the idea that the end is nothing but a recapitulation of the means employed in order to attain it, highlights the bleeding wound of contemporary Marxism. One cannot speak of Marxism without speaking of Stalinism and vice versa. Refusing to admit this complex relation results in repetition of old blunders and tragic misunderstandings.

The fate of the *Short course*, masterfully analysed by Leszek

Kolakowski, illustrates the metamorphoses of ideology. The sacred writ was totally abandoned after the tyrant's demise and his once-revered theoretical pronouncements were derided as the climax of mediocrity. Ironically, former worshippers were particularly active in the demolition of Stalin's glory. Ideology *is* power and once power has changed its strategy, ideology faithfully follows it. This is not to gainsay the tremendous impact of ideological deception and self-deception. Ideology is mental pabulum for the subjects of totalitarianism:

> The *Short course* was not merely a work of falsified history but a powerful social institution — one of the party's most important instruments of mind control, a device for the destruction both of critical thought and of society's recollections of its own past.[21]

In Soviet-type regimes, truth is a social value fraught with political meanings. The objectivity of truth, its universally compelling nature, is denied in the name of *partiinost*, the Leninist principle of partisanship. The truth of the proletariat is declared to be the opposite of the bourgeois alleged science. History was at a standstill, natural rights seemed forever forfeited, and the long-celebrated individual was at a loss to distinguish himself from the shapeless, atomised mob which had superseded the civil society.

The unique source of truth remains the thought of the Supreme Leader: Stalin's catechism was considered divine precisely because it was authored by Stalin. In his *History and class consciousness*,[22] Georg Lukács postulated the epistemological superiority of the proletariat in the process of simultaneous comprehension and transformation of the historical totality. The Soviet ideology went even further and stipulated the privileged epistemological status of the charismatic party leader. The Marxist terminology was preserved but the intellectual intentions were basically altered.

The symbols of internationalism were usurped by the Stalinist bureaucracy which pretended to embody the only legitimate version of Marxism. The cult of the general secretary was rooted in the cult of the party as an almost sacred institution. In Stalin's own words, the party is the embodiment of unity of will and action, incompatible with the existence of factions. Its strength depends on the willingness to proceed to endless, unmerciful purges:

The source of factionalism in the party is its opportunist elements . . . Our Party succeeded in creating internal unity and unexampled cohesion of its ranks primarily because it was able in good time to purge itself of the opportunist pollution, because it was able to rid its ranks of the Liquidators, the Mensheviks. Proletarian parties develop and become strong by purging themselves of opportunists and reformists, social-imperialists and social-chauvinists, social-patriots, and social-pacifists.[23]

It was of utmost importance for Stalin — and for the Stalinist generation in the Bolshevik party — to impose an undisputable monopoly over truth. The political monolith has to find its mental counterpart in the unfaltering faith. As already shown, heresies had to be stamped out and independent thought, particularly Marxist independent thought, was unfailingly harassed. Ironically, this was Stalin's highest homage to theory, an oblique way of acknowledging the extraordinary force of ideas. Even before reaching social *Gleichschaltung* (uniformisation), Stalin was interested in creating a total captivity of the mind. The moral perversity that underlies Stalinism, depicted by Czeslaw Milosz as 'Ethical Ketman', culminates in the dissolution of all traditional bonds of loyalty and attachment between individuals:

Informing was and is known in many civilizations, but the New Faith [Marxism-Leninism] declares it a cardinal virtue of the good citizen (though the name itself is carefully avoided). It is the basis of each man's fear of his fellow man.[24]

Under fully-fledged, mature Stalinism, ideas were judged, i.e., punished or rewarded, in accordance with their practical-political implications. Pragmatic functionalism replaced dialectics, and an overall tendentiousness substituted Marxist universalism.

The advent of the millenium, as announced by the founding fathers of the doctrine, was a final goal to be circumscribed by pragmatic (geopolitical) limitations. With Stalin, Lenin's most successful even if not the most faithful disciple, *Realpolitik* triumphed over any consideration inspired by social idealism. All the rest, including the romance of anti-fascism, the myth of the Spanish Civil War, and other episodes related to what André Malraux once called *l'illusion lyrique* (the lyrical illusion), were barely tolerated anachronisms, a misleading tribute paid to 'the lost treasure of the revolutionary tradition' (Hannah Arendt).[25] Ignoring this substitution amounted to deliberate blindness and cost many Marxist believers exacting sacrifices.

Stalin's myth, a theoretical justification for irrepressible radical longings, took its toll over many intellectuals in this century. Unfortunately, their naïveté was equalled only by their abhorrence of the liberal-democratic *status quo*. Even the demolition of that myth, its exposure by Khrushchev and the end of Soviet hegemony in world Communism could not persuade certain unrepentant believers that the evil was hidden deep within the doctrine, that it was Marx who had inaugurated this experiment in 'social pedagogy'. It was Marx who gave the most articulate form to the modern nostalgia for communitarianism and paved the way for the later attempts to totally subordinate the individual to the englobing collectivity. In his *Theses on Feuerbach*, however, Marx gave vent to his apprehensions about any form of pedagogic dictatorship:

> The materialist doctrine that men are products of circumstances and upbringing, and that, therefore, changed men are products of other circumstances and changed upbringing, forgets that it is men who change circumstances and that it is essential to educate the educator himself. Hence, this doctrine necessarily arrives at dividing society into two parts, one of which is superior to society. The coincidence of the changing of circumstances and of human activity can be conceived and rationally understood only as revolutionary practice.[26]

Stalin's main enemy was the principle of difference. His strategy, so effective that no epigone has dared to question it, consisted of uniformising the ideology through its canonisation. Theoretical debates were encouraged only insofar as they underwrote the officially sanctioned truth. It goes without saying, Stalin was the ultimate arbiter and his verdict was extolled as sacred wisdom.

Marxism turned into a mystical exercise, with devout zealots, initiatic rites and procedures, esoteric dogmas where the latent meaning was always something essentially different from the manifest expression. Adherence to this sect was regarded as an enviable privilege and those who were accepted paid this allegiance to a chosen brotherhood with the willing emasculation of their critical faculties. Mountains of pages have been dedicated to this debasement of reason, but the fact of the matter is that one is still puzzled by the fascination exerted by a rudimentary metaphysics on spirits well acquainted with the most sophisticated achievements of Western cultural legacy. The case of Georg Lukács, to take the most intriguing one, speaks of the endless readiness of the intellectuals to indulge in self-deceit and masochistic self-denials.

The underlying structure of Stalin's myth, its infra-rational substance, was all the more unfathomable because of the ostentatious celebration of reason. The cult of Reason, entertained by French and German radical philosophers and political thinkers, was carried to an extreme in Stalin's bewildering statistics of terror. The image of man as a mechanism put forward by French *philosophes*, found its strange echo in this all-pervading technique of socially-oriented murder. That was the acme of radical utopianism, when nothing could deter or resist the perpetual motion of foul play. Marxist eschatology was substituted through Stalinist demonology. The public discourse was saturated with frightening images of deviators, heretics, spies, agents, and other scoundrels. A phenemonology of treason was devised to justify the carnage and there was no paucity of intellectuals to support this morbid scenario. Louis Aragon, Pablo Neruda, Paul Eluard, even Sartre and Merleau-Ponty, were disposed to trust and endorse the Stalinist fabrications. Too few were those like Arthur Koestler and Albert Camus who openly engaged in a struggle with the Stalinist ideology and the system it was serving.

An almost perfect form of totalitarianism, Stalinism represented a perpetual subversion of traditional morality. It can be even described as an ethical revolution: good and evil, vice and virtue, commendable and reprehensible deeds, all were drastically revalued. Long-cherished distinctions between moral and immoral behaviour were treated as irrelevant, mere petty-bourgeois prejudices, and were consequently jettisoned as relics of the past. A new vision of man's moral realm was imagined, one that would fit in Stalin's dreams of the totally planned and administered society. Ideology and morality were fused and one could barely think of reacting against this abusive identification.

In Stalin's mind the purges were means of political consolidation and authority-building, a springboard for newcomers and time-servers. They were bound to secure the human basis for effective control over society. In one of his most poignant essays published before World War II in *Partisan Review*, Philip Rahv put forward a thorough interpretation of the mechanism that led to the 'great terror':

> These are trials of the mind and of the human spirit . . . In the Soviet Union, for the first time in history, the individual has been deprived of every conceivable means of resistance. Authority is monolithic: property and politics are one. Under such circumstances it becomes impossible to defy the organization, to set one's will against it. One cannot escape it: not only does it absorb the whole of life but it also seeks to model the shapes of death.[27]

Stalinist neo-Machiavellianism carried Marxist ethical relativism to its ultimate consequences. This was the bitter conclusion reached by Koestler's hero Rubashov, and such a view would have certainly been espoused by many a Bolshevik luminary assassinated in the name of 'a tomorrow that beckons':

> We were the first to replace the nineteenth century's liberal ethics of 'fair play' by the revolutionary ethics of the twentieth century . . . Politics can be relatively fair in the breathing spaces of history; at its critical turning points there is no other rule possible than the old one, that the end justifies the means. We introduced neo-Machiavellianism into this country; the others, the counter-revolutionary dictatorships, have clumsily imitated it . . . We know that virtue does not matter to history, and that crimes remain unpunished; but that every error had its consequences and venges itself into the seventh generation.[28]

The cult of the organisation and the subordination of the individual to the decisions of the supreme leadership had always been present in the ethos of Bolshevism. Lenin's theory of the vanguard party, his insistence of centralism and 'iron discipline' as opposed to 'bourgeois liberalism' were the prelude to the rise of Stalinism. An organisation made up of professional revolutionaries abides by different rules than traditional political parties; only such a permanently 'mobilized army', guided by a presumably infallible Central Committee, may help revolutionary dreams come true.[29]

No rival was to be tolerated, no real dialogue with real or potential adversaries was to be accepted. The Communist International (Comintern), created on Lenin's initiative in 1919, exported this intolerant logic to foreign countries and contributed to the emergence of political groups totally dedicated to the implementation of the Leninist programme of world revolution. Within the Comintern parties, as in the Soviet Union, the rules were dictated by Stalin and his acolytes. The main effect of the 'Bolshevisation' process of Western radical socialist parties was the suppression of their independence and the submission to the Moscow headquarters. The Marxist concept of internationalism was replaced by the Stalinist one: unconditional solidarity with the USSR was proclaimed by the general secretary as the touchstone of true internationalism. In the last analysis, the meaning of this thesis was that all communist parties had to accept Stalin's views exactly as devout Christians follow the indications of the Church. Party and leader became identical primarily as a result of ideological manipulation bound to foster the supremacy of the leader:

> The rise of Stalinism between 1928 and 1938 involved a process of change far more deep and pervasive than is generally realized. It was the metamorphosis of the original Communist or Bolshevik movement-regime into a new movement-regime of the fuehrerist type.[30]

Without the purges the system would have looked radically different. In other words, both victims and beneficiaries of the murderous mechanism were lumped together by this sacrificial ritual. For some of the Bolshevik militants liquidated or deported during the great purge, the terrorist ordeal amounted to *necessary* self-deprecation and self-abasement. Moreover, it was an opportunity to attain the long-expected absolution for those moments of 'derailment' when they had dared to oppose Stalin. Who were the actors of the show-trials? By what criteria were they selected? To meet what secret requirements?[31] How was the logic of the terror to be related to the Bolshevik mind and particularly to Lenin's ruthless dialectic?

From sacrifice to despair

Stalin's fundamental objective was to establish a sense of tribal community, a kind of mystical adulation surrounding his own figure. Rather than a community of hope, he was interested in strengthening a consensus based on fear and resentment. What

23

linked the individual to his fellow citizen was first and foremost this universalised anguish. Everything else (lies, cowardice, cynicism, betrayal, amorality) was rooted in this all-pervasive, all perverting sense of anguish. No communication was possible between terrified social atoms. In the murky climate of totalitarianism the individual is downgraded to a simply monadic condition.

The social space was blocked, reduced to mechanical gestures, stereotyped behaviour, and demagogic exhortations. As previously emphasised, Marxism, a doctrine conceived in direct opposition to bureaucratic alienation and a philosophy of subjective emancipation, was turned into a subservient instrument for the conservation of the new form of domination. It was precisely this decrepit Marxism that suited the tastes and needs of the Stalinist apparatchik, a social category whose mind was perfectly grasped by Robert Conquest:

> . . . not merely among the political leadership but even in the lower ranks of the cultural bureaucracy and elsewhere, there is a cadre of men with closed minds, wholly saturated with the prejudices, the illusions, and the inordinate pretensions of a low-grade and limited dogma.[32]

Stalin coveted the paeans and odes of the apparatus since, like most tyrants, he was aware of the horror provoked by his politics; in Gibbon's words, quoted by Robert Conquest:

> Persecutors must expect the hatred of those whom they oppress; but they commonly find some consolation in the testimony of their conscience, the applause of their party, and, perhaps, the success of their undertaking.[33]

Now, the pangs of conscience were not Stalin's main weakness, but there is no doubt that he enjoyed being called the greatest military strategist of all times, a universal, Renaissance-like genius, and, of course, a 'coryphaeus of science'. It was not enough to him that he had turned Marxism into a theoretical mockery. To quench his thirst for glory, Stalin wanted to be regarded as the most accomplished Marxist theorist since Lenin, equal, or even superior, to the founding fathers.

No doubt, Stalin was not competitive in the field of grand theory. A vulgar Marxist at the level of conceptual debates,

appreciated by Lenin for his proficiency in sweeping simplifica-
tions of otherwise obscure issues, Stalin was nevertheless superior
to his rivals in terms of astuteness and perspicacity, of ability to
manipulate both ideas and people. His was a science of conspiracy
and intrigue that certainly outwitted anything his enemies in the
Bolshevik party could have imagined. 'He is Genghis Khan' —
this was the horrified confession murmured by Bukharin to
Kamenev in a moment of total hopelessness. Unlike the Bolshevik
'old guard', Stalin was not restrained by any moral standards. His
former colleagues were astounded by this incredible chameleonic
ability. Stalin's superiority over his rivals flowed precisely from
this strict, unflinching commitment to absolute power. Under
Stalin, and for Stalin, power became an end in itself, but it was
with Lenin — as Rosa Luxemburg had brilliantly indicated in her
critique of the Russian revolution — that this devolution of
Marxism had started. Lenin did not hesitate to annihilate his
enemies, to thwart — by any means, be they noble or ignoble —
any project bound to curtail his domination. What actually
triumphed in Lenin's contemptuous dismissal of formal democracy was an obdurate Jacobin tradition, a line of political thought
for which illuminated minorities are entitled to discard and flout
the willingness of silent or vocal majorities. First Leninism, and
later Stalinism, carried to chilling perfection Rousseau's sophistries about the providential lawgiver, the almost divine legislator
endowed with infinite powers to understand the 'sense of history'.
Like Saint Just, they dreamt of 'a tyranny of virtue to prevent the
recurrence of a tyranny surrounded by vice'.[34]

Rosa Luxemburg, who was herself well-trained in the mysteries
of dialectics, felt the enormous danger involved in the attempt of
the Bolsheviks to stifle any form of dissent. It may be worth
quoting some of her most acerbic critical considerations on triumphant Leninism: 'Freedom only for the supporters of the government, only for the members of one party — however numerous
they may be — that is not freedom. Freedom is always freedom for
the man who thinks differently.' And to make her point more
unambiguous, she added:

> With the suppression of political life in the whole country, the
> vitality of the Soviets too is bound to deteriorate. Without
> general elections, without complete freedom of the press and
> of meetings, without freedom of discussion, life in every
> public institution becomes a sham in which bureaucracy

alone remains active. Nothing can escape the working of this
law. Public life gradually disappears; a few dozen extremely
energetic and highly idealistic party leaders rule, and the elite
of the working class is summoned to a meeting from time to
time to applaud the speeches of the leaders and to adopt
unanimously resolutions put to them. *Au fond* this is the rule
of a clique — a dictatorship it is true, but not the dictatorship
of the proletariat, but of a handful of politicians.[35]

What followed was indeed the establishment of the dictatorship of
a clique, a Mafia-like structure bound to eliminate any residual
traces of popular spontaneity and keep the whole society under
tight control.

Marx's caveat about the possibility of splitting society into two
groups — one of those 'in the know' and one of simple agents of
power, Orwell's 'interior party' versus the larger, diffuse one —
was disregarded by Lenin. In the Bolshevik mind, success,
palpable efficiency, was the sole criterion of truth. Lenin was not
interested in the truth of the losers. He inaugurated the cult of
victory against all odds, and Stalin was indeed his loyal heir when
he proclaimed that there is no fortress the Bolsheviks could not
storm.

Until the Bolshevik takeover, Lenin's endeavours consisted of
incessant hairsplitting polemics with other social-democrats. He
was possessed by revolutionary faith and lambasted any effort to
abate the radical pathos of the avant-garde. Primarily because of
his intransigence and tactical imagination, Lenin triumphed over
adversaries better prepared as Marxist theorists. He managed to
isolate Plekhanov and defeated illustrious Marxists like Martov,
Dan, and Akselrod. Later, when the Bolshevik party imposed its
dictatorship, *raison d'état* and party truth needed to become
identical.

Lenin died too early, but there are few doubts that he would not
have shown more mercy for heretics than his successor. His
methods could have been different, but the intolerance was intrinsically the same. The nineteen conditions for affiliation to the
Comintern, no less exacting than requirements established by
medieval religious orders, are an epitome of Lenin's exclusiveness,
of his aversion for any spontaneous development of the revolutionary movement. Needless to add, until his conflict with the
triumvirs (Stalin, Zinoviev, Kamenev), Trotsky was not a
supporter of intra-party democracy. Communists usually discover

the virtues of democracy only after they lose the privileges associated with power. Defeat in such political struggles is often conducive to reassessment of both methods and goals. Outcast prophets like to posture as adamant fighters for freedom of discussion and hypocritically regret their previous blindness. As a matter of fact, it is somewhat disturbing to notice how similar statements of defeated (or purged) communist leaders may sound. Certainly, we speak here of genuine avowals, not of the extorted confessions made during Stalinist frame-ups. They all claim they have struggled for the good of mankind. They were all partisans of a better world, immaculate heroes engulfed by the forces of evil. Therefore, one cannot deny that Isaac Deutscher made some good points in his otherwise idiosyncratic remarks about embittered ex-communists. It is true that some ex-communists have tended to overstate their discontent with the 'God that failed', but it is no less true that our understanding of the communist political culture would be fatally impoverished without the illuminating testimonies of intellectuals like Manès Sperber, Arthur Koestler, or Ignazio Silone. Deutscher accused disillusioned communists of failing to make vitally important distinctions. As a radical socialist, and an ex-Trotskyite, he could not accept the virulence of Arthur Koestler's or Boris Souvarine's anti-communist stances. Referring to this alleged manichean distortion characteristic of the 'ex-Communist's conscience', Deutscher wrote:

As a Communist he saw no difference between fascists and social-democrats. As an anti-Communist he sees no difference between nazism and communism. Once, he accepted the party's claim to infallibility; now he believes himself to be infallible. Having once been caught by the 'greatest illusion', he is now obsessed by the greatest disillusionment of our time.[36]

It is no secret that most of the intellectuals who joined the Stalinist camp in the thirties did it because they could not see a better, more effective, alternative to Nazism. No wonder therefore that many committed anti-fascists felt betrayed by Stalin's collaboration with Hitler and reappraised their original faith. For instance, two German former communists, who had spent the war years as refugees in the United States, published in 1947, under the pen-name Ypsilon, a fascinating report about the tribulations of militants associated with the Comintern. Their account is

27

particularly important since it depicts in colourful vignettes the biographies of such professional revolutionaries like Boris Savinkov, Georg Lukács ('Sorcerer's Apprentice'), Ernst Thälmann, Heinz Neumann, Willy Münzenberg ('Hearst of the Comintern'), Jacques Doriot ('Renegade of the Revolution'), André Marty ('Underground General'), and many others. Ypsilon aptly described the psychology of terror in the famous Hotel 'Lux', the Holy See of international communism, a Moscow residence for the bigwigs of the Comintern. Between 1936–9, Hotel 'Lux' turned into a real pandemonium or, in Ypsilon's words, it 'became a purgatory':

> All the ties of friendship and of common conviction that formerly had united men had become knots of friction. The terror made primitive savages out of 'pure' and 'impure' alike. They fought for dear life, friend denouncing friend, husband his wife, wife her husband, father his son and son his father.[37]

The authors had experienced those times of wretched despondency and could not but underwrite Ignazio Silone's terrible indictment of that revolutionary generation:

> We know the story of the hermit who, in order to give himself wholly to God and renounce his earthly desires, castrated himself with his own hand. He was, it is true, delivered from certain inner conflicts; but at the same time he lost the energy of his love for God, and he was forever more incapable of returning to normal life. The case is the same with many Communist bureaucrats who have lost their faith in the always changing party line and who, as a result of their spiritual self-mutilation, can never return to normal humanity.[38]

The total commitment to the organisation is the vital principle of the Bolshevik ethos. Lenin and his votaries walked actually in the footsteps of Bakunin and Nechaiev, the Russian anarchists of the nineteenth century, for whom the individual is nothing compared to the general willingness of the radical group. Boris Souvarine pointed to this portentuous affinity when he wrote in 1937:

> The Bolsheviks are the inheritors of this conception, and they

28

adjusted it to their needs and to their epoch. For them, the world is divided in two parts: the Party and the rest. Being expelled from the party amounts to being banished from this planet. To avoid this, they are ready for all the turpitudes, according to their amoral morality, they are ready to debase themselves, to make whatever public declarations while preserving mental restrictions, to denounce each other, to take *perinde ac cadaver* oaths of obedience and submission, only to resume whenever possible their intrigues.[39]

Coming from someone who was one of the founders of the French Communist Party, who had known Lenin, and had closely watched Stalin's suppression of all oppositions, this severe judgement should be taken seriously by all those interested in comprehending the communist mind.[40]

Bolshevism managed to capitalise upon a certain psychology of compliance with superior decisions, the masochistic sentiment that life is meaningless without the party. The infantilisation of the militants was the precondition for the inducement of a real voluptuosity in enslavement. Ironically, this indulgence in heteronomy was characteristic of those who believed they were making history. They were indeed *aficionados* of revolution as a cataclysmic collision between the forces of good and evil, and could not realise the depth of the chasm between their dreams and the lurid reality of Stalinism. And each time this moment of realisation was to come, they could not stand it as rational beings but rather as neurotic lovers, prone to hysteria and suicide. History as a black hole, an inescapable dead end, this is the ultimate vision of the apostate.

Stalinism as an ideological institution

The decay of Marxism in Soviet-type societies is both a disturbing and instructive story. It tells us about the confines of human reason and more precisely about the ambivalence of dialectical reason. The kingdom of reason itself, first sacralised by Marxism, then vandalised by Stalinism, has to be therefore debunked, brought back to earth, robbed of its mythological nimbus. In his early philosophical writings Marx proclaimed communism to be the *genuine* resolution of the conflict between man and nature and between man and man:

. . . the true resolution of the strife between existence and essence, between objectification and self-confirmation, between freedom and necessity, between the individual and the species. Communism is the riddle of history solved, and knows itself to be this solution.[41]

It was precisely this Promethean drive, this prophetic certitude, that appealed to those who could not bear the onus of the existing order and were longing for the millenium. Marxism can be described as the modern embodiment of the chiliastic expectation, a philosophy that abjures its philosophical status and attempts to become a science, namely a science of the supreme historical spasm supposed to bring about an ideal order where man would cease to be a prisoner of blind necessity. There is, to be sure, a hubris in this Marxist claim to universal knowledge, and Kenneth Minogue is right in stressing its ominous implications:

A condition of things in which all strife between essence and existence had been resolved might possibly be a thing of beauty, but there would be no one to contemplate such beauty, since the separation between beauty and its contemplator would also be among the things resolved. It is not a possible condition for human beings, and this means that ideology poses an *essentially* insoluble problem for the West. In pronouncing the rottenness of a civilization, it is actually declaring a hatred of any possible human life. What it proposes is the cosmic equivalent of a suicide pact.[42]

It was not classical Marxism, but its Leninist offspring which immediately paved the way for Stalinism and its repellent practices. After all, Marxism was the result of a certain trend within Western culture, one that emphatically abhorred the humiliation of the individual. True, Marx was obsessed with the supremacy of totality but his dream was that of a humanised order, not the penal colony. It was, however, Marx's radicalism which, by omission or commission, allowed Lenin to reinvent Marxism in such a manner as to permit the onslaught on subjectivity. The utopia of a unified, cohesive, non-contradictory society was pregnant with the totalitarian experiment unswervingly pursued by Lenin and Stalin. The tenet of class struggle, which for beter or worse is the kernel of Marxist social philosophy, was the alibi for the final solution of the class problem. In his posthumously published masterpiece *Life and fate*, Soviet writer Vassily Grossman has shown how ruthlessly this operation was fulfilled.[43]

Stalin was not concerned with sophisticated dialectical schemes. His was an utterly simplified, almost crude, social doctrine, a liturgy permeated with mystical undertones, resentful phantasies, and venomous prejudices. He could not live without combatting, i.e. smashing, an enemy, and that enemy was all the more dangerous since, according to Stalin, the evil had managed to infiltrate the Bolshevik citadel itself. There was a scent of envy in Stalin's indictment of the defeated opposition: that vermin, despicable and cowardly, was nevertheless able to create a parallel power, all sorts of diabolical centres, to perfidiously survive as the Soviet Union's second, underground party. To be sure, Stalin was not mesmerised by his propaganda but he was nonetheless convinced that the extermination of all opposition was the only way to ensure the survival of the Soviet system.

During the Comintern years, Soviet ideology and Stalinism became synonymous. Each of Stalin's pronouncements, each statement, letter, or even telegram, was celebrated as a new glorious achievement in the development of Marxism-Leninism.

Political terror, as mentioned, was accompanied by ideological terror. Orthodoxy ruled unchallenged, and the Stalinist ideological apparatus took great care to hunt any virtual heresy. And since the party doctrine was in perpetual change — dialectics was of course invoked to justify this blatant opportunism — thought had to be moulded and remoulded following the same pattern. Memory had to be continuously expurgated, reshaped in accordance with the latest insight of the *vozhd*. No scruples or cumbersome principles were allowed to obstruct this permanent readjustment to the imperatives of the day.

The main goal of the ideology was to strip *homo sovieticus* of those lingering ethical criteria that could have favoured indulgency in critical questions. The mind had to become acritical. Doubts were socially deleterious and therefore proscribed. Critical interrogations necessarily resulted in police interrogations. No one has better described the moral disaster represented by Stalinism than Nadezheda Mandelstam, the widow of one of Russia's greatest poets who died in a transit camp near Vladivostok. In the following passage she mentions her thoughts following conversations with Anna Akhmatova, another prominent poet and a victim of Stalin's hostility to culture:

At this period, [after the dictator's death] astonished how people — in particular Russian emigrés — utterly misunderstand our life, Akhmatova often repeated a phrase which infuriated me: 'They are envious of our suffering.' Such failure to understand has nothing to do with envy — it comes from the impossibility of imagining our experience and also from the deluge of lies by which reality has been twisted out of all recognition . . . But the main thing was that there was nothing to envy. There was absolutely nothing at all uplifting about our suffering. It is pointless to look for some redeeming feature; there was nothing to it except animal fear and pain. I do not envy a dog that has been run over by a truck or a cat thrown from the tenth floor of a building by a hooligan. I do not envy people, like myself, who suspected a traitor, provocateur, or informer in everyone and did not dare utter their thoughts even to themselves for fear of shouting them out in their sleep and giving themselves away to the neighbours on the other side of the thin wall that divide our apartments. There was, I can tell you, nothing to envy.[44]

It would be hard to find more telling an account of Stalin's atrocious times.

The stultification of Marxism under Stalin was linked to its complete appropriation and distortion by the Soviet party. It was incorporated in the Soviet ideology — a conglomerate of apocryphal Slavophile and fatuous positivistic ideas — and was therefore deprived of its original impetus. A certain conservative, anti-Western Russian philosophical tradition was appropriated by Stalinism, particularly in the cult of the party-state and the limitless disdain for the rights of the individual.[45]

Ossification in the form of prescriptive orthodoxy was the fate of institutionalised Marxism at least until Stalin's death. Party ideologues like Mark Mitin or Pavel Yudin, authors of Stalin's *Short biography*, enjoyed absolute power over what was defined as the ideological front. They had been the champions of Stalinism within the Institute of 'Red Professors', the ideological citadel in the late 1920s.[46] Mikhail Suslov himself, Zhdanov's successor as grand master of Stalinism after 1948 and for decades a professional kingmaker in the Kremlin, was also a graduate of that institution.[47] People like Mikhail Suslov, Boris Ponomariov, Pyotr Pespelov, Mark Mitin, Pyotr Fedosseyev, Fyodor Konstantinov, Mikhail Rozenthal, or Pavel Yudin were not interested in the

development of theory. Their unique concern was ideological conformity, the total regimentation of the intellectual sphere.

At the opposite pole, beyond the pale of orthodoxy, there were
attempts to save the original impulse of Marxism, to defend the
promise of all that Marx had truly believed in '. . . reason in
action, the establishment of a harmoniously, rationally organised
society, the end of the self-destructive struggles that distorted the
visions and the acts of mankind . . .'[48] This utopian project of an
ultimate reconciliation (*Versöhnung*) between man and community
inspired the works of writers like Theodor W. Adorno, Max
Horkheimer, Karl Korsch, Walter Benjamin, Ernst Bloch, all
united in the conviction that oppression will not have the final
word. They were committed to that magic quality of remembrance
and refused to acquiesce in the principle of reality as formulated by
the powers that be. *Nicht mitzumachen*, not to cooperate with the
forces of barbarism, was for such thinkers a moral imperative in
those unbearably dark times. As Hannah Arendt put it in her
introduction to Walter Benjamin's *Illuminations*:

> Like a pearl diver who descends to the bottom of the sea, not
> to excavate the bottom and bring it to light but to pry loose
> the rich and the strange, the pearls and the corals in the
> depths, and to carry them to the surface, this thinking delves
> into the depths of the past — but not in order to resuscitate
> the way it was and to contribute to the renewal of extinct ages.
> What guides this thinking is the conviction that although the
> living is subject to the ruin of time, the process of decay is at
> the same time a process of crystallization, that in the depth of
> the sea, into which sinks and is dissolved what once was alive,
> some things suffer a 'sea-change' and survive in new crystal-
> lized forms and shapes that remain immune to the elements,
> as though they waited only for the pearl diver who one day
> will come down to them and bring them up into the world of
> the living — as 'thought fragments', as something 'rich and
> strange', and perhaps even as everlasting *Urphänomene*.[49]

The ambition of Stalinism as an ideological institution was precisely to rule out the temptation of memory. Nothing was preserved of the dialectical refinement of Hegelian-Marxism, of
young Marx's impassioned philosophical musings. On the contrary, the more aseptic the style, the more vapid the alleged
demonstration, the more enhanced were the theorist's chances to

be regarded as a reliable propagandist. To reach the upper echelons of the ideological apparatus one had to act as a jukebox: slogans had acquired a life of their own and individuals became mere mouthpieces for those hackneyed cliches. Frontiers between party propaganda and Marxist philosophy were deliberately blurred. Axiological presuppositions were programmatically disregarded, and the only remaining pseudo-philosophical register was the litany of Stalin's presumed dialectical breakthroughs, actually an oversimplified variant of Engels's and Lenin's naive materialism.

As for Western attempts to imagine alternatives to Soviet ideology, they were isolated and meagre, with few resources and little appeal. Western Marxism became increasingly aristocratic, self-enclosed, ostentatiously radical and attracted to nebulous utopias. A whole jargon was created by French existentialism to justify political engagement, a term repeated by Sartre *ad nauseam* and bound to suggest a way to surmount the antinomies of contemplative life.

Disgust with their own society made those intellectuals to indulge in adamant support for the USSR and what they worshipped as the 'cause of peace and progress'. Referring to this readiness to endorse the worst Stalinist aberrations, Kolakowski wrote: 'Hypocrisy and self-delusion had become the permanent climate of the intellectual Left.'[50] He drew this conclusion with regard to the interwar period, but the Western leftist myopia became even more outrageous after World War II, when the Soviet Union emerged triumphant over the Nazi beast, and this victory was proclaimed a living proof of the viability of Stalin's politics.

It was with Stalin that a self-styled ideological construct became the permanent counterpart to systematic extermination of whole social categories. Stalin's works, collected until his death in thirteen volumes, were considered the supreme Marxist achievement, the *terminus ad quem*, the final station of philosophical development. Soviet ideology was reduced to monotonous repetitions of Stalin's formulae. Marx, Engels, Lenin, were quoted only insofar as their works could be figured as anticipations of Stalin's breathtaking innovations: it was he who had expanded the scope of dialectical laws, albeit he actually glossed over the Hegelian-Marxist interpretation of negation; it was also he who had spelled out in the most elaborated and articulate fashion 'the universal truth of Marxism-Leninism', whatever that formula may have meant. Stalinism did not need to be mentioned *expressis*

verbis since all the efforts of orthodox Marxists converged to underwrite Stalin's propositions as almost divine behests.

Too few were those who declined to participate in those bloody
pageants. Antonio Gramsci himself, in his *Cuaderni*, the prison
notebooks, otherwise a monument of lucidity, dodged any direct
confrontation with Stalin's myth. Fascinated as he was with the
dynamics of modern political illusions, interested in Georges
Sorel's philosophy of myth, violence, and rebellion, Gramsci
seemed unaware of the most nefarious consequences of myth-
making in the Marxist political area.[51] Most Marxist thinkers were
too concerned with Hitler's *Machtergreifung*, the Nazi takeover of
power in January 1933, to keep an eye on the abysmal decline of
revolutionary theory in the USSR. To their honour, one should
mention here the names of Karl Wittfogel and Franz Borkenau,
forerunners of an independent approach to matters Marxist (and
Leninist) to be later developed in the works of such authors as
Claude Lefort and Cornelius Castoriadis, indefatigable explorers
of the Stalinist bureaucratic elephantiasis.[52]

It would not be unjust to say that Hitler's rise to power perfectly
served Stalin's interests. Under those emergency conditions, it was
obvious that any opposition to Stalin amounted to objective support for Nazi Germany. Unless one was really prepared to become
a victim of the Comintern's besmirching machinations, one was
compelled to keep deadly silence until better days would come. It
would be, however, unfair to forget those who raised their voices
aginst the all-pervasive lie: Arthur Koestler, André Gide, Ignazio
Silone, Victor Serge, Manès Sperber, Panait Istrati, Max
Eastman, James Burnham and, of course, those American anti-
Stalinist radicals grouped around *Partisan Review* (Philip Rahv,
William Philips, Dwight MacDonald, Sidney Hook, Edmund
Wilson, Lionel and Diana Trilling). Those intellectuals con-
sciously ran the risk of being vilified and blamed for all the sins of
the world only to remain loyal to their own conscience. One did
not need special qualifications to tell the truth: it was sufficient not
to regard ethical values as superfluous, to have the courage of
making the distinction between vice and virtue, between nightmare and utopia.

It is difficult to believe that all those who persevered in their
Stalinist commitment could not conceive of other choices. After
all, *Darkness at noon*, Koestler's masterwork, became a best-seller
after World War II, but it dealt with social and psychological
realities well-known to the Cominternist generation. It was

nevertheless more comfortable to cling to old phantasies than to try to get rid of those ideological shackles. Surprising as it may sound, projection into despotism seems a peculiar intellectual disease, a phenomenon all the more baffling since it is associated with a social stratum supposed to defend the autonomy of mind. The schizophrenic behaviour of radical intellectuals — on the one hand professing the values of the *Geist*, on the other accepting the subaltern status bestowed upon them by the party — cannot be explained only at the sociological level. One can even say that Karl Mannheim's noocratic ideal, the dream of a *freischwebende Intelligenz* (the free-floating intelligentsia), was founded on an overly optimistic appraisal of the relationship between intellectuals and power.[53]

The political aberrations of radical intellectuals in this century have been determined by self-hatred, a perpetual anxiety with regard to one's professional calling, and a refusal to contemplate responsibility as a personal duty. Power and decision, authority and prestige, were relegated to the party; the individual was spared any cumbersome troubles and worries. As for those witnesses — Whittaker Chambers was perhaps one of the most famous and unfortunate among them — who dared challenge these peremptory certitudes, their lot was to be cursed and pilloried as abject villains. There was no golden middle way available under those abnormal circumstances. The spasm of deliverance from the spellbinding power of Stalin's myth was followed by the despair of total solitude. The witnesses were persecuted: remember Arthur Koestler's confession about the attempts of the French Communist Party to lynch him in the late 1940s, or the onslaught organised by the literary weekly *Les Lettres Françaises* against Viktor Kravchenko, the Soviet defector who had exposed the Stalinist system of labour camps, or so many other leftist campaigns against those who denounced the Stalinist imposture? They had to expiate for their alleged betrayal through ceaseless harassment and attempts at character assassination.

The myth of unity, the authority of the Stalinist church had to be safeguarded against all odds. As for those who wanted to ruin it, their lot was to undergo the vendetta of the messianic community. They were troublemakers, a living confirmation that the figure of difference had endured, regardless of massive witch-hunts and endless purges. Their survival was the proof *a contrario* of the ultimate ineffectiveness of Stalin's favourite political weapon. Purges could not be considered successful until the very suppression of the last attempt to assert one's own autonomy. Trotsky's concept of the permanent revolution was thus perversely appropriated in the Stalinist celebration of the permanent purge.

Leszek Kolakowski makes a convincing point in describing Stalinism as a 'combination of extreme rigidity and extreme flexibility'.[54] Stalin felt no contrition in rewriting history in accordance with his ever-changing priorities. His pragmatic *Weltanschauung* was rooted in an unquenchable need for legitimacy. Had Trotsky been a hero, then what of a hero would Stalin have made? It was utterly important therefore to diminish, then to bring down, all the other legends only to enthrone the legend *par excellence*: that of the visionary guide, the omniscient *vozhd* whose sole concern was of course the happiness of the people. After painstaking attempts to grasp the nature of Stalinism, Lev Kopelev came to the following conclusion:

> Like the dwarf Zaches in Hoffmann's tale, he (Stalin) obtained the magic power to attribute other people's achievements and deeds to himself and to blame his crimes and vile acts on others. Thus, by 'postdating', he became a leader and a theoretician of the Revolution, a troop commander in the Civil War, the author of those thoughts and manager of those events that at one time created the popularity of Lenin, Trotsky, Bukharin, Tukhachevskiy, Kirov, and others. Killing his rivals, he pillaged — he plundered their thoughts and projects. And for the disasters and defeats brought on by his orders and ukases, his cowardice and ignorance, he punished his obedient servants and executors: Postyshev, Kossior, Yagoda, Yezhov, Voznesenskiy, the people's commissars, generals, Party bosses, and rank-and-file apparatchiks. It was this way even in the early period of his despotic rule, in 1929–30, and it continued until the final weeks of his life when, totally paranoid and afraid of every shadow, he was ready to start a new war.[55]

No term was more abused by modern revolutionary rhetoric than happiness. Concrete facts were to be averted in theoretical disquisitions; in order to be renewable, the theory had to rid itself of solid points of reference. The individual had to give up any hopes of immediate reward and invest his expectations in the hazy, unfathomable image of the communist future.

37

Notes

1. See Isaac Deutscher, *Marxism, wars, and revolutions* (London: Verso, 1984), p. 100.
2. See Adam Ulam, 'The Price of Sanity', an interview conducted by George Urban in G. R. Urban (ed.), *Stalinism. Its impact on Russia and the world* (Cambridge, Mass.: Harvard University Press, 1986), p. 113.
3. See Arthur Koestler, *The yogi and the commissar* (New York: Macmillan, 1946).
4. See Anthony Giddens, *The constitution of society. Outline of the theory of structuration* (Berkeley and Los Angeles: University of California Press, 1984), pp. 192 and 217–18; Louis Althusser, *For Marx* (London: Verso, 1979).
5. See Michel Heller, *La machine et les rouages. La formation de l'homme soviétique* (Paris: Calmann-Lévy, 1985).
6. See Ferenc Fehér, Agnes Heller and György Márkus, *Dictatorship over needs* (New York: St. Martin's Press, 1983), p. 190.
7. See Gustav A. Wetter, *Dialectical materialism. A historical and systematic survey of philosophy in the Soviet Union* (London: Routledge and Kegan Paul, 1958); Herbert Marcuse, *Soviet Marxism* (London: Routledge and Kegan Paul, 1958).
8. See Stephen Cohen, *Bukharin and the bolshevik revolution* (Oxford, New York: Oxford University Press, 1980); Nikolai Bukharin, *Selected writings on the state and the transition to socialism* (Armonk, N.Y.: M. E. Sharpe, 1982).
9. See Robert C. Tucker (ed.), *The Marx-Engels reader* (New York and London: Norton, 1978), pp. 193–200.
10. See Leszek Kolakowski, *Main currents of Marxism*, Vol. 3, *The Breakdown* (New York: Oxford University Press, 1978), p. 85.
11. See George Urban, 'Portrait of a dissenter as a Soviet man. A conversation with Aleksandr Zinoviev', *Encounter*, April 1984, p. 21; even more provocative reflections were spelled out by Zinoviev in his book *Le héros de notre jeunesse* (Paris: Julliard/L'Age d'Homme, 1984). It seems that according to Zinoviev no one can escape the ensnaring force of ideology: 'We fought against that society, but we did it as members of that society. We are both its product and the product supposed to combat it. But that has to be done inside it. And for it' (p. 34).
12. See Robert Conquest, *The harvest of sorrow. Soviet collectivization and the terror famine* (New York: Oxford University Press, 1986).
13. See Alvin W. Gouldner, *Against fragmentation. The origins of Marxism and the sociology of intellectuals* (New York: Oxford University Press, 1985), pp. 260–1.
14. See Zbigniew K. Brzezinski, *Ideology and power in Soviet politics* (New York: Praeger, 1962), p. 68. For an excellent survey on the contemporary relevance of the totalitarian paradigm, see the volume *Totalitarismes*, edited by Guy Hermet in collaboration with Pierre Hassner and Jacques Rupnik (Paris: Economica, 1984).
15. See Max Horkheimer, *Dawn and decline* (New York: Seabury Press, 1978), p. 239.
16. See F. Fehér *et al.*, *Dictatorship over needs*, p. 195.

17. See Mihailo Marković, *From affluence to praxis* (Ann Arbor: University of Michigan Press, 1974), p. 206; Gerson S. Sher, *Praxis. Marxist criticism and dissent in socialist Yugoslavia* (Bloomington & London: Indiana University Press, 1977).

18. See Karl Korsch, *Marxisme et contre-révolution* (Paris: Ed. du Seuil, 1975): Douglas Kellner, 'Korsch's revolutionary historicism', *Telos*, no. 26, Winter 1975–6; while still in Romania I published fragments of my research on Korsch: see Vladimir Tismaneanu, 'Korsch's Hegelian-Marxist radicalism', *Romanian Journal of Philosophy*, no. 3, 1977, pp. 349–56.

19. *The Marx-Engels reader*, p. 485.

20. See Andre Glucksmann, *Cynisme et passion* (Paris: Grasset, 1981), p. 241.

21. Kolakowski, *Main currents of Marxism*, p. 95.

22. See Georg Lukács, *History and class consciousness* (London: Merlin Press, 1971): Agnes Heller, ed., *Lukacs Reappraised* (New York: Columbia University Press, 1983).

23. See T. H. Rigby, ed., *Stalin* (Englewood Cliffs: Prentice Hall, 1966), p. 35.

24. See Czeslaw Milosz, *The captive mind* (New York: Vintage Books, 1981), p. 76.

25. See Hannah Arendt, *On revolution* (Middlesex, New York: Penguin Books, 1977).

26. See *The Marx-Engels reader*, p. 144.

27. See Philip Rahv, *Essays on literature and politics, 1932–1972* (Boston: Houghton Mifflin, 1978), p. 288.

28. See Arthur Koestler, *Darkness at noon* (New York: Bantam Books, 1970).

29. See V. I. Lenin, 'What is to be done' in *Collected Works*, Vol. 5 (Moscow: Foreign Languages Publishing House, 1961), p. 509.

30. See Robert C. Tucker, *The Soviet political mind. Studies in Stalinism and post-Stalin change* (New York: Praeger, 1963), p. 18.

31. The unsurpassed account of the annihilation of the Bolshevik elite remains Robert Conquest's *The great terror. Stalin's purge of the thirties* (New York: Collier Books, 1973).

32. See Robert Conquest, *Russia after Khrushchev (New York: Praeger, 1965)*, p. 56.

33. Ibid., pp. 52–3.

34. See James Billington, *Fire in the minds of men. The origins of revolutionary faith* (New York: Basic Books, 1980), p. 70; for the relation between Rousseauism and Marxism, see Bernard Yack, *The longing for total revolution* (Princeton: Princeton University Press, 1986); for a captivating investigation of revolutionary prophetism, see Melvin J. Lasky, *Utopia and revolution* (Chicago and London: Chicago University Press, 1976).

35. Cf. Lasky, *Utopia*, p. 120; see also George Lichtheim, 'Rosa Luxemburg', *Encounter*, June 1966, pp. 55–60; Francis L. Carsten, 'Freedom and revolution: Rosa Luxemburg' in Leopold Labedz (ed.), *Revisionism* (New York: Praeger, 1962), pp. 55–66. Taking into account Luxemburg's unequivocal statements on the Bolshevik revolution, it is quite surprising that some authors still try to minimise her criticism of the

Leninist anti-democratic methods. See, in this respect, the entry on Rosa Luxemburg in Tom Bottomore (ed.), *A dictionary of Marxist thought* (Cambridge, Mass.: Harvard University Press, 1983), pp. 293–4.

36. See Isaac Deutscher, 'The ex-communist's conscience' in *Marxism, wars and revolutions*, p. 55.

37. See Ypsilon, *Pattern for world revolution* (Chicago and New York: Ziff Davis, 1947), p. 243.

38. Ibid., p. 222. For a comprehensive source on successive cominternist generations, see Branko Lazich and Milorad Drachkovich, *Biographical dictionary of the Comintern*, new revised and expanded edition (Stanford, CA: Hoover Institution Press, 1986).

39. See Boris Souvarine, *A contre-courant, Ecrits, 1925–1939* (Paris: Denoël, 1985), especially pp. 208–359.

40. For Souvarine's role in the early history of the French Communist Party, see Edward Mortimer, *The rise of the French communist party, 1920–1947* (London and Boston: Faber and Faber, 1984), pp. 19–130.

41. See Karl Marx, 'Economic and philosophic manuscripts of 1844' in *The Marx-Engels reader*, pp. 66–125.

42. See Kenneth Minogue, *Alien powers. The pure theory of ideology* (New York: St. Martin's Press, 1985), p. 222.

43. See Vassily Grossman, *Life and fate* (New York: Harper & Row, 1986); with regard to Grossman's personal tragedy, see Simon Markish, 'A Russian Writer's Jewish Fate', *Commentary*, April 1986, pp. 39–47.

44. See Nadezhda Mandelstam, *Hope abandoned* (New York: Atheneum, 1974), pp. 249–50.

45. For the Russian counter-enlightenment line of thought, see Richard Pipes, 'Solzhenitsyn and the Russian intellectual tradition', *Encounter*, June 1979, pp. 52–6.

46. For precious biographical details on those Stalinist ideologues, see Abdurakhman Avtorkhanov, *Stalin and the Soviet communist party. A study in the technology of power* (New York: Praeger, 1959).

47. For Suslov's career, see Boris I. Nicolaevsky, *Power and the Soviet elite* (New York: Praeger, 1965), pp. 253–75; Roy Medvedev, *All Stalin's men* (Garden City: Anchor Press/Doubleday, 1985), pp. 61–81.

48. See Isaiah Berlin, 'Benjamin Disraeli and Karl Marx', in his *Against the current. Essays in the history of ideas* (New York: The Viking Press, 1980).

49. See Hannah Arendt's 'Introduction' to Walter Benjamin, *Illuminations* (New York: Schocken Books, 1969), pp. 50–1.

50. See Kolakowski, p. 116.

51. With respect to Gramsci, see, *Selections from the prison notebooks* (New York: International Publishers, 1971); Luciano Pellicani, *Gramsci. An alternative communism?* (Stanford, CA: Hoover Institution Press, 1981); for revolutionary myth and violence, see Georges Sorel, *Reflections on violence* (London: Collier-Macmillan, 1970); Isaiah Berlin, 'Georges Sorel', in *Against the current*, pp. 296–332, for a penetrating analysis of the 'Sorelification' of Marxism.

52. See Karl A. Wittfogel, *Oriental despotism, a comparative study of total power* (New York: Vintage Books, 1981); Franz Borkenau, *World*

communism (Ann Arbor: University of Michigan Press, 1971).

53. See Karl Mannheim, *Ideology and utopia* (Routledge & Kegan Paul, 1960).

54. See Kolakowski, p. 117.

55. See Lev Kopelev, *Ease my sorrows* (New York: Random House, 1983), p. 244.

2
Soviet Ideology and Eastern Europe

For them what counted was their theory, the victory of Marxism-Lenin-
ism on a world scale. To that end all means were good, everything
worked, everything was profitable. You could praise Ivan the Terrible,
and hold church services, and invent Russian priorities, but the goal
was still the same — world revolution.

Lev Kopelev

The meaning of Zhdanovism

Expansionism was embedded in the deep structure of Stalinism.
The low living standards of the Soviet population and the
discontent with the permanent purges had to be compensated by
the sense of external triumph and the mystique of great power
achievements.

Stalin's plans for Eastern Europe consisted not only of the
political domination over that area. The Soviet dictator was aware
of the existence of centrifugal forces that could easily contaminate
even the Soviet occupation forces. On the other hand, it was
crucially important to put an end to the ideological relaxation of
the war years. The climate of the anti-fascist coalition and Stalin's
pledges to observe the rules of pluralism in the Soviet-occupied
territories had encouraged many people to believe that the future
of Eastern Europe would look different than the bleak Soviet
model. It was precisely against these illusions that Stalin decided to
unleash a new ideological and political war.[1]

The idea of a 'popular front' in culture, Georg Lukác's ideal
expressed during his polemics with Hungarian propaganda czar

42

József Révai and other Comintern doctrinaires, had to be inclemently uprooted. A new wave of theoretical and political radicalism was subsequently unleashed as an ideological counterpart to the exacerbation of international antagonisms and the beginning of the Cold War.[2] The system cannot survive without successive ideological offensives. Ideology is the main ingredient, and consistent injections of faith are indispensable to keep up the moral of the 'troops'.

Zhdanovism was thus the response of the bureaucratic apparatus to the challenges of the post-World War II situation. It was primarily a strategy of withdrawal within the bloc's frontiers, and a reaction against the threat of proliferation of pluralist temptations. Associated with the name of Andrey Zhdanov, Stalin's faithful lieutenant and the main spokesman for party orthodoxy, this attempt to restore the institutional supremacy of the party was bound to further consolidate Stalin's myth.[3] Zhdanov's power in the party was delegated by Stalin and it is hard to believe that he had managed to reach such an independent status as to initiate a politics of his own, different, or even opposed, to the dictator's preferences. It would be more reasonable to assume that Zhdanovism merely expressed and underlined Stalin's own idiosyncrasies and apprehensions linked to the breakup of the wartime alliance and the Western rejection of Soviet imperialist claims. It would be appropriate to consider Zhdanovism as one of the hypostases of fulfilled Stalinism, mainly characterised by ideological conformity and unyielding dogmatism on international issues. Intransigence was *l'ordre du jour*, the imperative of the day, and Andrey Zhdanov, the leader of the Leningrad party organisation, personified this new upsurge of fanaticism.

The old, well-tested tactic of the scapegoat was meted out on such writers as Anna Akhmatova and Mihail Zoschenko who were accused of anti-Soviet attitudes.[4] On the other hand, it was fundamental for the Soviet empire to secure the rapid ideological *Gleichschaltung*, the regimentation of the satellised countries. Stalin could not accept any form of autonomy on the part of East European communist parties. In addition to other objectives, Zhdanovism aimed to re-establish the old cominternist sense of discipline within the subordinate parties in countries like Czechoslovakia, Poland, or Yugoslavia. This was the reason for the foundation of the Cominform in September 1947, a most fateful event for the peoples in Eastern Europe. It was Zhdanov who first spoke at the Cominform meeting about the division of the world into two main camps: one, headed by the United States, intent upon provoking a new world war, and the other one, the 'camp of peace and democracy', led by the Soviet Union.[5] Solidarity of the communist parties was particularly worth promoting under such threatening circumstances when, according to Zhdanov, the 'imperialist circles' were fomenting belligerent conspiracies against the Soviet bloc:

> . . . the present position of the Communist Parties has its shortcomings. Some comrades understood the dissolution of the Comintern to imply the elimination of all ties, of all contact between the fraternal Communist Parties. But experience has shown that such mutual isolation of the Communist Parties is wrong, harmful, and in fact unnatural.[6]

It was obvious that Zhdanov's fulminations indicated a turning point in Stalin's strategy toward the people's democracies. He may have introduced some personal notes in emphasising certain themes but, as a Soviet Communist Party Secretary, he was basically his master's voice. Justifiably associated with Zhdanov's name, this politics was nevertheless the product of Stalin's increasingly suspicious mind. The enemy's fifth column had to be exposed. To attain this goal all means were serviceable: 'The object was not only to restore ideological purity but to raise it to fresh heights, at the same time isolating Soviet culture from all contact with the outside world.'[7]

In the ideological field, the main target was rootless cosmopolitanism, a spectre that was to haunt the ageing dictator's last years. Zhdanov's performance in August 1946 against Anna Akhmatova and Mihail Zoshchenko recommended him as Stalin's most reliable underling. The decree on the literary journal *Zvezda* and *Leningrad* on 14 August 1946, by the Central Committee of the All-Union Communist Party, marked the beginning of a ruthless obscurantist campaign largely known as the *Zhdanovshchina*. The decree echoed Zhdanov's wrathful indictment of Akhmatova's lyrical poetry and Zoshchenko's satirical pieces. In his inimitable style, the cultural satrap indulged in vilification of the two writers: he called Zoshchenko a 'lampoonist', 'a philistine', 'vulgar' and 'the dregs of literature', whereas Anna Akhmatova was vilipended as 'a whore' and 'a crazed lady rushing to and fro between bedroom and chapel'.[8] Melancholy was to be combated as a 'decadent symptom', and Soviet culture was urged to exalt the 'positive hero', the radiant and uplifting figure of the Stakhanovite (the norm-breaking worker), the dedicated *kolkhoznik*, the vigilant security police officers, etc. Needless to add, this relentless militantism involved the duty to excoriate all 'the vestiges of bourgeois ideology'. Tolerance and leniency in the ideological realm were branded as impardonable political offences. In Zhdanov's manichean mind, there was no room for diversity. He carried the Stalinist logic of party-mindedness to its most reprehensible consequences. Terms like responsibility and culpability became interchangeable. The right to error was emphatically denied and the narrowest interpretation of *partiinost* was proclaimed mandatory for all Soviet intellectuals.

Lenin's theses on party literature were canonised and philosophy was reduced to mere parroting of Stalin's statements. The few decent Soviet philosophers were forced to withdraw into the less exposed field of the history of philosophy, but even there the ideological earthquakes could not be totally avoided. The authors of Stalin's *Short biography*, leading members of the ideological apparatus, became the party's only authorised spokesmen on theoretical issues. Lamentable political leaflets were declared paramount accomplishments, whereas real Marxist research was asphyxiated. Georg Lukács himself was forced by Révai, the Hungarian Zhdanov, to indulge in repeated (and nauseating) rituals of self-criticism. The party needed this morbid exorcism in order to warrant its most eccentric decisions. The level of cultural production was perplexingly low: schematic plots in the novels, endless epic versifications, assaults on 'intimist', i.e. real, poetry, lyricism as such accused of 'objectively' serving the counter-revolution.

Stalin's narcissism had to be titillated by odes, hymns, epopees. His *Short biography* and the notorious *Short course*, whose authorship was now attributed to Stalin himself, became objects of collective adoration.

The enslavement of mind had to be total and irreversible. No area was to escape this overall crusade: the grand inquisitor needed humble subjects, entirely subjugated by the totalitarian mechanism. Stalin's view of Soviet citizens had been bluntly expressed in one of his speeches after the end of World War II when he mentioned the 'common people, those who have little rank and unenviable title, . . . the cogs in the great machine of state without whom, to be brutally frank, all of us marshals and front and army commanders are not worth a cent.'[9]

Under the catchword of the 'struggle against formalism', all varieties of artistic experimentation and efforts at innovation were sentenced to death. No deviation from the ossified norms of socialist realism was allowed to persist. Soviet art (and its pale imitations in the people's democracies) could barely be distinguished from the Nazi neo-classical monumentalism inspired by the dogma of *heroisch-völkischer Realismus* (heroic-popular realism). Stalinist and Nazi triumphalist aesthetics were indeed the two sides of the same coin. They were both rooted in aversion for the high culture of bourgeois elites, and they were both instinctively inimical to the spirit of modernity. No wonder that both comrade Zhdanov and Dr Goebbels despised the cultural avant-garde in which they could not but see political anarchy, cultural decadence, and moral perversity.[10]

Was there any poetry, any redeeming feature in the mystique of Stalinism, as Aleksandr Zinoviev would have us believe? Was it a distorted response to basic popular needs and aspirations, with Stalin playing the role assigned to him by objective historical forces? In his paradoxical way, Zinoviev invokes the 'objective laws of social roles':

> . . . this form of the struggle for power and for the organization of power is an objective necessity of history and not a subjective feature. Stalin was not more power thirsty than other leaders. Whoever would have been in his place would have acted the same way.[11]

As a matter of fact, Stalinism was a modality to satisfy unfulfilled dreams of revenge over an allegedly rotten, corrupted liberalism. It was also a form of unscrupled exploitation of the meanest instincts of the individual caught in the cobweb of the atomised society. Hannah Arendt had certainly thought of this dimension when she elaborated her model of the totalitarian system.[12]

After having destroyed all the nuclei of the civil society, all centres of independent thought and action, Stalinism could not rely but upon the amorphous, shapeless population. Moral abulia is the prerequisite for this political order whose advent had been anticipated by Nietzsche in his most pessimistic prophecies about the revenge of the masses. Stalinism appealed — and still appeals — to the atavistic impulses in human nature; it is the social mask of regression into barbarism or, to quote Bernard-Henri Lévy, it is 'barbarism with a human face':

. . . every time a religion is embodied and the sacred is wedded to the earth, every time it is made the ground of politics instead of its heaven and distant goal, barbarism and murderous madness are not far away. The totalitarian State is not a State without religion; totalitarianism is the religion of the state. It is not atheism but literally idolatry.[13]

That such a fate was to befall Marxism, once proclaimed inheritor to German classical idealism, is perhaps regrettable but not entirely surprising. At the moment Marx had decided that the proletariat was supposed both to abolish and to realise philosophy, he paved the way for further simplification and mutilation of his doctrine:

> The *emancipation of Germany* will be an *emancipation of man*. *Philosophy* is the *head* of this emancipation and the *proletariat* is its *heart*. Philosophy can only be realized by the abolition of the proletariat, and the proletariat can only be abolished by the realization of philosophy.[14]

No direct relation can exist between a philosophy and a class, and postulating the opposite amounts to granting a *carte blanche* to professional mountebanks, political sorcerers, and would-be dictators.

According to reliable witnesses, during his last year Stalin was convinced about the imminence of a new world war.[15] Preparations for such an eventuality should therefore include the struggle for a homogeneous rearguard, in other words an uncompromising crackdown on all potential trouble-makers. Stalin's vassals in Eastern Europe slavishly followed his indications and they competed with one another to emulate their idol's lesson. How else can one interpret the hallucinating, almost surrealistic, succession of show-trials in Eastern Europe? How else can one explain the mind-boggling sadistic instincts which allowed people like Klement Gottwald, Mátyás Rakosi, Gheorghe Gheorghiu-Dej or Walter Ulbricht to indulge in the most abhorrent practices? A new theory of the double truth was concocted by these masters of self-deception. According to this self-serving view, they were mere instruments of history, and therefore their personal convictions — inasmuch as they had any — did not matter at all. What really mattered was the collective truth, the iron axioms of class struggle as dictated by Stalin.

47

Zhdanov's doctrine of the two camps was the ultimate formulation of this exclusive logic. The world was forever divided, hell and heaven were insurmountably separated and any attempt to imagine a middle road, a *tertium datur*, amounted to bringing grist to the mill of the enemy.

The campaign against Georgiy Alexandrov's *History of west european philosophy* belonged to the same struggle. A party philosopher and a long-time ideological apparatchik, Alexandrov had allegedly underrated the revolutionary meaning of Marxism and thereby promoted a 'vegetative spineless' view of the dynamics of philosophical ideas. Dialectical materialism had to be presented as the absolute beginning of a new era in the history of human thought. Acknowledging its indebtedness to bourgeois predecessors was an unforgivable sin. In all communist countries, little Alexandrovs had to be invented in order to meet the revengeful lust of local Zhdanovites. All the bricks of the cultural edifice had to be recomposed and Marxism — certainly a most impoverished, totally sterilised version of it — was to be the sole accepted outlook. Speaking in March 1956 before the session of the Council of Culture and Art, Jan Kott, a well-known Polish drama historian and critic, strikingly pointed out the devastating effects of Zhdanovism:

> We have been trying to explain reality and not to learn the truth; to explain and justify at any price, even the price of truth. Thus modern history became a great mythology before our eyes . . . Whenever the facts stood in the way, the facts were changed. If genuine heroes were obstacles, they evaporated. Literature that was not allowed to speak about crimes, literature which had to keep silent about trials which shocked men's minds and which were the daily reality for years, literature which had a sealed lip and wandered even further and deeper into lies, created a more and more fictitious vision of reality. The false theory of the mechanical rotting of art in bourgeois society in the imperialist epoch was accompanied by a theory of the automatic flourishing of art in socialist society . . .[16]

In a similar vein, Antoni Slonimski, a distinguished Polish poet, suggested that mature Stalinism was almost unequalled in its rabid adversity to free thought:

The history of philosophy knows few periods in which intolerance has so greatly increased as that of the last few years. The persecution of critical thought at the beginning of the Renaissance or later, in the seventeenth and eighteenth centuries, appears to have been almost idyllic when compared to the times we have recently witnessed . . . Only a true democratization of public life, restoration of public opinion, and the return from fideism to rational and unfettered thought can save us from Caesarism.[17]

Obscurantism was the mainstay of this perpetual offensive. Mature Stalinism amounted to an incredible explosion of irrationalism covered by pretentious hymns to the victories of Soviet science. It was indeed, as Kolakowski put it, a 'reactionary' attempt to thwart any effort to westernise Soviet culture. Stalinist ideology and its tributaries in the satellised countries became imbued with the most repellent themes of traditional Slavophilism. Needless to add, that was another semantic fraud, since genuine advocates of the Slavophile *Weltanschauung* had been long deprived of the right to speak out their ideas and sent to experience 're-education' in the Gulag.

Dialogue was forbidden and Western creations were *a priori* suspect, regarded as poisonous products of a decadent civilisation. Zhdanov and Goebbels nourished the same pathological aversion for Western avant-garde and the same hostility to anything related to cultural modernity. The pompous, overwhelmingly grandiose style of Stalinism and the Hitlerite morbid aestheticisation of politics stem from the same disgust with the negative values supposedly endorsed by high culture. Zhdanovism represented the triumph of kitsch in the field of Marxist ideology. It was the most complete systematisation of the anti-intellectual obsessions of a déclassé elite pretending to voice the proletarian cultural interests:

If the term 'reactionary' has any meaning, it is hard to think of a more reactionay phenomenon than Marxism-Leninism in the Stalin era, which forcibly suppressed everything new and creative in science and in every other form of civilization.[18]

To be sure, Marxism was only an alibi: the gist of the matter was to emphasise the superiority of Stalinism to any other current of thought. The instrumental reason culminated in the total integration of the individual into the totalitarian web. To make use of Ferenc Fehér's appropriate formula, the Stalinist *bestiarium* carried to an extreme the onslaught against reason. Zhdanovism was the instrument for the accomplishment of this process of de-enlightenment: 'The culture created by Stalin, attenuated but left fundamentally unaltered by his heirs and successors, is barbaric precisely in the sense that in it there is no strict line of demarcation between the bestial and the non-bestial.'[19]

In this apotheosis of senselessness there was only one guiding principle, one way to avoid the punishment inflicted by the system on those suspected of heretical propensities: total fanaticism, or rather the simulation of out-and-out radicalism. Dialectical laws were presented as the perfect confirmation of Stalin's unequalled force of premonition as well as of his superhuman insights.

The intellectual morass was accompanied by the direct intervention of the police in the so-called debates. Those who dared to challenge the party line in genetics, physiology, or cybernetics were sent to concentration camps. Lysenko's scientific hoax named agrobiology was proclaimed the only dialectical, i.e. the only tolerable, biological conception.[20] In a similar vein, Olga Lepeshinskaya, a former canteen caretaker for the Bolshevik elite during Lenin's exile years in Geneva, became a celebrated scientific luminary of late Stalinism. She was anointed an 'eminent biologist', the 'annihilator' of Virchow's teachings, and went out of her way to thank the Supreme Leader for his interest in natural sciences. On 1 January 1951, Lepeshinskaya published in *Pravda* a dithyrambic piece glorifying Stalin's scientific acumen:

> Fulfilling the plans of Lenin and Stalin, Soviet scientists uphold in their everyday work the principles of the Bolshevik party spirit in science. This principle became the motto not only for me, an old Bolshevik, but also for the many thousands of young scientific workers, educated by the party of Lenin and Stalin . . . Guided by principles laid down by Comrade Stalin, we have studied the development of complex life units (cells) from the simpler forms of living matter, from albuminous bodies capable of metabolism. In this way, Virchow's idealist theory . . . has been experimentally refuted and a new dialectical materialist cell theory has been created — a theory which teaches us that every cell consists of living matter and that beyond the cell, there is a lower and simpler form also consisting of living matter.[21]

The positivistic dimension of Marxism was thus replaced by a mystical conviction that politics could dictate the result of scientific research. The Marxist claim to scientificity backfired. It allowed for this bizarre and tragic turn of the doctrine into a tribunal of thought. In its last stage, Stalinism became a major obstacle to the very survival of Soviet science. It was more than philosophy that underwent the consequences of this ideology run amok. The whole sphere of the superstructure was disfigured and threatened with extinction.

Speaking about mature Stalinism, we have to think of certain unmistakable characteristics of that system. Seweryn Bialer rightly considers that in its late years, Stalinist totalitarianism displayed the following features:

> the system of mass terror; the extinction of the party as a movement; the shapelessness of the macro-political organization; an extreme mobilizational model of economic growth, tied to goals of achieving military power, and the political consequences thereof; a heterogeneous value system which favored economic status, and power stratification, fostered extraordinary cultural uniformity, and was tied to extreme nationalism; the end of the revolutionary impulse to change society and the persistence of a conservative *status quo* attitude toward existing institutions; the system of personal dictatorship. [22]

I would only emphasise, in addition to these characteristics, the pharaonic structure of political power, and the identification of the dominant ideology with the myth of the infallibility of the *vozhd*, i.e. of the General Secretary. Furthermore, Stalin's decision to restructure the party leadership during the Nineteenth Congress in 1952, as well as the plans to resume the practice of show-trials against members of the top hierarchy, indicate a well-conceived design to maintain society in a state of continuous fever. It was precisely the insecurity of **all** strata of the apparatus, including people associated with KGB (the Ministry of State Security) that led to the partial thaw immediately following the dictator's death in March 1953.

In the Soviet Union and in Eastern Europe, hopelessness was the universal state of mind. People felt lost and helpless, forever abandoned to the wayward decisions of an insane despot.

It would be no exaggeration to call this state the **mythocratic**

society, when the Egocrat, as Solzhenitsyn called Stalin, imposed his delirium as the main criterion of social normalcy. Cosmogony, genetics, literary criticism, linguistics, aesthetics, all were unified under the aegis of Stalin's indisputable genius. They were all required to partake in the same plan to reconstruct human nature, to surpass any limitations, be they social, natural, or psychological. It was a most distressing time for all those who were fighting for survival behind the 'iron curtain'. This is a term nowadays derided by historians who believe that Stalin was not the *primum movens*, the originator, of the cold war. But for those who experienced those years in Eastern Europe, who were trembling from dawn to dusk and fearfully watched during the nights the strange steps on the stairway, for whom historical optimism sounded outrageously hollow since the figure of the future had been frozen in the nightmare of endless servitude, the iron curtain was a bloody, inescapable reality. They strove to outlive their civical death. *La mort dans l'âme*, terrified by the spectre of death, denizens of the Soviet empire acted like prisoners waiting for the imminent execution. Some resisted, but most of them followed the system's most appalling precept: abandon all hope, ye who enter here . . .

Those conditions were particularly propitious for the social success of scientific impostors and moral gangsters like the notorious Trofim Lyssenko. He had understood the 'social necessity' and formulated a pseudo-theory of evolution bound to suit Stalin's disturbed mind. Lyssenko maintained that in certain circumstances, acquired characteristics could be inherited from one individual organism by its progeny. His aim was to assert the infinite possibilities of Soviet science: everything can be transformed, nothing is eternal and unchangeable, everything can be adjusted to the extent that there is willingness to do so. External conditions became a fetish, while the 'immutable substance of heredity' was exposed as an 'imperialist concoction'. Mendelism-Morganism-Weissmanism became the nemesis of Soviet biologists guided by Lyssenko's teaching. According to this intellectual charlatanry, human intervention was possible and desirable at the level of genetic processes. That was genetic engineering in its magical form, the answer to Stalin's willingness to impose his schemata over the coming generations. Scholars who did not comply with this pseudo-science were deported to the *gulag* as enemies of the people.

Ideological constraints were most traumatic in the human

sciences where any autonomous research was practically banned. Biology followed next since, in Engels's view, it represented the main field of controversy between idealism and materialism. Psychology, sociology, epistemology simply vanished. They were denied scientific status and their proponents were severely reprimanded. Pedagogy was reduced to the methodology of permanent re-education and its assumptions, formulated by Anton Makarenko, another dilettante lionised by Stalinist propaganda, suggested that human personality is fundamentally the result of social influences. Hence, it was possible to modify it to suit the dynamic, ever-changing needs of the regime.

Ideological reification under mature Stalinism was unparalleled. In the people's democracies the situation was even worse since there Stalin's vassals imposed Russian values as the only source of inspiration and eliminated any national schools of thought. Traditions were re-interpreted to adjust to the Soviet distinction between progressive and reactionary directions. Everything linked to the Russian (Soviet) culture was automatically proclaimed worthwhile, whereas presumably western-oriented disciplines and schools of thought were outlawed. In Romania, for example, the Bucharest School of sociological monographic research led by Dimitrie Gusti was dissolved.[23] In Hungary, Georg Lukács was forced into abject self-criticism. Its result was his philosophical abdication and the embarrassing sociologism of a book like *Die Zerstörung der Vernunft* (*The destruction of reason*). In Poland, sociology became an almost clandestine profession, whereas Marxist hacks vituperated against elitism in aesthetics and neutralism in praxiology. The situation was somewhat different in East Germany, where Ernst Bloch continued his investigations into the phenomenology of hope. The less virulent nature of intellectual purges in the GDR can be attributed to that country's special role in the Soviet empire. Walter Ulbricht's regime had not been totally sovietised and the ruling communist party (the SED) did not belong to the Cominform. Stalin had not abandoned the project of a unified, neutralised German state, and the regime had to postpone total regimentation.

The scope of Stalin's area of interest was astounding: from philology to political economy, he felt he had a word to say and obedient scribes rushed to extoll his epoch-making contributions. All the cultural domains had to bear the imprint of his universal genius. Consequently, they were all devastated by this avalanche of arrogant ignorance. In its full-fledged form, Stalinism was to be expounded as *mathesis universalis*, the sole and all-encompassing theory of nature and society. Not even cybernetics, albeit so important for military research, was spared the ideological intoxication and was described by the official *Philosophical dictionary* as a 'reactionary, bourgeois pseudo-science'.

The toll Stalinism took on Soviet culture and science is incalculable. Recovery was therefore painful and dramatic, not only in the USSR, but in the people's democracies as well. The bureaucrats had too many vested interests to defend and preserve and therefore they consistently opposed attempts to question traditional ideological shibboleths. In their view, ideology had to remain basically untarnished in the process of scientific renaissance following Stalin's death. All the aberrations were disingenuously attributed to a single man, in a dialectical reversion no less mendacious than the previous worshipping rituals.

Stalin, the once venerated God, was to become, at least for several years, the embodiment of ultimate evil. Blatant platitudes and conspicuous lies had been praised for decades as the climax of intellectual creativity. They were now deplored by people who had been instrumental in the ideological campaigns of the late 1940s and early 1950s. Mikhail Suslov, who had been Zhdanov's heir as main ideological supervisor, presided over the simulacrum of de-Stalinisation in Soviet social sciences. Pyotr Pospelov, another Stalinist ideological apparatchik, was charged to head the commission that prepared Nikita Khrushchev's 'secret' speech for the Twentieth Congress. Boris Ponomariov, another Stalinist sycophant, was the head of the editorial board charged to write the party history and Lenin's biography after 1956. The same continuity in the ideological apparatus could be noticed in the satellite countries. In Romania, where the wind of de-Stalinisation was tenaciously resisted by the party leadership, Leonte Rautu, a former editor of Radio Moscow, remained a prominent figure in the propaganda field until the early 1980s. Similar examples can be provided from all the other Soviet bloc countries. Suffice it to think of people like Zoltan Komocsin, Istvan Szirmai, and György Aczel in Hungary, Kurt Hager and Hanna Wolf in the GDR, Artur Starewicz and Andrzej Werblan in Poland, Jiri Hendrich in Czechoslovakia, *et al.* The presence of the Cominformist generation at the top of the propaganda machine even after the shock of de-Stalininsation could be noticed also in the two leading West European parties, the French and the Italian ones, where Jean Kanapa and Giancarlo Pajetta continued to hold influential positions as members of the Politburo and close advisors to the respective general secretaries.

The ideological apparatus

The values and the methods of the ideological elites in Soviet-type regimes were shaped in accordance with Stalin's desires. They were the dictator's creatures, moulded in Stalin's own image. Their biographies were colourless and lacked any moment of real distinction. Speaking about Eastern Europe, one would notice that the ideological watchdogs were recruited from the Muscovite factions of the ruling parties. In Hungary, József Révai, who had once been one of Lukács's promising disciples, became the scourge of intellectual life. Révai was a member of the Hungarian delegations to various Cominform meetings and enthusiastically implemented the Zhdanovist strategy.[24] In Romania, the tandem Iosif Chisinevschi-Leonte Rautu forced the national culture into a mortal impasse. The Latin legacy and the pro-Western orientation of the Romanian culture were rabidly opposed in the name of an absurd emphasis on allegedly traditional Romanian-Russian links.[25] Similar denial of genuine national traditions and an apocryphal sense of internationalism were promoted by ideological bureaucracies in Czechoslovakia. The same hacks who applauded the judicial murder of avant-garde writers linked to surrealism and the ban on Kafka's work were ready to brand cosmopolitanism as the deadliest sin. What they understood by this was made clear by Václav Kopecky, the man who played Zhdanov's role in Czechoslovakia: 'Cosmopolitanism means world citizenship', maintained Kopecky in a February 1952 speech. 'We know that this conception, which implied the deadening of one's relationship to the native land, to one's own people, and the acceptance of the mentality of a nonnational world community, originated as an ideological product of the capitalist development . . .'[26]

If in the field of economic management there was some room for young people with real skills — Dmitriy Ustinov's career under Stalin is indicative in this sense — ideology had to remain immune to any attempt at experimentation. In the cultural arena the task of the apparatchiks has always been indoctrination and thereby manipulation. Authentic debates in the rarefied Soviet ideological cosmos were unthinkable. Mikhail Suslov bemoaned this situation in his speech at the Twentieth Congress, but he was himself the main artisan of the ideological crusades of late Stalinism.

All devices were convenient when it came to uprooting the vicious deviationist temptations. 'Bourgeois nationalism' was fused with 'rootless cosmopolitanism' in the diabolical figure of the malignant enemy. In the meantime, socialist nationalism — Stalin's immortal contribution to the development of Leninism — was thriving. The members of the ideological army were willingly officiating the rites of the cult. Deprived of their own personality, they were glad to identify with and invest in Stalin's super-personality. After the terrorist dissolution of the ego it was normal for the apparatchiks to project themselves into Stalin's myth as an institutionalised superego. The cult of personality went far beyond the Byzantine traditions. It involved a desperate search for compensation, the ecstasy of voluntary servitude to the only achnowledged source of authority. It is this emotional infra-structure of mythocracy that explains the enduring commitment of the apparatus to the preservation of Stalin cult. In a thoughtful essay on 'The rebirth of the Stalinist cult', Viktor Zaslavsky refers to a relatively recent judgement about Stalin. It expresses the views of the Brezhnevite *nomenklatura*, but it is also indicative of a larger nostalgia for Stalin's times of apparent order and stability:

> . . . he never opposed Lenin, invariably considering himself Lenin's pupil and follower. Stalin did not introduce anything into Marxist-Leninist teaching which was not essentially in harmony with its basic conclusions . . . During Stalin's years our party steadily and unswervingly followed the basic Leninist course, always turning to the masses and regarding their support as essential to the viability of its policies.[27]

In the satellised countries, ideological persecution and naked police terror led to the decimation of the old intelligentsia. There were some solutions for survival, including reconciliation with the powers that be. On the other hand, there were also some resolute people who refused the pact with the usurping power. Those who indulged in compromises had to resort to all sorts of rationalisa-tions, to self-flagellation, and other masochistic practices. No one has better grasped the devious channels that led to the captivity of the mind than Czeslaw Milosz. The narcotic power of the 'new faith' emanating from Moscow was particularly deleterious among intellectuals:

There is a species of insect which inject its venom into a cater-pillar; thus inoculated, the caterpillar lives on though it is paralyzed. The poisonous insect then lays its eggs in it, and the body of the caterpillar serves as a living larder for the young brood. Just so (though Marx and Engels never foresaw this use for their doctrine), the anaesthetic of dialectical materialism is injected into the mind of a man in people's democracies. When his brain is duly paralyzed, the eggs of Stalinism are laid in it. As soon as as you are a Marxist, the Party says to the patient, you *must* be a Stalinist, for there is no Marxism outside of Stalinism.[28]

Souls and minds were perverted and the language of domination was internalised by the victims of domination. The ultimate aim, the *telos* of Stalinism, the law of its well-functioning as a *bestiarium*, was precisely, as Ferenc Fehér put it, the imprisonment of the body by the soul:

But since 'soul' (the dominant ideology) became a ruthless guardian of every subject and of all aspects of social life, all institutions, doctrines, habits, norms have lost their culture-creating validity precisely because they had originally a general humanistic claim. Therefore it is not accidental that the only cultural creation in this society has been coming for decades now only from dissidents who are writing about the bestiarium and whose outraged question is precisely this: what have you done to our people?[29]

The Soviet ideology, that commingling of social triumphalism, Russian chauvinism, Leninist messianism, and unabashed contempt for the West, took over all the states annexed, *de facto* or *de jure*, to the Stalinist heartland. In October 1952, during the last CPSU Congress attended by Stalin, the future of East-Central Europe could not have looked grimmer.

The ideological elite, which is not mandatorily made up of intellectuals but can incorporate them to a significant extent, is a product of mature Stalinism. The Stalinist mandarins capitalised on the support provided by certain collaborationist groups within the old intelligentsia as well as on the moral capitalation of leftist intellectuals like Bertolt Brecht, Pablo Neruda, Louis Aragon, Elsa Triolet, Ilya Ehrenburg, and other luminaries of the Popular Front shock brigade. The ideological apparatus is indeed a segment of the ruling class, with the parvenu features overly swollen. The parvenu mentality was the spiritual foundation of Stalinism:

> A parvenu has no peace of mind as long as he sees about him representatives of the intellectual culture of the former privileged classes, which he hates because he is shut out from it, and which he therefore decries as bourgeois or aristocratic . . . Stalin was the idol of parvenu Russia, the incarnation of its dreams of glory. The parvenu state must have a pyramid of power and a leader who is worshipped even while he scourges his subordinates.[30]

Any form of sophistication, any attempt to open the doors towards dialogue was branded a capitulation. Stalinism was the triumph of the monologue, the revenge of the lowest strata in the apparatus, the victory of all-embracing mediocrity over any form of distinction.

No Western ahcievement was spared, no obstacle could hamper the insatiable destructive urges of the zealots. Culture was the main enemy and the most trivialised Marxism became the spearhead of this neo-barbarous offensive. It seemed that the worst aberrations of the Nazi *Rassenwissenschaft* (the 'science of race') were to be reiterated in the excess of the Stalinist *Klassenlehre* (the 'class science'). Quotations from publications of those times could be haphazardly selected to illustrate the amplitude of the intellectual catastrophe. They could certainly enrich an anthology of human degradation and moral baseness. Aleksandr Zinoviev's paradoxical explanation of Stalinism, irritating as it might sound to certain manichean ears, actually touches some of the most unsettling issues. Was Stalinism an outgrowth, a monstrous deviation from an otherwise wholesome ideology? All historical evidence suggests the opposite view: Stalin was indeed the human measure of an epoch and a mentality, the criminal by-product of a criminal system. A system that — it should be emphasised — managed to unify victim and torturer, to blur the distinctions between them, to abolish traditional moral taboos and set about a different code, with different prescriptions and prohibitions. Cowardice, turpitude, infamy were turned into virtues through a process of semantic alchemy. By the same token, loyalty, honour, individual dignity were stigmatised as vestiges of the *Ancien régime*, poisonous sentimentalisms unworthy of the 'new man'. If nothing else, this myth of the 'new man' is the main heritage contemporary communism has preserved from its Stalinist epoch.

Notes

1. See Zbigniew Brzezinski, *The Soviet bloc. Unity and conflict* (Cambridge, Mass.: Harvard University Press, 1967), pp. 3–151.
2. With regard to the Cold War and its impact in Eastern Europe, see Hélène Carrère d'Encausse, *Le grand frère. L'Union Soviétique et l'Europe soviétisée* (Paris: Flammarion, 1983).
3. For a fascinating, though sometimes debatable, interpretation of Zhdanovism in the context of the rivalry between various Kremlin factions, see William O. McCagg, Jr., *Stalin embattled. 1943–1948* (Detroit: Wayne State University Press, 1978).
4. See Lydia Tchoukovskaia, *Entretiens avec Anna Akhmatova* (Paris: Albin Michel, 1980); for an unforgettable portrait of Akhmatova, see Joseph Brodsky, *Less than one* (New York: Farrar Straus Giroux, 1986), pp. 34–52.
5. See McCagg, *Stalin embattled*, pp. 278–9.
6. Zhdanov's speech at the Cominform foundation meeting in September 1947, quoted by Brzezinski, *The Soviet bloc*, p. 60.
7. Kolakowski, *Main currents*, pp. 121–2.
8. See Julia Wishnevsky, 'The fortieth anniversary of the "Zhdanov Decree"', Radio Liberty Research, RL 301/86, 11 August 1986.
9. Quoted by McCagg, *Stalin embattled*, p. 76.
10. See George L. Mosse (ed.), *Nazi culture. Intellectual, cultural, and social life in the Third Reich* (New York: Grosset & Dunlap, 1966).
11. See Aleksandr Zinoviev, *Le héros de notre jeunesse*, p. 122.
12. See Hannah Arendt, *The origins of totalitarianism*, particularly her discussion of the relation between power and ideology.
13. See Bernard-Henri Lévy, *Barbarism with a human face* (New York: Harper & Row, 1979), p. 137.
14. *Marx-Engels reader*, p. 65.
15. See Teresa Toranska, *Oni. Des Staliniens polonais s'expliquent* (Paris: Flamarion, 1986), especially the in-depth interview with former propaganda chief and Stalin's main agent in Poland, Jakub Berman, pp. 198–344.
16. See Paul E. Zinner (ed.), *National communism and popular revolt in Eastern Europe*. A selection of documents on events in Poland and Hungary, February–November 1956 (New York: Columbia University Press, 1956), pp. 48–9.
17. Ibid., pp. 49–54.
18. Kolakowski, *Main currents*, p. 135.
19. See Ferenc Fehér and Agnes Heller, *Eastern left, Western left* (Atlantic Highlands: Humanities Press International, 1986), p. 266.
20. For Lyssenko's spectacular career under Stalin and Khrushchev, see Zhores Medvedev, *The rise and fall of T. D. Lyssenko* (New York: Columbia University Press, 1969); for recent Soviet reassessments of the

anti-scientific drive of mature Stalinism, see Vera Tolz, 'Khrushchev's son-in-law writes about Soviet science under Stalin', Radio Liberty Research, RL 228/86, 11 June 1986, pp. 1–7.

21. Quoted by Nikolay Valentinov (Volsky), *Encounters with Lenin* (London: Oxford University Press, 1968), pp. 85–6.

22. See Seweryn Bialer, *Stalin's successors* (New York, Cambridge: Cambridge University Press, 1980), p. 10; for a classical analysis of Stalinism, see Carl J. Friedrich and Zbigniew Brzezinski, *Totalitarian dictatorship and autocracy* (New York: Praeger, 1961).

23. See Vladimir Tismaneanu, 'Miron Constantinescu or the impossible heresy', *Survey*, vol. 28, no. 4, Winter 1984, pp. 175–87.

24. For Stalinism in Hungary, see Charles Gati, *Hungary and the Soviet bloc* (Durham: Duke University Press, 1986); as general sources, see Brzezinski, *The Soviet bloc* and Ivan Volgyes, *Politics in Eastern Europe* (Chicago: Dorsey Press, 1986).

25. With regard to Romania, see Ghita Ionescu, *Communism in Romania* (London: Oxford University Press, 1964); Michael Shafir, *Romania* (Boulder: Lynne Rienner, 1985); Vladimir Tismaneanu, 'Ceausescu's socialism', *Problems of communism*, January–February 1985, pp. 50–66.

26. Quoted by Edward Taborsky, *Communism in Czechoslovakia* (Princeton: Princeton University Press, 1961), p. 140.

27. See Viktor Zaslavsky, *The neo-Stalinist state* (Armon, N.Y.: M. E. Sharpe, 1982), p. 4.

28. See Czeslaw Milosz, *The captive mind*, p. 220. A perceptive analysis of the identification of estranged Western intellectuals with left-wing totalitarianism is provided by Paul Hollander, *Political pilgrims* (New York: Oxford University Press, 1982).

29. See Fehér and Heller, *Eastern left, Western left*, p. 266.

30. See Kolakowski, *Main currents*, pp. 144–5.

3

The Decay of Stalinism

'No,' said the priest, 'it is not necessary to accept everything as true, one must only accept it as necessary.' 'A melancholy conclusion,' said K. 'It turns lying into a universal principle.'

Franz Kafka — *Before the law*

In spite of its presumptuous arrogance, Stalinism was beset by insuperable contradictions. Certainly, it was paranoid, exclusive, hypersuspicious, in short the apotheosis of abscurantism. Its main problem, however, was the cancerous personalisation of authority and, taking into account Stalin's psychology, the increasingly frightening role of the political police. Stalin's henchmen were themselves paralysed with fear and stampeded at any whim of the dictator, failing to fathom his shockingly arcane decisions.

The system could not work in the long run against the apparatus. Some outrageous features of extreme Stalinism were to be jettisoned after the corypheus' demise, but certainly not its main content, the power monopoly of the communist party. In his sullen, uninspiring way, Leonid Brezhnev offered a perfect illustration of the Stalinist mind: 'We have a party, a governing party. What do we want an opposition for? People are always talking about freedom. What does it mean?'[1]

Glorious as they were for the *nomenklatura*, Stalin's times were also years of anguish and confusions, of an excruciating scare. During the great purge, but particularly after 1949, no one felt secure in Stalin's entourage and the members of the ruling gang — as Khrushchev later admitted — were uncertain about their own chances of survival. In Stalin's eyes everyone was a potential traitor and it hinged on him, and him alone, to decide over the life and death of his underlings. Everyone risked falling entrapped in Stalin's intrigues. As if possessed by resentment for the whole of mankind, the senile dictator was drawing wolves in his secluded *datcha* in Kuntsevo, indulging in phantasms of forthcoming vendettas, new bloody purges and ultimate repression. He viscerally despised the lackeys surrounding him in the Politburo: where were the flamboyant Trotsky, the hysterical Zinoviev, the soft-spoken Kamenev, the sharp-tongued Radek, and especially where was Bukharchik, Nikolay Ivanovich Bukharin, whom Lenin had once called the favourite child of the whole party? Stalin was now forced to domesticate toothless 'kittens', lamentable, nauseating Liliputians.

Stalin's last days must have been terribly sad and infinitely melancholy. The sombre romance of factional struggles was over, Tito had been excommunicated, the Zionist conspiracy exposed, but he was still anxiously contemplating the future. His heirs lacked any stamina. They were spineless executants who could not think in world historical terms. Devoid of his guidance, they would certainly undo the magnificent totalitarian edifice. Stalin's speech to the Nineteenth Congress in October 1952 was a hopeless outcry, the dictator's fearful theoretical and political testament. This caveat was shrouded in the jargon of 'progressivism', but Stalin's misgivings about his successors could be hinted from the organisational transformation of the party leadership. The Stalinist barons, people like Georgiy Malenkov, Vyacheslav Molotov, Nikita Khrushchev, Kliment Voroshilov, Lavrentiy Beria, Anastas Mikoyan, or Lazar Kaganovich, were joined in the highest echelon by representatives of the 'third Bolshevik generation', ready to fulfil the exterminating tasks assigned to them by the 'boss'. Suslov, Brezhnev, Patolichev, Ignatiev, Pervukhin, Shepilov, to mention only some of the stalwarts of the new power elite, were encouraged to topple the old clique.

In his final weeks, in a final murderous convulsion, Stalin strove to engineer new show trials, more inflaming, more 'pedagogical', more far-reaching than all the previous ones. The 'doctor's plot', unmasked thanks to comrade Stalin's watchfulness, was to become his swan song. He died too early and most of the 'traitors' outlived him unpunished. From his mausoleum glass coffin, however, the 'old commandant' was still supervising events in the Kremlin, still pulling the strings, mobilising one faction against the other, overshadowing the pigmies who pretended to be better Leninists than he had been. The greatest genius of mankind, the fourth sword of

Marxism, could not rest in peace. Nothing was to happen in the Leninist party, and for that matter within world communism, without reference to what Soviet writer Konstantin Simonov once called the 'accursed question' of Stalin and Stalinism.

Lavrentiy Beria, the former chief policeman, would be executed, Malenkov demoted, Khrushchev risen to heaven, lionised, then ousted, and so on, but Stalin's question would go on haunting the communist memory and imagination. There would be no exaggeration in saying that true communists were only those who refused to acquiesce in Nikita Khrushchev's devastating anti-Stalin campaign. To be sure, it was Khrushchev himself who once put it quite bluntly; according to him, Stalin had been first and foremost a Marxist-Leninist, and his 'errors' — the communist euphemism for crimes — had been perpetrated in good faith. A committed Marxist-Leninist he had been indeed, and it was a matter of scandalous ingratitude on the part of his heirs to confiscate the glorious titles they had so lavishly bestowed on him while alive and all-powerful.

Demonising Stalin and exonerating Lenin is a cheap device. Stalin was not only a true Leninist, but also a legitimate inheritor of a certain authoritarian trend in the Marxist revolutionary movement. Cornelius Castoriadis is right in pointing to other avenues stemming from the Marxist project, but this does not contradict the affinity between the Bolshevik radicalism and Marx's dream of total revolution.[2] No matter that Stalin was an illiterate in terms of Marxist philosophical culture. Everybody in the Bolshevik party could have underwritten David Riazanov's pungent remark about Koba's (Stalin's party nickname) more than problematic relation to revolutionary theory. He nevertheless understood the Marxist concept of political power, the implications of political struggle first within the revolutionary movement, later in the first socialist state, and eventually on a global scale. It is primarily thanks to Lenin and to Stalin, his faithful disciple, that Marx is now more than another chapter in the history of Western social utopias.

Even more than Lenin's, Stalin's was a sacred name for successive communist generations whose political coming of age was fulfilled in deep veneration for the fatherly figure in the Kremlin. In other words, he superseded not only God, but also traditional, ancient human links. Belonging to the Stalinist fraternity was for millions of communists the most uplifting experience. Thus, the erosion of critical intelligence was gradually and successfully achieved. People like Nikolay Rubashov, the hero of Koestler's *Darkness at noon*, was still able to grasp the sense of traditional ethics. Like Bukharin, Radek, or Pyatakov, he had been a witness of the beginnings, therefore he was not emblematic for the Stalinist militant faith. Members of the Leninist promotion, those who were propelled to the highest rungs of the ladder after Lenin's death in January 1924, belonged to the new category of followers spellbound by Stalin's myth. When executed as despicable agents, instead of cursing, they were blessing the name of their assassin. Such a God could not die off easily.

Stalin's cult, with its Byzantine-orthodox undertones, was readily embraced by legions all over the world. He was celebrated with religious fervour, his works were arduously revered, his life was depicted in hagiographic colours. An instrument to acquire and conserve legitimacy, the cult was also a religious ersatz, a stimulant for unavowable mystical propensities, the elating opportunity to fill in the painful spiritual vacuum — the mystical *Armut des geistes* (poverty of spirit) — many intellectuals experienced after their break with traditional religions. Secular salvation requires its own eschatology and Stalinism functioned as the mental balsam bound to placate doubts and foster definitive convictions. To quote the title of Nikolay Ostrovskiy's famous socialist realist novel, *Thus steel was tempered* . . .

Many of these intellectuals could later overcome this neurotic identification; others would be continuously tormented and look for new substitutes. The case of French Marxist philosopher Roger Garaudy is symptomatic in this respect. He could never go beyond a superficial, and sometimes sentimental, denunciation of Stalinism and eventually failed to discover a better ideological platform than Kaddhafi's 'revolutionary Islamism'.[3] An opposite case was Ernst Fischer, an Austrian Stalinist doctrinaire, who broke with the Soviet orthodoxy and became an advocate of Marxist revisionism.[4]

In Stalin's cult therefore culminated not only a self-styled version of Great Russian nationalism allied with vulgar-positivistic Marxism but also an irrepressible human need for communion and cosmic unification. Stalin's liturgical Marxism, with its rudimentary teleology, was arduously espoused by people who would have sworn otherwise that dialectical materialism was the opposite of any fanaticism. One example should suffice to suggest the level of sycophancy practised by Stalinist scribes:

Comrade Stalin, the great master of the sciences, has given a systematic exposition of the foundations of dialectical and historical materialism as the theoretical basis of Communism, in a study unsurpassed for its depth, clarity and vigour. The theoretical works of Comrade Stalin were admirably described by the Central Committee of the All-Union Communist Party (Bolsheviks) and the Council of Ministers of the USSR in an address to Comrade Stalin on his seventieth birthday: 'Great leader of science! Your classic works developing the theory of Marxism-Leninism in relation to the new age of imperialism, proletarian revolution and socialist victory in our country are a tremendous achievement of humanity, an encyclopedia of revolutionary Marxism. From these works Soviet men and women and leading representatives of the working people of all countries derive knowledge and confidence and new strength in the battle for the victory of the cause of the working class, finding in them answers to the most burning problems of the contemporary struggle for Communism.' Comrade Stalin's brilliant philosophical work on *Dialectical and historical materialism* is a powerful means of knowledge and revolutionary transformation of the world and an irresistible ideological weapon against the enemies of materialism and the decaying ideology and culture of the capitalist world, doomed to inevitable overthrow.[5]

All the clichés characteristic of the Stalinist wooden language can be easily recognised in this psalmodic recitation of the General Secretary's theoretical achievements.

Lenin's authority within the Bolshevik elite was undisputed. Stalin's coming to power had, on the contrary, been thorny, tortuous, utterly dangerous. The more power he acquired, the more compelled he felt to deny any legitimacy to his adversaries. According to the carefully manufactured myth, Stalin was right from the very outset; Trotsky had been wrong *ab initio*, too.

It was nonsensical in communist circles under Stalin even to think Trotsky could have been right at least on some minor issues. Communist faith is one and indivisible. One crack and the whole castle could crumble. No wonder therefore that Khrushchev's attack on Stalin infuriated hardened Stalinist militants. A personage like the French Communist leader Maurice Thorez owed his whole career to Stalin and had come to identify himself, emotionally and intellectually, with the Soviet dictator. In this respect he was emblematic of the whole Cominternist elite, and his reticence to follow in Khrushchev's footsteps was shared not only by the unreconstructed Albanian Stalinist leader Enver Hoxha, but also by other exponents of the international communist aristocracy.[6] There were of course many leaders who later admitted they had not known about the extent of Stalinist atrocities, and others who confessed that though they had known, they preferred to keep silent to defend the sacred cause. According to a reliable source, Ana Pauker, the Romanian communist leader who had been expelled from the top hierarchy during the rabid anti-'cosmopolite' campaign in 1952, read Khrushchev's 'Secret' speech in 1956 and had one comment: 'Nothing is false in this document, except things were far worse . . .' It seems to be the rule that communists discover reality — if they ever do — only when stripped of power. Even Jeanette Thorez-Vermeersch, Maurice Thorez's widow and a life-long Stalinist, complained about the lack of democracy in the party leadership after she was forced out of the Politburo in 1968.

The social function of ideology has remained the same even after Stalin's death. It is still a cardinal principle of justification for the power monopoly exerted by the ruling caste and a method of moral anaesthetisation of the population. Like in Stalin's times, political socialisation in Soviet-type regimes is unthinkable in the absence of the ideological factor. Ideology has to cement the social fabric, to instil a sense of commitment to the main values professed by the system. The fact that these values are conspicuously overruled in the day-to-day behaviour of the *nomenklatura* does not alter the nature of the official ritualistic monologue.

Soviet Marxism — and its reverberations in the other oligarchic-collectivistic societies — is the incarnation of the intellectual pretence of the ruling elite. This social stratum cannot do without ideology and desperately clings to it. As Wolfgang Leonhard rightly emphasises, moral idealism has long since vanished from Soviet society, primarily as a result of the obvious discrepancy between the claims of the ideology and the reality of Soviet life: 'The fact that Marxism-Leninism is an obligatory subject in all Soviet institutions of higher education (440 hours of lectures and seminars are devoted to it) did not stop the erosion of ideology; it actually contributed to it.'[7]

In the *German ideology*, Marx and Engels maintained that the dominant ideas in a given society are the ideas of the dominant class. In accordance with this thesis, it follows that the ruling ideology in Soviet-type regimes is the ideology of the bureaucratic caste, the system of beliefs, mental habits, myths, representations, and values bound to warrant the dictatorship of the *nomenklatura*. Needless to say, it is a mystified reflection of reality and the Marxist category of false consciousness suggests the misleading nature of this ideology. The party bureaucrats are viscerally inimical to truth and the role ascribed to ideology is to obfuscate, to cover and to disguise reality. Ideology furnishes the masks needed for the perpetuation of the historical travesty called Soviet-type socialism. Totalitarian regimes cannot survive but in the form of the ideological state, a point made clear by Heinrich Himmler when he announced the advent of the *Weltanschauunsgstaat*, the worldview state.

In his *History and class consciousness*, young Lukács strove to demonstrate that proletarian class consciousness, as configured in Marxist philosophy, is tendentially coincident with historical truth as such. In other words, it was in the systematic version of the proletarian class consciousness, i.e. in the radical Marxist *Weltanschauung*, that historical reason acquired its ultimate verification and confirmation. It was in the party doctrine, Lukács maintained, in the Bolshevik ideology, that class self-understanding and societal self-comprehension would become identical.[8] The much celebrated perspective of totality, Lukács's seminal point in his early dialectical disquisitions, amounts therefore to bowing to the collective wisdom of the party, as crystallised in the works of the General Secretary. In Thomas Mann's *Magic mountain*, the ex-Jesuit Naphta, whose ideas strangely echo young Lukács's messianic radicalism, indicates the rationale for this revolutionary mysticism:

> The world proletariat . . . is today asserting the ideals of *Civitas Dei* in opposition to the discredited and decadent standards of the capitalist bourgeoisie. The dictatorship of the proletariat, the politico-economic means of salvation demanded by our age, does not mean domination for its own sake and in perpetuity; but rather in the sense of a temporary abrogation, in the sign of the Cross, of the contradiction between spirit and force; in the sense of overcoming the world by mastering it; in a transcendental, a traditional sense, in the sense of the Kingdom. The proletariat has taken up the task of Gregory the Great, his religious zeal burns within it, and as little as he, may it withhold its hand from the shedding of blood. Its task is to strike terror into the world for the healing

of the world, that man may finally achieve salvation and deliverance, and win back at length to freedom from law and from distinction of classes, to his original status as child of God.[9]

It would be difficult to better formulate the meaning of the Marxist chiliasm and the purpose of the Leninist revolutionary crusade. Regardless of Lukács's conscious objectives, his youthful master-piece had paved the way for future perversions of the mind.

It was not only Lukács, but also Antonio Gramsci, the Italian communist doctrinaire, who facilitated, by omission or commis-sion, Stalin's task and the fateful degradation of Marxist philosophy. For Gramsci, as for Lukács, the 'collective intellec-tual', in other words the communist party, incarnated historical rationality, critical consciousness, and radical willingness. It was therefore perfectly logical, and even necessary, for 'advanced' members of the intelligentsia to turn into 'organic intellectuals of the proletariat'.[10]

In Soviet-type regimes, ideology is the main underpinning of political power. Virtual and actual terror have to be ideologically motivated. Irrespective of its credibility, ideology has to be pre-served, a self-congratulatory expression of the ruling class's vanity, a shield against any form of scepticism or malaise. Under Stalin, ideology was enrapturing, mobilising, enthralling. Its alienated nature was hard to directly grasp. It managed to per-meate the very cells, the most intimate fibres of the social fabric. An alien power, to be sure, but nonetheless a comforting, reassur-ing, strengthening one. One could easily write an essay about ideological fallacies and abortive dreams of redemption in this century.

Instead of clarifying the substratum of social reality, Marxism turned into Soviet ideology further occulted it. Ideology managed to devour reality in the name of an all-embracing project of univer-sal happiness. Under Stalin, political reason and moral unreason were unified in the name of an instrumental definition of truth. In their masterful history of the Soviet Union, Mikhail Heller and Aleksandr Nekrich explain the rise of totalitarianism through the ideological imperatives contained in the Leninist utopian blue-print. The idea of an apocalyptic cleavage in history, the Marxist promise of a 'leap from the realm of necessity into that of freedom', are perennial obsessions for the Soviet political mind. Lenin's radical Jacobinism was followed by Stalin's totalitarian pedagogy. Ideology, hackneyed as it may appear to sophisticated Western experts, remains the sole symbolic support of the *status quo*, a sacred table no leader would dare to defy. Ideology cannot be simply annulled because it represents the only well-tested means of socialisation in the Soviet system:

> Ideology has a most important function in the Soviet system. Just like the stern father of a lazy and disobedient child, ideology teaches Soviet citizens how to understand events in the world around them, how to behave, how to relate to their families, neighbours, and strangers.[11]

The Marxists have failed to come to terms with this embarrassing situation. They have missed, even in the most refined investigations, the specificity of the Soviet regime, which is like none other precisely because of the pre-eminence of ideology. This was pointed out by Raymond Aron who showed that it was the ideological intentionality that explained the original nature of totalitarianism.[12] Drawing the necessary conclusions from this fact, Alain Besançon agrees with Solzhenitsyn who, in the *Gulag archipelago*, called the Soviet system an ideological regime.[13] Even Louis Althusser could not advance more than philological notes on the concept of Stalinism without weighing the mortal effects of ideology over the body politic as a totality.

The undermining of radical praxis through ideological manipulation was acknowledged by heretical Marxists like Cornelius Castoriadis, Claude Lefort, Edgar Morin, by the members of the Frankfurt School (at least by Adorno and Horkheimer), but was obstinately denied by official Marxism. Soviet ideology sticks to the rusty orthodoxy and Leninism is regarded as the only scientific theory of revolution. Boris Ponomariov, who was for decades the main Soviet expert on international communism, pointed to what he defined as the organic unity between Marxism and Leninism:

> Lenin's teaching is indissolubly linked with the 'origins', and the ideals left by the founders of Marxism. The new elements that Lenin introduced into Marxism, far from constituting a 'break' with Marx's ideas, are their further creative development, their creative application in the process of comprehending and generalizing new historical experience. Leninism is a direct extension and continuation of Marxism. It is the Marxism of the modern era that is transforming the world

and itself developing continually through generalization of the revolutionary experience gained to date.[14]

The fate of Marxism in Soviet-type societies was determined by the institutionalisation of ideology following its proclamation as a state doctrine. After that transfiguration, ideological heresy amounted to sedition. Ideas were supportive of, or hostile to the proletarian state: *tertium non datur*.

Science may elvolve in Soviet regimes. Social sciences, however, have to be simple mirrors of the party statements. Their margin of autonomy is precarious and their conclusions have to be dovetailed to fit the prevailing dogmas. The leaders' boundless narcissism requires their ceaseless glorification as visionary helmsmen. The social structure is not to be analysed with the methods of empirical research, but through rumination of the party documents. It is thus that the problems of social stratification, of the privilege-gap and the symptoms of political crisis are conspicuously absent from the published findings of official sociology in Eastern Europe. Certainly, the existence of contradictions is admitted, but they are not antagonistic. Even assuming they could become antagonistic — which is already an indication of unorthodox thought — the conscious factor, i.e. the communist party, is always present to solve them in due time. The bureaucratic jargon with its indigestible ready-made recipes precludes any understanding of ongoing social tensions and processes. Kolakowski's unequivocal conclusion is therefore legitimate: 'The official philosophy and social theory are merely the self-praising rhetoric of the privileged Soviet ruling class.'[15]

Intolerance of divergent views has remained a pivotal characteristic of Soviet Marxism. Mikhail Gorbachev's pathetic calls for *glasnost* (openness, frankness, transparence) notwithstanding, it seems clear that the ideology is petrified and cannot be drastically overhauled without provoking dismantlement of the hegemonic institutions. Attacks on revisionism have thus remained a permanent strand of Soviet (and East European) ideological life. Combating any rival interpretations of Marxism is regarded as a permanent duty: 'Thus the term "Western Marxism" is basically not geographical, but frankly ideological,' Doctor of Philosophical Sciences Professor I. Naletov informs us in the pages of *Pravda*.

It is not hard to grasp that a superficial mastery of the logic of Marxism-Leninism inevitably leads to dogmatic interpreta-

tions of it. In turn, dogmatism in the interpretation of particular propositions itself nourishes the revisions of Marxism.
Whether or not the 'Western Marxists' are aware of this fact,
it is clear that the disintegration or the 'pluralization' of
Marxism weakens its positions in the present-day ideological
struggle and is widely exploited by bourgeois ideologists in
their subversive actions against the socialist countries and the
international communist and workers movement.[16]

The autogenic constitution of Soviet ideology is stupefying:
hollow ideas nourish hollow ideas, sterile concepts miraculously
beget other sterile notions. Under Brezhnev, it was fashionable to
speak of developed socialism. Later, Andropov introduced some
correctives in this theory, and Gorbachev came with the concepts
of *glasnost* and *perestroyka* (restructuring). It does not take much perspicacity to see that these are actually cosmetic changes and the
Soviet ideology has remained unaffected by the chain of succes-
sions in the Kremlin. Viktor Afanasiev, the already-quoted editor
of *Pravda*, criticised the sluggishness of the Brezhnev era — euphe-
mistically depicted as 'a harmful evolution' — and indicated, in
the traditional subservient manner, the 'originality' of
Gorbachev's approach:

> The concept of developed socialism became divorced, as it
> were, from the realities of our life. It hovered above those
> realities. There started a game of definitions, various kinds of
> scholastic argument, and so on and so forth. A new concept
> was needed: a concept based on the real state of affairs . . .
> And the party provided that concept: the strategic course of
> acceleration of the country's social and economic develop-
> ment. That course was proclaimed at the April 1985 plenum
> of the CPSU Central Committee.[17]

Needless to add, Afanasiev had been one of the leading ideologues
of the now blamed Brezhnev epoch and had decisively contributed
to the theoretical inertia of those years.
Soviet ideologues never run out of clichés. They are not
interested in the credibility of the message they convey since they
know that alternative views cannot reach a large audience because
of the actions of the repressive apparatus (censorship, jamming of
foreign broadcasting, social marginalisation, prison sentences and
deportation for vocal critics of the system). Co-operation between

the ideological bureaucracy and the police is one of the basic characteristics of Soviet-type societies: 'The language of the official ideology may serve to legitimize the activities of the regime. But it is not taken seriously by anyone — not by those who rule, not by those who are supposed to propagate the accepted ideology. As a consequence, pure repression is the only effective instrument available to those who wish to control the population.'[18] Hidebound as it certainly is, ideology is fertile in at least one respect: it is always ready to reproduce itself along the same unchanged parameters.

The cognitive value of *Diamat* (dialectical materialism), as Leszek Kolakowski, Karel Kosik, Svetozar Stojanović, Mihailo Marković, Henri Lefebvre, or the members of the Budapest School have shown, is for all practical purposes nil. Soviet ideologues nevertheless cling to it, simulating faith and forcing younger generations to acquire a deep resentment for anything redolent of social theory. Perpetual repetition of pseudo truth makes truth itself barely believable. Contradictions, almost an obsession for Marxist ideological viziers, have remained a matter of scholastic perusal. No doubt, there have been debates about the struggle between the old and the new in social life, but as a rule it is the party who decides the reality of a given contradiction and the methods to solve it. The monolithic image has to be safeguarded against real diversity. Following the Stalinist logic, everything has to be homogeneous, otherwise it has to be curtailed, dovetailed, reduced to elemental unity. The struggle of the opposites, acknowledged by Stalin and his disciples, meant the struggle for an amorphous, almost cadaveric unity. Class ideology has thus turned into self-justification for the domination exerted by a political coterie over the whole society. Under Stalin, apocryphal Marxism succeeded in smothering the original emancipatory promise of dialectics. What remained of Marxism after this devastating purification was a catechism made up of aseptic quotations, the ambiguous description of communism (borrowed from Marx's *Critique of the Gotha programme*) plus the Leninist debased epistemology. The entire Marxian legacy was abandoned and substituted through a lamentable vulgatum, the pinnacle of fatuous imposture.

There were some philosophers in the West who were well aware of this ultimate poverty of historicism. Karl R. Popper deciphered the origin of the Marxist authoritarian impulse in the secret structure of Platonism and Hegelianism. He dedicated his book on the pitfalls of social engineering and messianic historicism to the memory 'of the countless men and women of all creeds or nations or races who fell victims to the fascist and communist belief in Inexorable Laws of Historical Destiny'.[19] Maurice Merleau-Ponty regarded the misadventures of dialectics in this century as emblematic for the fate of a philosophy aiming to become world-wide, to unify immanence and transcendence in the frenzy of 'revolutionary praxis'.[20] In the United States, Sidney Hook consistently exposed the colossal intellectual abuse perpetrated by Stalinism.[21] Such warnings were however glossed over, and the crowd of zealots pursued their path *ad majorem Stalini gloriam*, for the eternal glory of the Kremlin generalissimo. The dissection of faith, of blind utopianism, was masterfully undertaken by Melvin J. Lasky in his *Utopia and revolution*, a book written in the spirit of Albert Camus for whom 'Tout révolutionnaire finit en opresseur ou en hérétique'. ('every revolutionary ends up either as an oppressor or as a heretic').[22]

Millenial expectations, deep-seated frustrations and resentments, the voluptuosity of immediate action, immersion in the transindividual community, all these were compelling driving forces in the constitution of adamant communist beliefs. No one has better expressed the intellectual and emotional infrastructure of communism than Leszek Kolakowski, for whom this ideology, the substratum of an entire cultural formation, appeared and evolved as a secular alternative to the religious yearning for an absolute, the tormenting need for redemption:

> This need, one can assume, is part and parcel of all civilizations, but its existence does not explain why, at certain times and in certain places, it emerges in the form of intense historical convulsions, engulfing enormous numbers of human beings and leading to unexpected and violent upheavals which turn existing orders upside down. Communism is an example of such a convulsion, which grew out of the desperate need for ultimate salvation and a new epoch.[23]

The real *aficionados* of communism were immune to criticism and reluctant to take into account the most glaring evidence precisely because they were captive to the ideological straitjacket, engulfed in that poisonous quagmire mentioned by Arthur Koestler in his autobiography. They could be indignant about any iniquity carried out by the so-called class system, but had no eyes to see the emergence and the rigidification of the most abhorrent dictatorship precisely in the name of the fight against class antagonisms.

The Hegelian-Marxist search for total negativity, a passionate longing described by Max Horkheimer as *die Sehnsucht nach dem Ganz Anderen* (the longing for something totally different), was surreptitiously converted into a ruthless experiment in social engineering. Initial ideals were irrevocably desecrated as a result of this operation. In other words, after Stalin the very ideal of communism looked decisively tarnished. It had been tainted with the innocent blood of millions of victims, it had been disfigured and, for all intents and purposes, turned into its opposite.

It seemed clear that a thoroughgoing critique should go beyond moralistic denunciation of the horrors of the Stalinist epoch. What was required consisted of a soul-searching operation to be accomplished by those who had been spellbound by dialectical fireworks. It was tremendously important to rediscover the incendiary power of such concepts as reification, bureaucracy, spontaneity, radicalism; to inject a new force and a new meaning into them. What mattered for the rebellious intellectuals was to hasten the implosion of the ruling ideology. The ideological masquerade was to be exposed in its obscene nudity and the premiss for this was the regeneration of the long since abandoned humanist programme.

Critical intellectuals in East-Central Europe were intent upon imposing the resurgence of the other Marx. What they aimed at was to make use of Marx against Marxism, to rescue the dialectic from the dogmatic chains defended by mummified bureaucrats. Times were ripe for rebellion and critical intellectuals were aware of this situation. The burden of Stalinism had to be weighed before it was thrown into the dustbin of historical anomalies.

Those were also times propitious for inordinate illusions, for the resurrection of electrifying pipedreams. It seemed that a new birth was possible for the values of freedom and justice and East European intellectuals embarked on this fight with all their hopes and resources of confidence. In his *Poem for adults*, Adam Wazyk, the Polish writer, gave vent to this excitement provoked by the rediscovery of truth:

> We make demands on this earth,
> for the people who are overworked,
> for keys to open doors,
> for rooms with windows,

for walls which do not rot,
for hatred of little documents,
for holy human time,
for safe homecoming,
for a simple distinction between words and deeds.
We make demands on this earth,
for which we did not throw dice,
for which a million perished in battle:
for a clear truth,
for the bread of freedom,
for burning reason,
for burning reason.

We demand these every day.
We demand through the party.[24]

Notes

1. Quoted by Mikhail Voslensky, *Nomenklatura* (Garden City: Doubleday, 1984), p. 243. See Voslensky's discussion of the dictatorship of the *nomenklatura*, pp. 243–318.

2. See Cornelius Castoriadis, *Crossroads in the labyrinth* (Cambridge, Mass.: MIT Press, 1984); *Domaines de l'homme* (Paris: Seuil, 1985).

3. See Roger Garaudy, *Crisis in communism* (New York: Grove Press, 1970); *Marxism in the twentieth century* (New York: Scribners, 1970); for the evolution of French Marxism, see Michael Kelly, *Modern French Marxism* (Baltimore: Johns Hopkins University Press, 1982).

4. See Ernst Fischer, *An opposing man* (London: Allen Lane, 1974).

5. V. M. Pozner, *J. V. Stalin on the basic features of Marxist philosophical materialism* (1950), quoted by L. Kolakowski, *Main currents of Marxism*, pp. 147–8.

6. See Philippe Robrieux, *Maurice Thorez. Vie secrète, vie publique* (Paris: Fayard, 1975).

7. See Wolfgang Leonhard, *The Kremlin and the West* (New York: Norton, 1986), p. 57.

8. See Andrew Arato and Paul Breines, *The young Lukács and the origins of Western Marxism* (New York: Seabury Press, 1979); Istvan Deak, 'The Convert', *New York Review of Books*, 12 March 1987.

9. See Thomas Mann, *The magic mountain* (New York: Vintage Books, 1969), p. 404.

10. For a critical account of these disturbing issues, see Walter L. Adamson, *Marx and the disillusionment of Marxism* (Berkeley: University of California Press, 1985).

11. See Mikhail Heller and Aleksandr Nekrich, *Utopia in power: the history of the Soviet Union from 1917 to the present* (New York: Summit Books, 1986), p. 657.

12. See Raymond Aron, *Démocratie et totalitarisme* (Paris: Gallimard, 1965), p. 291.

13. See Alain Besançon, *Présent soviétique et passé russe* (Paris: Hachette/ Pluriel, 1986), p. 147.

14. See B. N. Ponomarev, *Marxism-Leninism in today's world* (Oxford and New York: Pergamon Press, 1983), p. 147.

15. Kolakowski, *Main currents*, p. 151.

16. I. Naletov, 'From a single piece of steel: on some attempts to revise Marxism', *Pravda*, 5 September 1986.

17. 'Pravda chief editor discusses domestic issues', FBIS, Soviet Union, 16 June 1986, p. R10.

18. Leszek Kolakowski in discussion with Stanislaw Baranczak, *Salmagundi*, no. 70–1, Spring–Summer 1986, p. 229.

19. See Karl R. Popper, *Poverty of historicism*.

20. See Maurice Merleau-Ponty, *Les aventures de la dialectique* (Paris: Gallimard, 1955).

21. See Sidney Hook, *Revolution, reform, and social justice. Studies in the theory and practice of Marxism* (Oxford: Basil Blackwell, 1976).

22. See Melvin J. Lasky, *Utopia and revolution*, p. IX.

23. See Leszek Kolakowski, 'Communism as a cultural formation', *Survey*, Summer 1985, vol. 29, no. 2, p. 147.

24. See Paul E. Zinner (ed.), *National communism*, p. 48.

4

The Search for Renewal

We have put an end to this system, or we are putting an end to it once and for all. Great appreciation should be expressed to the 20th Congress of the CPSU which so greatly helped us in the liquidation of this system.

Wladyslaw Gomulka

To understand the disarray of the ruling circles in Eastern Europe in the years following Stalin's demise, it is appropriate to point out the crucial meaning of the Soviet Communist party's Twentieth Congress in February 1956. It was perhaps the most traumatic event in the history of world communism since Trotsky's defeat by Stalin in the 1920s. The confusion of the Soviet bureaucratic oligarchy was limitless: they had abhorred Stalin's overbearing, whimsical despotism, but at the same time they were not prepared for (or interested in) genuine de-Stalinisation. To be sure, the Soviet hegemonic team was less homogeneous than one would have imagined and it was precisely this factionalism that allowed for the Khrushchevite iconoclastic approach. It is now a documented fact that First Secretary Nikita Khrushchev encountered strong opposition to his initiative of disclosing some of the worst crimes perpetrated against Soviet party and government cadres. Stalin's former acolytes perceived Khrushchev's onslaught on the late dictator's memory as an attempt to topple their pre-eminence in the party. Molotov, Kaganovich, Malenkov, Voroshilov and Bulganin justifiably suspected Khrushchev of harbouring the plan to carry out a fundamental elite turnover. A new image was required for the party leadership, a new language of power had to be discovered, that would favour the emergence of a self-styled social consensus in the Soviet Union. In other words, it was urgent to create mobilisational techniques based on confidence rather than on terror.

Previous ideological axioms were reassessed. As a result of the breathing space created by the Twentieth Congress, it seemed that all established dogmas could be openly questioned. The ethical paralysis of late Stalinism was replaced by a kind of perpetual moral anguish, a feverish quest for those basic principles that would supposedly warrant genuine communist commitment. With its earth-shattering denunciation of the Stalinist cult, with the blunt, though partial, exposure of the repression against the party apparatus, Khrushchev's *Secret Speech* paved the way for the resurrection of heretical tendencies stifled during the heyday of Stalinism.[1] Furthermore, this dynamite-like text seemed to vindicate Tito's anti-Stalinist stances. Willingly or unwillingly, it made *tabula rasa* out of the whole mythological superstructure of the Stalinist system. The logical consequence of Khrushchevism, to be further elaborated by the doctrinaires of the 'return to Leninism', was the distinction between the early, presumably healthy, uncorrupted stage of the Soviet system, and the latter, Stalinist one, decisively marked by Stalin's morbid personality.

Anti-Stalinism could thereafter legitimately become the catchword of liberal factions within the ruling elites. It would be inaccurate to deny any significant divisions between leading communists. Overlooking these factious squabbles would result in failure to anticipate schisms and breaks so characteristic of the communist political culture. This does not imply, however, that such conflicts indicate the competition between different worldviews, rivalry between advocates of distinct political platforms, or any other form of pluralism. They are rather imputable to subjective factors, including personal ambition, opportunism, fear of change, etc. At least in the years that followed the Twentieth Congress, there were in the leading teams in Eastern Europe and the USSR tensions and splits with long-term implications for the future of those countries. It would be foolish, however, to deny that all those conflicts were eventually futile, that all those who had believed in the reformability of the system from within were terribly disillusioned with the Jesuitism of the ruling caste.

The issue of the disenchantment of the revisionist generation is a fascinating topic in itself. Those people have bitterly experienced the progress-reaction cycles in the history of Soviet-style regimes: the exhilaration of de-Stalinisation was to be followed by the grey, apparently endless winter of re-Stalinisation. The reaction against Stalinism was associated with the rehabilitation of the individual as both a political and philosophical category. East European anti-Stalinism was a subjectivistic, normativist, individualist rebellion against the tyranny of totality, the metastasis of the party-state power. It was a protest movement bound to rehabilitate the category of subjectivity against alienated ideas and mystified ideals. It dared to utter unorthodox interrogations about the legitimacy of communist dictatorship and reminded the party doctrinaires of the initial claims of Marxism as a philosophy of emancipation. The much-trumpeted partisanship invoked by official Marxism was exposed as a smokescreen, a shelter for the most depressing pragmatism.

It was the merit of the Yugoslav 'humanist socialist' School to have indicated the functionalist infrastructure of Stalinism.[2] Other philosophers associated with revisionism highlighted the underlying assumptions of Stalinism and its historical determinations. It was — and it still is — important to circumscribe the area of vested interests Stalinism strove to protect, to discriminate between moral and sociological interpretations. Zinoviev's anti-normativism, previously alluded to, is therefore warranted: if we limit ourselves to a mere denunciation of Stalinism, if we keep on blaming Stalin as the most vicious criminal of all times, we risk missing the central point, i.e. the social significance of both the man (Stalin) and the system associated with his name.

Breaking with the dogma

The constitution of revisionism as an alternative modality of thought in the communist countries was linked to the attempt to clarify the meaning of Stalinism. Trying to make sense of this issue means getting embroiled in a labyrinth of verities and counter-verities with direct political implications.

There are sociological and there are psychological explanations of the Stalinist regime: for Adam Ulam, Stalin incarnated the ultimate historical evil, while for Isaac Deutscher such a moral view would be *déplacé*: Stalin's cruelty was monstrous, to be sure, but it was the expression of an impersonal sociological necessity. Robert C. Tucker thinks that Lenin's work had been betrayed by Stalin, that there was no inexorable development leading from the founder of Bolshevism to the man who pretended to be his only true disciple:

. . . Leninism is not some monolithic doctrine. It is internally heterogeneous. There are different Leninisms. Stalin appealed to a Leninism that was . . . the worst from the humanistic point of view — all that was most brutal in the record of Lenin's impact on history. Others appealed to what was more humanistic in Lenin's legacy. I maintain that the historian must be aware of the plurality in Lenin and Leninism.[3]

Boris Souvarine, Arthur Koestler, George Orwell, or Manès Sperber were convinced that Stalin belonged to the Borgia family of spirits. In other words, they emphasised the pathology of Stalinism and linked it to the abnormal appetite for power of Lenin's successor. In their view, Stalin took advantage of the totalitarian features of the Soviet system: the militaristic organisation of party and society, the prevailing role of the secret police, the dissolution of the civil society, the ideological straitjacket imposed on culture, education, and science. These are structural characteristics of the system created by the Bolsheviks. In accordance with this interpretation, Milovan Djilas is convinced there was a necessary continuity from Lenin to Stalin:

One may accuse Stalin of many things, but not of betraying the power that Lenin constructed. Khrushchev did not understand that. He proclaimed Stalin's power a 'mistake', a retreat from Lenin and Leninism . . . Although some of the methods changed, Lenin's power continued in Stalin. And not only his power. But it was power that was essential. That power — somewhat altered — continues today.[4]

Was then Stalinism unavoidable, pre-ordained, deeply embedded in the Leninist project? Or was it, like many revisionist philosophers would maintain, a horrible deviation from the pristine Leninist doctrine? Was the 'revolution from above' a Thermidorean reaction of rather the fulfilment of the Bolshevik neo-Jacobin strategy? In other words, was Stalin the arch-traitor to Lenin's cause, as it has been maintained by people like Trotsky, Paul Levi, Ruth Fischer, or was he its most faithful advocate, as generations of Stalinists, from Molotov, Thalmann, and Thorez, to Enver Hoxha and Mao Zedong have incessantly proclaimed? Stalin's role in the history of Marxism is certainly no less important than that ascribed to Lenin, since a philosophy pretending to discover in *praxis* the highest criterion of truth must accept to be judged in accordance with its practical performance and consequences. We do not refer here to existentialism, phenomenology, neo-Thomism, or personalism: our concern is about a doctrine that vaunted practical effectiveness as its *differentia specifica*, its claim to originality, and whose historical avatars sealed the fate of millions in this century.

Many Western observers focus on the irrational nature of the Stalinist terror in the 1930s. But one might justifiably wonder whether the very act of the Bolshevik seizure of power in October 1917 was a logical one. Certainly, it was the only alternative to resignation with a peripheral political status, and the Bolsheviks gladly succumbed to the dictatorial temptation. The logic of survival, formulated by Lenin in his justification of the 'red terror' and of the suppression of the Kronstradt rebellion, was pushed to an extreme in Stalin's apparently insane practice. Within the Bolshevik mental framework, Stalin was both consistent and rigorous. We can thus conclude that Stalinism was not the betrayal or mutilation of Bolshevism, but its fulfilment, its logical outcome.

Trotsky may have bemoaned the bloody excesses against the opposition, but he never questioned the principle of a command economy and the legitimacy of the power monopoly exerted by the Bolshevik party. The opposition was blocked in the mental province of the party spirit. For the Trotskyites, as for Bukharin's followers, the party was the repository of truth. Trotsky used to say that history has not discovered a better vehicle to embody revolutionary truth. 'Right or wrong, it's my party', this moral — or pseudo-moral — axiom is indicative of Bolshevik delusions, of the readiness to indulge in self-debasement and endless humiliations only to strengthen the 'vehicle of truth'.

The Russianisation of Marxism, a process initiated by Lenin, culminated in Stalin's appropriation of the expansionist goals of the Russian empire. Marx, who had been intensely critical of the Russian imperial behaviour, would have been shocked faced with this czarist socialism.

Leszek Kolakowski's concise formulation is worth quoting: 'Stalinism came into being as a continuation of Leninism, based on the Russian tradition and a suitably adapted form of Marxism.'[5] Firstly, one has to grasp the specific Russian nature of Leninism. It certainly was a form of unabashed historical voluntarism, but of a different species than, say, the revolutionary syndicalism of Georges Sorel or Ervin Szabó. The long conspiratorial traditions of Russian social radicalism culminated in Lenin. Richard Pipes is therefore right in pointing to Lenin's *What is to be done* as a watershed in the history of Russian social-democracy. The Western-oriented gradualist approach, represented by people like Georgiy Plekhanov, the 'old man' of Russian social-democracy, and the Menshevik leaders Pavel Akselrod and Yuliy Martov, was challenged by Lenin's messianic activism:

> He dissociated himself from all those forces, the alliance with which in the preceding five years he had regarded as essential for the triumph of socialism: the labor movement; the liberals; even Plekhanov and the other patriarchs of the movement. He saw himself as the only genuine revolutionary — a leader with followers but no longer any allies. Around him were nothing but reactionaries, opportunists, traitors.[6]

Lenin's predecessors, intellectually, not only chronologically, were Chernyshevskiy and Tkachev, thinkers who had praised revolutionary asceticism and sectarian conspiracies. They belonged to a generation that scorned Western-oriented liberalism. Leninism, the only successful Russian version of Marxism, was inherently anti-Western and imbued with an almost religious sense of national predestination. It had borrowed from the Russian populist tradition the myth of the beleaguered radical fraternity and an exclusive elitism.[7]

The mental fortress of Bolshevism was therefore the most suitable environment where Stalin's passion for intrigues and conspiracy come to full blossoming. The soft-spoken Mensheviks were for him contemptible opportunists. Lenin alone was the 'eagle of the revolution', and the mind of the Georgian ex-student of a theological seminary was inflamed by the Bolshevik cult of willingness. For many Russian dissident intellectuals, this line of explanation represents an unacceptable extrapolation. Solzhenitsyn, for example, would not admit any Russian responsibility for Leninism, let alone for Stalinism.[8] The root of the evil would lie, in good Dostoyevskian tradition, in the corrupting influence of the West. Certainly, Solzhenitsyn is never that simplistic, but he is somewhat tempted to underrate the persistence of autocratic, anti-individualistic features in the Russian political culture. Lenin may have hated Dostoyevsky, but his successors have seemed fascinated by the theory of the God-carrying people as put forward by the author of the *Demons*. Providential nations need providential leaders, and Stalin was ready to obey history's (or God's) behest . . .

Stalin had to re-invent Marxism to turn it into the ideology of the Soviet empire. Leninism itself was not perfectly suited to such purposes: it was still too internationalist, too imbued with Western values and prejudices. In Zhdanov's anti-cosmopolite campaigns, references to Lenin, when they occurred, were only perfunctory. It was nevertheless Leninism that constituted the ground for further developments: the ethical values may have changed, but the technology of power was not basically different in the hands of the new ruling class.

The rise of revisionism

In the irresistible avalanche of attacks on Stalinism that followed the Twentieth Congress, intellectuals were to act as the real radical avant-garde. The tragic awareness of the basic injustice of the system led to an empirical discovery of their social calling. The revisionist generation was primarily interested in restoring what they still believed to be the humanist core of Marxist social philosophy. István Eörsi, a leading Hungarian oppositional writer, has recently tried to explain his motivation in joining the anti-Stalinist, revolutionary camp in 1956:

> First of all, I took part in these events as a true Communist, believing firmly that Rákosi and Stalin were traitors. I attended meetings outside the parliament building and listened to people. After the Russians came, I collaborated in illegally published newspapers and the like; finally, I became a liaison officer between the Writers' Revolutionary Committee and the Workers' Council in Budapest.[9]

This is an emblematic itinerary for intellectuals who had once invested in the romance of Marxist internationalism and were bitterly disappointed by Khrushchev's revelations. They felt they had been abused by Stalinist propaganda and returned to original Marxism to find an antidote to all forms of fanaticism.

It was the main role of disenchanted communists to elaborate programmes for democratic renewal in countries like Hungary and Poland. Far from being a destructive event, the disclosure of the real fulcrum of Stalinism, i.e. the exposure of the necessary relationship between dictatorial domination by the communist party and the bureaucratic degeneration of the revolutionary project, was actually the beginning of a new era in the history of Marxism. It was necessary therefore to proceed to a drastic reassessment of all Marxist postulates.

Times were asking for an unambiguous break with the morally suicidal idealism of pseudo-revolutionary romanticism. Rehabilitating the concept of socialism, believed revisionist Marxists, implied a restoration of human dignity and amounted therefore to a genuine axiological revolution, an *Umwertung aller Werte* (transvaluing all values). The logic of revisionism went beyond internal party squabbles:

> The appearance of revisionism in Communist countries was not simply a symptom of the dissatisfaction of intellectuals prevented by the Party from using their eyes and brains. It was indicative of wider discontents which the intellectuals, bound by the doctrinal framework, articulated in a more or less mystified form. It reflected not only the conflicts between the Party bureaucracy and the intelligentsia, between the *apparatchiki* and the intellectuals, but general social tensions and national unrest.[10]

Emancipation from the mental captivity was not possible without transcending the Stalinist ideological carcass. 'Stalin's ghost', to make use of Sartre's metaphor, was pertinacious and its overcoming was to take long years of intellectual guerrilla warfare. It involved tantalising doubts and excruciating self-denials, soul-searching interrogations for leftish intellectuals already disgusted with the prevailing orthodoxy. Initially, the ruling groups failed to grasp the scope and the sea-change implications of this intellectual upheaval. They treated the revolted intellectual like a pedagogue who would castigate a spoiled, but certainly gifted, child. Georg Lukács was allowed to surround himself with a group of promising young Marxist philosophers, all obsessed with sensitive historical topics and tormented by what they rightly perceived as a chasm between Marxist theory and socialist reality.

In East Germany, Ernst Bloch became the leading voice of Marxist dissent and Wolfgang Harich was his favourite disciple.[11] *Das Prinzip Hoffnung* — hope as a philosophical principle, the negative counterpart to the supremacy of integrative positivism — seemed destined to explode as a practical possibility within the tangible political realm.[12] Intellectual action seemed the only way to put an end to the widening gap between the alienated political values and the needs of the individual. Philosophical categories, as mentioned, were endowed with explosive force. The grim faces of the priests, to make use of Kolakowski's insightful metaphor, could not prevent the critical intellectuals, the jesters becoming the vital centre of the agora. The public space was rediscovered and the spurious uniformity of the Stalin epoch irremediably fell apart.

Old methods of intimidation could not work any more: intellectuals were convinced that the system could be humanised only by adamant opposition from within. This was the main assumption of revisionism: the conviction that the struggle opposed two camps with the same ultimate values. What mattered was to improve the system, not to overthrow it. It was therefore important to preserve channels of communication with the leading bureaucracy, to simulate certain affinities, to combat communist abuses making reference to the communist original promises. This ambivalence constituted both the strength and the weakness of revisionism. Its ambition was to formulate an alternative to the distortions of Leninism (or Marxism), not to re-think, to re-elaborate, social philosophy after almost one century of Marxist fallacies.

Raymond Aron's disquieting investigations into the mythological foundations of historical materialism were no more popular in East European revisionist circles than on the Left Bank in Paris. Marx was considered an ally, and even a most valuable one, not the target of the operation of demystification. Stalinism was regarded as a malignant outgrowth, a result of Russian backwardness, a tragic tribute paid to the victory of the revolution in a less developed country. Georg Lukács, Ernst Bloch, Italian neo-Gramscians, Polish, Hungarian, and Czech revisionists, Yugoslav philosophers of the Praxis group, all were united in the conviction that the fate of the revolution would have been essentially different had the German uprisings been successful in 1919 and the early 1920s. In other words, they firmly held the belief that Lenin's victory in Russia and the defeat of revolution in Western Europe had been a most portentous event. Furthermore, the devastating dogmatism of the Stalin era was attributed to Russian Byzantine-autocratic traditions rather than to Marxism as a theoretical foundation of the closed society. Instead of being questioned, historicism was extolled by humanist Marxists. The myth of progress and the dogma of the proletariat's special mission remained unaltered by the revisionist offensive.

85

This project was thus intrinsically utopian, since it was rooted in unfulfilled desires and quixotic expectations. No doubt, the chimera of the universal class, of the revolutionary happening supposed to bring about the millenium *hic et nunc*, had been calcined in the ordeal of Stalin's terror. However, revisionist intellectuals could not cut off the umbilical cord that linked them to the Marxist semantic matrix. For them, as for the young Lukács, Bolshevism was first and foremost a moral problem. Morality is certainly a significant issue at stake in the struggle against totalitarian domination, but it is overdetermined — as Louis Althusser would put it — by political values and actions. It was in the political field that Marxism went bankrupt and its ethical collapse was therefore inescapable. Attempting to restore the hidden (or betrayed) humanist dimension of Marxism turned out to be nothing but an additional illusion harboured by heretics in Soviet-style societies.

The rottenness of the system was detected in the kernel of its ideology. Getting rid of ideological blinkers required the courage to overcome Marxist hypnotic rationalisations. Transcending false consciousness entails exposing the instrumentalisation of consciousness on behalf of a politically, that is party-defined, truth. Human objectivity was opposed to the class perspective and party-mindedness was debunked as the substratum of ideological schizophrenia.

Knowledge, under any circumstances, is related to self-knowledge. Individual and social interests and needs decide over the nature, orientation, and dynamics of the cognitive process. Subject and object cannot be defined as eternal, immutable entities, value-free and indifferent to human action. Historically they shape each other, merge tendentially in the figures of politics, religion, morality, culture; in other words their interaction creates the sphere of history as the self-realisation of man. It was Stalin's goal to congeal both knowledge and action, to postulate ultimate truths meant to be taken for granted *sub specie aeternitatis*.

The revisionist onslaught questioned therefore not only the sphere of practical reason but also that of the *reinen Vernunft*, the theoretical realm. To acquire a dignified status the intellectuals have to define practical rules for the survival of the spirit. The Stalinist pressure on the 'life of the mind' (Hannah Arendt) was disastrous not only because it annihilated the critical tradition of radical thinking — what Alvin Gouldner called the 'culture of critical discourse' — but also because it introduced the criterion of functional truth as the only valid one in the field of praxis (including cognitive praxis).

Trying to make up for the lost values, endeavouring to regenerate a hidebound theoretical paradigm, a desperate search for ancestors and a no less agonising quest for ethical legitimacy: these were the main ambitions of the revisionist undertaking. Speaking about the condition of the Polish intellectual, Stanislaw Baranczak noted the distance between the revisionist hopes and the post-Marxist awareness of the reality of communism:

The long road that lay ahead can be defined as a gradual process of shaking off misconceptions and illusions as to the nature of the ruling system — from the naive 'revisionist' belief, which still prevailed in the late fifties, that the system could be 'humanized' or improved from within, without changing its fundamental premises, up to the clearsighted awareness, characteristic of recent times, that totalitarian inhumanity is an innate and unavoidable component of the system.[13]

The towering shadows of young Marx, Franz Mehring, Rosa Luxemburg, Antonio Gramsci, Karl Korsch, the early books by Lukács and Bloch, all were fused in this yearning for spiritual revival. Was all this in vain, a noble but fruitless exercise in futility? Leszek Kolakowski's sinuous experience is a vivid symbol of the irrepressible need to go beyond the limited perspective offered by neo-Marxist revisionism.[14] One can only hope that his intellectual trajectory will be one day described by a gifted biographer of ideas who will emphasise the philosopher's endless fight with the angel of utopianism.

In the feverish effort to assert their status as a radical opposition to the ruling caste, critical intellectuals were aiming to surpass their unbearable feelings of estrangement and insert themselves in a real political movement. What they wanted to acquire through political radicalisation was a redeeming freedom from alienation. They could not underwrite the official conception of the revolutionary party which they described as an ankylosed institution. New forms of organisation had to be invented that would restore the dignity of radical thought. Critical intellectuals conceived of themselves as agents of revolutionary change in the field of ideas and mentalities. In this, they clashed with the party's pretence to exert total control over the ideological sphere. No wonder therefore that purges were unleashed by the ruling elites to eliminate the virus of autonomous thought.

After the illusions of his revisionist period, Kolakowski does penance and underwrites a sceptical, almost conservative, view of history. His interpretation of revolutions echoes some of the gloomiest passages in Kafka's diary. Nothing good should be expected from these elusive explosions of freedom. More often than not the *heroici furori*, the feverish revolutionary exploits, result in the establishment of new despotisms. After that, the few nostalgics of the original project are viciously slandered and the new privileged elite imposes its crackdown on the whole society. For Kolakowski, revolutions are eventually senseless, farce and tragedy are intertwined in their bloody texture, and violent means cannot but engender unjust norms and systematic atrocities:

> Throughout history the masses had been used, under various ideological banners, to overthrow the privileged classes of the day; the result, however, was only to replace them with new masters who at once set about oppressing the rest of society no less efficiently than their predecessors. The despotism of the new class in Russia was not an exception, but an illustration of this universal law.[15]

Would Leszek Kolakowski maintain this viewpoint with regard to the Polish self-limited revolution of the early 1980s, when Solidarity became the symbol of a national will for renewal? Is it possible to dismiss the legitimacy of genuine revolts against tyranny because of previous experiences of abysmal failures to establish a less unfree society? In the above-quoted passage, Kolakowski is far away from Hannah Arendt's more sanguine assessment of revolutionary chances in history. Until her death, Hannah Arendt was hopeful about the probability of a genuine revolution, a movement bound to re-assert the rights of the 'social sphere'.[16] She was convinced that the workers' councils would be the form able to solve the antinomies of the political sphere. The Hungarian insurrection in October 1956 convinced Hannah Arendt that the councils, as spontaneously created bodies, belonged to the 'lost treasure of the revolutionary tradition' to be thought through and rehabilitated against all usurping bureaucratic powers. With due respect for this master of political thought, it is astonishing to read the following description of Hannah Arendt's reaction to events in Portugal in 1975, where a violence-prone minority, undeniably dominated by a staunchly Stalinist communist party, was preparing a showdown with the democratic forces: 'Arendt had toward the Portuguese revolution just the sense of wonder and enthusiasm she was reading about in "good old Kant", who had written many notes to himself about the fountainhead of modern revolutions — the French.'[17]

The concept of revolution lies at the centre of modern political thought, and the rationale for revolt cannot be trenchantly discarded. It is however disheartening to notice the need of the intelligentsia to find out time and again other causes for emotional attachment and political identification. Adorno and Horkheimer were perhaps closer to truth than Hannah Arendt in their refusal to invest in any of the promises of the utopian communities. Regardless of Kolakowski's manifest lack of affinity with the Frankfurt philosophers, the latter partake of the same horror of sacralised violence. The revolutionary experience of this century is far from being unequivocal. First, there were the class and racial revolutions, which resulted in unspeakable horrors for millions. The later Third World revolutions, with their anti-imperialist rhetoric, have further complicated the issue. By an ironical twist of its initial thrust, Marxism has become the ideological camouflage for revolutions in countries where the industrial proletariat has not come of age and representative democracy remains a mere desideratum.

Notes

1. For the dramatic implications of the Twentieth Congress, see the selection of documents edited by the Russian Institute, Columbia University, *The anti-Stalin campaign and international communism* (New York: Columbia University Press, 1956).

2. See Wolfgang Leonhard, *Three faces of Marxism. The political concepts of Soviet ideology, Maoism, and humanist Marxism* (New York: Paragon Books, 1979); Rudi Supek and Branko Bosnjak (eds), *Jugoslawien denkt anders. Marxismus und Kritik des etatischen Sozialismus* (Vienna and Frankfurt: Europa Verlag, 1971); Svetozar Stojanović, *Between ideals and reality — a critique of socialism and its future* (New York: Oxford University Press, 1973).

3. See G. R. Urban (ed.), *Stalinism*, p. 162 ('A Choice of Lenins?' Interview with Robert C. Tucker).

4. See Milovan Djilas, *Parts of a lifetime* (New York: Harcourt Brace Jovanovich, n.d.), p. 316–17.

5. See Leszek Kolakowski, *Main currents*, p. 159.

6. See Richard Pipes, 'The origins of Bolshevism: the intellectual evolution of young Lenin' in Richard Pipes (ed.), *Revolutionary Russia*

(Cambridge, Mass.: Harvard University Press, 1968), p. 51.

7. See Alain Besançon, *The rise of the gulag. Intellectual origins of Leninism* (New York: Continuum, 1981).

8. For an assessment of Solzhenitsyn's world-historical views, see Alain Besançon, 'Solzhenitsyn at Harvard', *Survey*, Winter 1979, vol. 24, no. 1, pp. 133–44; for the writer's more recent opinions on the relation between Soviet communism and Russian history, see Alexander Solzhenitsyn, 'Our Pluralists', *Survey*, Summer 1985, vol. 29, no. 2, pp. 1–28.

9. See 'Hungarian oppositionalist insists on his own road', Radio Free Europe, Hungarian SR, 30 September 1986, p. 14.

10. See Leopold Labedz, 'Introduction' in L. Labedz, *Revisionism*, p. 22; Jean-Paul Sartre, 'Le fantôme de Staline', *Les Temps Modernes*, November–December 1956–January 1957.

11. See Heinz Kesten, *Aufstand der Intellektuellen* (Stuttgart: Seewald, 1957); Melvin Croan, 'East German revisionism' in L. Labedz, *Revisionism*, pp. 238–56.

12. With regard to Ernst Bloch, see the recent translation of his *The principle of hope* (Cambridge, Mass.: MIT Press, 1986); Jurgen Ruhle, 'The philosopher of hope: Ernst Bloch' in L. Labedz, *Revisionism*, pp. 166–78; Leon Wieseltier, 'Under the Spell of Paradise', *The New York Times Book Review*, 23 November 1986, p. 44.

13. See Stanislaw Baranczak, 'The Polish intellectual', *Salmagundi*, Spring–Summer 1986, p. 223.

14. For Kolakowski's biography, see Robert A. Gorman (ed.), *Biographical dictionary of neo-Marxism* (Westport, Conn.: Greenwood Press, 1985), pp. 232–4.

15. See Kolakowski, *Main currents*, p. 165.

16. See Agnes Heller, 'The Great Republic' in Fehér and Heller, *Eastern left, Western left*, pp. 187–200.

17. See Elisabeth Young-Bruehl, *Hannah Arendt. For love of the world* (New Haven and London: Yale University Press, 1982), p. 466.

5

Poverty of Utopia

Every restriction of freedom of thought or opinion, even if made for the sake of the most splendid ideology, must inevitably lead to the corruption of those responsible for it.

Milovan Djilas (1953)

The history of Marxism in the states that fell under Soviet control in the aftermath of World War II can be divided into various stages. The initial period was marked by the domesticist promises of the communist leaders, and there was a limited tolerance in the cultural sphere. Wladyslaw Gomulka in Poland incarnated this attempt to create a model of socialism that would not be the carbon copy of Stalin's regime. In other East European countries, communist personalities proclaimed their intention of experimenting with models of the new society different from the Soviet one. It can be assumed that Stalin encouraged this idea of diversity to placate the apprehensions of potential opponents to a violent revolutionary solution. Otherwise, there is no reason to credit the Soviet Union with an interest in allowing its faithful underlings to engage in pluralistic dialogue with other political parties. In all his public statements, Stalin tried to reassure Western powers of his commitment to the observance of democratic rules. Master of deceit, the Soviet leader declared the export of revolution a historical nonsense. This era came to an end with the creation of the Cominform in September 1947 and the overall regimentation of ideological life in all satellised countries. The Soviet model became mandatory; the most prominent advocates of domesticism were singled out as anti-Soviet nationalists. This was the fate of Gomulka in Poland, Traicho Kostov in Bulgaria, Lászlo Rajk in Hungary, and

Lucretiu Patrascanu in Romania. They were scapegoats for Stalin's failure to lure the West and dictate the rules of political and economic games in Europe. It is thus well-known that the Prague communist coup in February 1948 was expedited by the interest expressed by many Czech politicians in the advantages of the Marshall Plan. On the other hand, the Yugoslav communist leaders refused to submit to Stalin's whims and rejected their country's transformation into a Soviet semi-colony. After 1948, a new stage began in the history of East and Central Europe. Political lynching, irrespirable conformity and encouragement of the lowest mob instincts were to prevail.

From 1948 to 1954, the complete Stalinisation of the so-called people's democracies resulted in the thwarting of any unorthodox views. The general tone was given by the leading articles in *Pravda* and all the ideological machines in the other communist countries merely reproduced the Stalinist tune. After Stalin's death, the third stage was associated with the cultural 'thaw' in the Soviet Union and a certain relaxation in the cultural policy in the other countries of the bloc. The official attacks against dogmatism, usually linked to internecine struggle in the highest party circles, eased the task of those intellectual groups intent upon revising and renewing the basic tenets of the revolutionary doctrine.

Anti-Stalinist revisionism emerged in the fight waged by communist intellectuals against the party ideological bureaucracy. This current was particularly active and influential in Poland and Hungary, but its reverberations were noticed throughout the whole Soviet bloc. The Stalinists were right in pointing to the seditious force of revisionism. This current led to the desacralisation of the established dogmas and subsequently was to play an active part in the political upheavals in 1956. Revisionism, the spectre decried by Soviet ideologues, had a corrosive effect on the sham unanimity of the Stalinist systems. It was an antidote indispensable for the awakening from the deadly lethargy of *Diamat*. According to Kolakowski, who was one of the most articulate spokesmen for the revisionist platform, this current was almost extinguished after 1965 and came to an end about 1968. It was precisely the Prague Spring that both justified and nullified the revisionist hopes. Without anticipating further discussion of the reform movement in Czechoslovakia, it is worth noting that revisionism could provide only a partial alternative to the system. It was a hesitating, self-questioning, unassertive, and therefore self-destructive cultural and political movement. Certainly, revisionism faded away primarily because of the furibund counter-reaction of the communist bureaucracy, but it is nonetheless true that it lacked the necessary vitality to win in the violent showdown with the system. A product of the communist political culture, the Marxist revisionism of the post-Stalin era was doomed to vegetate at the periphery of political life. Refusing to comply with the abhorred new class, revisionist intellectuals wavered to cross the Rubicon and assume an unmitigated post-Marxist, or even an anti-Marxist, identity. Their social status and practical attitudes were thus determined and limited by the logic of domination, albeit they were adamantly denouncing it as mutilating and intrinsically aberrant.

Finally, the last phase, the twilight of Marxism as a source of inspiration even for those forces intent upon renovating the system from within, its metamorphosis into a mere appendage of the powers that be, a verbal counterpart to the political rituals of sclerotic totalitarianism, coincided with the Brezhnev era. Hélène Carrère d'Encausse rightly points out the long-term achievements of Brezhnev's mandate in power: what was accomplished consisted not only of a new sense of self-confidence for the members of the *nomenklatura*, but also — and in direct relation to the former — the coalescence of the imperial consciousness of the ruling class.[1]

In recent years, Soviet Marxism has turned into a mere apologetic for the power elite, whereas its East European branches have been vegetating in preposterous scholastic debates about the functions of historic materialism and the nature of 'really existing socialism'. Real events and authentic social dynamics do not belong in the sphere of interest of this aseptic gibberish. Innovative research was permitted, however, in economics, primarily because of the rulers' efforts to introduce a modicum of reforms.

From our perspective, the most exhilarating and productive period in the evolution of Marxism in Eastern Europe was that of full-fledged revisionism. It was significant not only because it brought to the fore provocative ideas and thus vivified and radical-ised the cultural atmosphere , but also because it impugned the faked consolidation of orthodoxy as a stable and allegedly unassail-able institution. Revisionism questioned the hegemony of the apparatus and belied its pretences to omniscience and impunity. Since it was primarily a moral outburst, a rebellion of what Hegel called *das unglückliche Bewusstsein* (the unhappy consciousness), revisionism was perpetually dissatisfied with the *status quo*. It was a principle of negation, 'the cry of the insulted being', as Marx would have put it, an attempt to give moral outrage a powerful social impetus.

The divisions within the upper echelons of the bureaucracy, bewildered by the Soviet vagarious politics following Stalin's death, could only facilitate the task of the revisionist thinkers. The theory of the 'double truth' and the narrow-minded principle of *partiinost* were exposed as deleterious for both the soul and the mind of the individual. Gyula Hay, a Hungarian writer belonging to the anti-Stalinist opposition, advocated the need for the whole truth:

> We are talking about the *full freedom* of literature. We understand by this the most absolute, the most unlimited freedom possible among people living in a society. In other words, nothing should be forbidden to literature that is not forbidden in the laws of the country . . . the writer, like anybody else, should be allowed to tell the truth without restrictions; to criticize everybody and everything; to be sad, to be in love, to think of death; not to wonder whether his work contains 'positive' and 'negative' elements in the prescribed proportion; to believe or disbelieve in the omnipotence of God; to doubt the accuracy of certain statistics of plans; to think in a non-Marxist way; or to think in a Marxist way even if his thought has not as yet figured among the officially proclaimed and obligatory truths; . . . to despise certain writings that persons of authority have found exemplary, and vice versa; to respect certain literary values, and to ignore certain literary values; etc., etc., etc. Who could deny that of all this, much was forbidden only a short while ago — forbidden, at least in practice, under the threat of sanctions — and that even today it is only tolerated instead of declared free. This is the freedom we writers have to demand, come fire and sword.[2]

The same position was voiced by leading intellectuals in other countries of the bloc. Even in the Soviet Union, during the first post-Stalin Writers' Congress and the 1956 ideological debates, influential cultural figures like Ilya Ehrenburg, Konstantin Paustovskiy, and Konstantin Simonov decided to bypass the limits of criticism ascribed by the party leadership. Great Russian writers like Boris Pasternak and Anna Akhmatova were hopeful about a possible loosening of the party's grip on literature. The nightmarish legacy of Stalinism became a central topic for the resuscitated mind of the intelligentsia. One of Pasternak's poems written after Stalin's death conveys this feeling of immense sadness for the loss of so many friends in the terrorist whirlwind:

My soul, you are in mourning
For all those close to me,
Turned into a burial vault
For all my martyred friends . . .[3]

The revisionist movement was primarily moral and philosophical, but it affected and revived the cultural mainstream. In a way, it was the promise of a counterculture whose main purposes and sentimental infrastructure were the antithesis of the official one. To quote Kolakowski's statement in *Nowa Kultura*: 'No one is exempt from the moral duty to fight against a system of government, a doctrine, or social conditions which he considers vile and inhuman, by resorting to the argument that he finds them historically necessary.'[4]

Revisionism attacked orthodoxy on its own ground, within the Marxist framework, and was therefore vulnerable to criticism coming both from the Stalinist headquarters and from anti-Marxist circles. Confining the discourse to a Marxist criticism of the system was advantageous as a way to pre-empt possible accusations of counter-revolutionary intentions. At the same time, it was frustrating and counter-productive in terms of a broad social appeal. Emancipation from domination should entail, or should even start with, emancipation from the jargon of domination. Otherwise, criticism suffocates in powerless moralism, certainly respectable, but nevertheless conspicuously ineffective.

Taking the measure of the degeneracy of Marxism, revisionists hesitated to embark on an overall struggle against the new class. They were persuaded that what mattered was to regenerate, to heal, to improve the ailing system. Revisionist thinkers were discontented with Khrushchev's naïve explanations of the Stalinist horrors, but it took them a long time to discover the origins of totalitarian terror in the very structure of both the system and the ideology. Illusions were still taking a massive toll on the revisionists' minds. As Adam Michnik pointed out in his 1976 essay on 'A New Evolutionism', the Achilles' heel of revisionism was precisely this virtual integration in the system:

The revisionist concept was based on a specific intraparty

perspective. It was never formulated into a political program. It assumed that the system of power could be humanized and democratized and that the official Marxist doctrine was capable of assimilating contemporary arts and social sciences. The revisionists wanted to act within the framework of the Communist party and Marxist doctrine. They wanted to transform 'from within' the doctrine and the party in the direction of democratic reform and common sense. In the long term, the actions of the revisionists seek to allow enlightened people with progressive ideas to take over the party.[5]

It is important to find an explanation for the coagulation of revisionist nuclei in certain communist countries. Such phenomena are linked to cultural traditions, but their full development depends on the aptitude — or failure — of the ruling circles to counter the critical currents. The Polish and the Romanian cases are each symptomatic. Belonging to Western Christianity, having experienced several traumatic attempts to destroy their national identity, the Poles were the least prone to comply with the rules of Stalinist autocracy. Romanians, no less hostile to Russian imperialism than the Poles and traditionally more than the Hungarians, had been subjected by the USSR to a most vexing treatment. The obdurate belief that time would work on their behalf, that piecemeal changes could be brought about through simulated collaboration with the system was however the tragedy of the Romanian intelligentsia.[6]

The peculiar Romanian tactic to ignore unpleasant reality and withdraw in mythical expectation of better days did not pay off. On the contrary, what followed was that Romanian intellectuals were absorbed by the totalitarian system and could not emulate their Polish peers at the moment of a possible confrontation within the system. As for the Polish intellectuals, they rediscovered their lost honour after the cumbersome interlude of the Stalinist years. Historical generalisations are always misleading and we owe to Adam Michnik penetrating insights into the psychological profile of the Polish intelligentsia. In his 'Conversation in the Citadel', Michnik discusses the dualism of romanticism versus positivism in Polish political thought and the alternatives of armed insurrection versus organic work as a part of the Polish practice of resistance. The political programme he puts forward tries to create a synthesis of the anti-totalitarian tradition. Michnik calls for a politics of activism, that would mean 'a realistic assessment of one's place in

the world'. It also means 'firmly holding on to the realities of life
and rejecting idealistic illusions'. This innovative approach to
politics would promote self-determination and emphasise the
moral values defended by the Catholic Church. It would also
reformulate the meaning of socialism as a form of ethical reconstruction of society based on the sacredness of individual rights.
Michnik approvingly quotes Kolakowski's anti-utopian definition
of socialism:

> We need a living tradition of socialist thought which in pro-
> claiming the traditional values of social justice and freedom
> appeals solely to human forces. But here we do not need the
> ideas of any socialism. We do not need crazy dreams of a
> society from which all evil temptations have been removed or
> dreams of a total revolution which all at once will bring us a
> bliss of final redemption in a world devoid of conflict. What
> we need is a socialism that will help us find our way in the
> complex reality of the brutal forces that operate in human
> history, a socialism that will strengthen our readiness to fight
> poverty and social injustice. We need a socialist tradition
> conscious of its own limitations, because the dream of final
> redemption is despair in the cloak of hope, the greed for
> power clothed in the gown of justice.[7]

The attitudes of the Romanian intellectuals have been carefully
analysed by Dorin Tudoran, a dissident poet and journalist who
was forced to emigrate in 1985.[8] Tudoran was one of the most
successful poets in his native Romania. As so many of his peers, he
had indulged in the illusion that the regime could be transformed
from within, without an open confrontation. The exacerbation of
the repression, the reprehensible features of Ceausescu's Balkanic
'Caesarism', convinced him that someone had to break the
enchanted circle of complicity. In Tudoran's perspective, the
intelligentsia is a class endowed with a special mission. But speaking of classes, one should bear in mind the special interests of these
collectivities. The Romanian intelligentsia has demonstrated a
guilty passion for short-term interests, hesitating to defend
precisely those values that could have placed her in the mainstream
of world history. In 1956, when in Budapest and Warsaw the dictatorship was in mortal danger as a result of social revolt, the
Romanian intellectuals as a group chose to remain silent. One can
think that for the Romanian intelligentsia 1956 was the great

occasion manquée, a missed opportunity to wake up from the moral dereliction induced by the system.

There were many causes that engendered Romanian stoic passivity and forced Poles into action. Among them, and not the least important, was the difference in radical traditions. Romania, unlike Poland, could not boast of an impressive history of socialist organisations. Moreover, the Polish Communist Party, sectarian and isolated as it was after its fateful 'Bolshevization', had been founded by prominent figures of European socialism and never been totally Stalinsed. During his persecution as a Polish Titoist, Wladyslaw Gomulka could rely on a certain number of followers within his own party, primarily those who had experienced the war years in Poland and who justifiably resented the takeover of the party leadership by the Muscovites.[9] The left in Poland had been a significant segment of the interwar intellectual life, whereas in Romania it maintained a minor stature and was dramatically out-weighed by the radical right. Lucretiu Patrascanu, one of the few genuine Marxist intellectuals belonging to the leadership of the Romanian Communist Party since the clandestine years, was denounced as a 'bourgeois nationalist' and a Titoist in 1948. Unlike Gomulka, he was tragically isolated within his own party and did not have the chance of prolonged controversies with his comrades. Unfortunately, there was not such a thing like a Patrascanu faction within the Romanian Communist Party. On the other hand, unlike László Rajk in Hungary or Rudolf Slánský in Czechoslovakia, Patrascanu refused to collaborate with his tormentors in the staging of a spectacular trial in Bucharest.[10] He was executed in April 1954, without ever confessing to imaginary conspiracies to overthrow the 'revolutionary order'.

In Poland, Trotskyism had been a temptation for a small but active group of leftist intellectuals. Similar 'heresies' were almost unknown among Romanian intellectuals, though one should per-haps mention the early Trotskyite affinities of Lucien Goldmann, the noted French critical Marxist who was born in Romania and was expelled from the RCP in 1936 because of his open disapproval of the first Moscow show trial. Another circumstance eased the job of Romanian Stalinists: they had got rid of the most execrated pro-Soviet elements during the 1952 purge (the elimination of the Ana Pauker–Vasile Luca faction), while Poland was, in 1956, still under the grip of the Cominternist (Muscovite) faction. Balkanic traditions and habits, Byzantinism and Oriental muddling through were also instrumental in the shaping of the Romanian Communist political culture.

The Failure of Titoism

Regardless of the overall assessment of Josip Broz Tito's political biography, Tito's life did not lack historical grandeur. He was triumphant where the giants of the October Revolution, people like Trotsky, Zinoviev, Kamenev, Rykov, and Bukharin, failed.[11] A victor in the anti-Nazi struggle for national liberation, Tito was a revolutionary hero in his own right. Moreover, he was the first Stalinist to challenge Stalin's claims to supremacy within world communism and in doing so he inaugurated the polycentric dynamics that would ruin the once monolithic unity. It was because of Titoism that Stalinism ceased to be the centre of the communist universe, though the Yugoslav heresy was rabidly denounced by people who would later walk in Tito's footsteps. Tito pioneered 'democratic socialism', albeit there is no doubt that he was the last to have aimed at the decline of Marxism as a world-conquering ideology.[12]

Josip Broz Tito, who had been formed in the theological disputes of the Comintern, was a seasoned Stalinist who wanted to be trusted by the man he had faithfully served. After the war, behind Tito's offended reaction to Stalin's insults was the conviction that he had not done anything against the Soviet interests. Tito consistently avoided antagonising the Soviet personnel in Yugoslavia. But he was not ready for total self-denial in relations with the Kremlin. He therefore refused the slavish surrender to Stalin's dictate and chose the thorny path of, first, de-Sovietisation and, later, de-Stalinisation.

By no means a theorist — Moša Pijade, Edvard Kardelj, and Milovan Djilas took care of these issues — Tito defied Stalin and challenged the Soviet arrogance. He was the architect of 'national Communism', a confusing term that led many western observers to conclude that the Yugoslav system had decisively broken not only with Stalinism, but also with Leninism. That was an enduring illusion, as erroneous as the belief that Yugoslav self-management was indeed an alternative to bureaucratic centralism. Certainly, Tito was compelled to make concessions, to allow more criticism and freedom of information in Yugoslavia than in any other communist country. But he never relinquished the party's hold on power and Alexandar Ranković's political police was perfectly competitive with similar organisations in Stalin's empire.

Yugoslav Marxism is rooted in Tito's angry response to the ignominious Cominform attack on his party. The cause of the

Soviet – Yugoslav split was not a conflict of visions, or a matter of ethical principles. It was rather the result of the struggle between the sovereign power and the vassal underdog. Rejecting Stalin's aggressive policy towards Yugoslavia led Tito to a theoretical break with his former idol. The Yugoslav communist elite abandoned Stalin only grudgingly, totally perplexed about the reasons behind the Soviet hostility.

Tito was aware that de-Stalinisation could be a dangerous, disruptive undertaking and those who were prone to exaggerations had to pay dearly for it. The case of Milovan Djilas, once one of Tito's closest collaborators, is more than telling in this respect. In his theoretical work, Djilas had taken too seriously the leader's democratic professions of faith and was therefore imprisoned by his former colleagues.

The Titoist schism was however the first visible fissure in the apparently inexpugnable Stalinist citadel. Tito's defiance of the Soviet rules paved the way for further attempts to resume 'national Communist' experiments. With the benefit of hindsight, Milovan Djilas can now discard national communism as a mere delusion, but at the moment of its emergence it could be taken for an alternative to the Stalinist oppression. Driven by the inner logic of political fight, Tito encouraged a general reassessment of the Marxist-Leninist tenets. The leading role of the party, the prevailing Leninist tenet, received a far broader interpretation in the writings of Yugoslav theorists than in the frozen postulates of Soviet Marxism. Genuine ethical concerns were, if not desired by the party, at least tolerated. Full-fledged Stalinism, with its paroxysmic voluntarism and cultural opacity, was excoriated by Yugoslav leaders. Tito himself uttered unequivocal condemnations of Stalinism, though he refused to sacrifice the main social and economic underpinnings of the regime. A pact with the intelligentsia, a historical compromise of sorts, further enhanced Tito's international image. Had Stalin wanted to get rid of Tito he would have had to defeat a genuine national resistance. This may have been the ultimate reason for Stalin's reluctance to make use of military force in his unabated attempts to overthrow the Yugoslav heretic leadership.[13] On the other hand, the Soviet dictator was increasingly convinced that a new world war had become inevitable, especially after 1950. The thrust of Stalin's actions in his last years was to initiate a cataclysmic purge, the outcome of which would have been the elimination of any Titoist germ in the satellised countries.

Yugoslav Marxists were urged to speak their minds, to rethink traditional categories and overcome false consciousness. In 1954, the Yugoslav chief ideologist Edvard Kardelj accused the USSR of having created a bureaucratic colossus. He defined the social nature of the Soviet regime as state capitalism. Tito's openness was nevertheless limited by a persistent opposition to any endeavour to question the very legitimacy of the Yugoslav regime. Dialogue was allowed only inasmuch as it did not endanger the party control over society. Until his death Tito made use of his absolute prerogatives to deter critical intellectuals from engaging in any thorough-going analysis of the system. He may have been by far more tolerant than other Communist leaders, but he was not a proponent of classic democracy. His ideal, that he partially managed to carry out, was an enlightened despotism, a semi-authoritarian, paternalistic regime, by all means less abhorrent than any other existing in the communist bloc.

Once the divorce from the Cominform was consummated, Tito was compelled to formulate an alternative doctrine, a counter-ideology bound to resist Stalinist vestiges and infiltrations. Titoism came into being as a desperate attempt to bestow both credibility and authority on a somewhat loose corpus of insights, apprehensions, and resentments. Later, Tito was to react idiosyncratically to the efforts to expand de-Stalinisation beyond the Leninist barriers.

Workers' self-management, the Yugoslav leaders' pet concept, turned out to be nothing but another manipulative device, and those who dared to voice their disappointment with the abortive liberalisation were brutally silenced. When faced with outspoken criticism, Tito was no more open-minded than any Stalinist leader. The brutal disbandment of the nucleus of critical thought created around the philosophical journal *Praxis* is emblematic in this respect.[14] Marxism had functioned as the ideology of the self-sufficient bureaucracy and it is precisely this fateful instrumentalisation that has presided over its degeneracy even under the less inauspicious Yugoslav conditions. It would be fair, however, to admit that Titoism granted far more elbow-room for critical thought than traditional Soviet-type regimes. It seems there was an unwritten contract between the regime and the intellectuals that stipulated the confines of heterodoxy. The goals and the legitimacy of the regime were not to become a matter of dissolving doubt, and criticism, exciting as that may appear, was nevertheless emasculated. In Yugoslavia, as in other communist regimes, the public space is governed by the party-state apparatus and Titoism could not put up with any undertaking meant to generate independent centres of thought and initiative. In one of his major ideological pronouncements, Tito referred to intellectual trouble-makers in no uncertain, directly ultimative terms:

> I was glad to hear some professors, university delegates to the Conference (in 1968), stress that there should be no place at the universities for those who do not agree with the policy of the League of Communists and with our social system in general . . . I am now waiting for practical measures, for action, for those who are corrupting our youth to be removed from their posts.[15]

It is interesting to note, on the other hand, the exploitation by Stalin and post-Stalin Soviet leaders of the Yugoslav scapegoat. All the economic difficulties within the bloc were attributed by the Cominform to imperialist conspiracies supported and carried through by Titoist agents. Later, Yugoslav revisionism was to become a catchword bound to englobe all heretical trends that could undermine the Leninist tenets.[16] From Stalin to Khrushchev and Mao, there was a consensual continuity with regard to the dangers implied in the Titoist approach. Certainly, the Sino-Soviet split modified the parameters of this enduring controversy and mollified any Soviet anti-revisionist zeal, but Titoism as an ideological challenge to the Stalinist paradigm has remained pariah within traditional communist milieux.[17]

As many critical Marxists were to discover during the repression that followed the Hungarian Revolution and the Polish October, Tito himself could be *persona grata* for Soviet leaders, but Titoism was both feared and execrated. Less egregious than late Stalinism, Soviet post-Stalin regimes could not stand the Titoist divergent trends within world communism. More than a different Marxism, Titoism was perceived in Moscow as a solidified form of resistance to Soviet hegemonism. Coming to terms with Titoism thus meant succumbing to an appeasing temptation which is viscerally alien to the Soviet political mind. Cohesion and uniformity have always been the Soviet purposes within the bloc and Titoism has been the palpable symbol of opposition to this strategy.

In Eastern Europe, Tito's victorious resistance to Stalin was regarded as a vindication of the assumption that Soviet hegemonism was not infallible. Certainly, most of those who staked their political career on Titoism, Imre Nagy included, could not have been aware of the Yugoslav leader's hidden agenda in his relations with the Soviets. Too passionate sometimes, British journalist Nora Beloff is however right in emphasising Tito's uncompromising allegiance to Leninist ideals. His opposition to Stalin and Stalinism stemmed primarily from his unswerving conviction that the Yugoslav interpretation of Marxism-Leninism was perfectly orthodox and subsequently unimpeachable. Until his death in 1980, Tito remained committed to his youth credo: a revolutionary belief in the advent of a classless society and an unyielding identification with the Marxist historical teleology. His deplorable behaviour toward the legal Hungarian Government headed by Imre Nagy was warranted in his eyes by the firm belief that socialism, be it of the Soviet variety, should be preserved at any cost. And socialism for Tito was synonymous with the one-party system that the Hungarian revolutionaries had succeeded in overthrowing.

As long as autonomy was not accompanied in Hungary by efforts to establish a pluralist system, Tito was ready to endorse the liberalisation. Any step further, any bold attempt to move away from the sacrosanct dogma of the leading role of the party, could not but irritate Tito. Since Hungarian revolutionaries bypassed his recommendations, he felt betrayed and consequently acted in qualified support for the Soviet crushing of the insurrection.

Titoism was intimately linked to Tito's personality. Certainly, even after his death, Yugoslavia does not look like the other communist countries, but she has lost the radical aura and seems caught in inescapable disarray. In April 1983, critical Marxist philosopher Svetozar Stojanović formulated the basic requirements for the introduction of political pluralism in Yugoslavia:

First, the LCY (the League of Communists) should undergo full democratization, including secret ballots for all party posts, with several candidates for each and the right to form factions within the party organizations. Secondly, the Socialist Alliance, the country's largest mass organization, should be separated from the party and become a genuine independent political organization based on voluntary membership; it would participate in power while recognizing the leading role of the LCY. Thirdly, the trade unions should also be separate from the party organization, becoming genuinely independent and a vehicle for the self-management system; strategic and key-sectors of the economy should remain nationalized, while the rest should be a mixed economy open to private initiative. Finally, the federal structure should be reformed and strengthened . . .[18]

Pointing to the ambivalent legacy of Titoism with its morally and politically numbing effects, Aleksa Djilas could conclude that 'an ideological dictatorship creates an ideological civilization, in which practical activity and action are difficult to bring to creation'.[19]

Tito's heirs are pale shadows of the regime's founder, and were it not for the need for an ideological ingredient to keep the pieces of the game together, Titoism would have been long abandoned as an antiquated dogma.

Self-management, which has become a fetish in contemporary Yugoslavia, is actually a political system under direct party control. The workers do not identify themselves with the so-called self-managing bodies, which are alienated institutions manipulated by the party bureaucracy and consistently reluctant to defend the workers' interests. There is no exaggeration in the following description of current conditions in Yugoslavia:

> Through the self-managing bodies, the party succeeded in increasing its control over the working class. Formally elected from below, self-managing bodies are actually nominated from above . . . The power of the bureaucracy is far less visible in the Yugoslav economy than in the economies of other Communist countries, since it is hidden in a complex web of self-managing bodies. The real culprits for the disastrous decisions that have ruined the Yugoslav economy find it easier to hide.[20]

In the era of global agreements and disagreements between superpowers, the ideology of non-alignment, Tito's most cherished concept, looks pathetically romantic and powerless. At their turn, the Yugoslav critical Marxists have discovered that subservience does not mitigate the despotic proclivities of the ruling caste. On the contrary, the more obedient the intellectuals' behaviour, the greater the pressure put upon them by the regime. Illusions about systemic self-improvement seem particularly farfetched in the post-Tito era when the leaders cannot offer but duplicitous statements with theoretical pretences. In a recent interview with the Belgrade bimonthly *Duga*, Ivan Maksimovič, a

Yugoslav economics professor and Marxist theorist, openly criticised the balance-sheet of 'really existing socialism':

Socialism promised things more as ideological concepts than
as real possibilities. Still, nobody anticipated that socialism
would increase nepotism and political bureaucracy and limit
rather than expand human freedoms. Bearing in mind the
traditions of great countries building socialism, we must try to
find out what freedom has actually meant in the history of
those countries. Empirically, the concept of freedom advocated in these countries has been very different from the
concept of freedom developed in advanced Western countries. In my opinion, the problem of freedom under socialism
therefore remains unsolved.[21]

Similar opinions were expressed by Nikola Milosević, the author
of a book with the symptomatic title *Marxism and Jesuitry*, published
in Belgrade in 1985. According to Milosević, the dictatorship
instituted by Lenin's party was worse than the tyrannies and autocratic dictatorships of ancient times:

I have proven unambiguously in my book that what the
Bolsheviks called 'the dictatorship of the proletariat' was in
many aspects not like the original Roman institution of
dictatorship. Roman dictators did not assume power by
employing force but rather by receiving it from legally elected
law-making bodies for a strictly limited period of six months;
in addition, they were not permitted to use state funds nor
were they allowed to change existing laws, that is, to introduce new ones. (Lenin's) so called 'dictatorship of the
proletariat', however, had none of these restrictions; and
therefore it was a dictatorship (in the classical Roman style)
only in name. Essentially, it was a sort of an oligarchic rule,
without legal restrictions on authority and with an absolutely
real possibility of developing, sooner or later, into a special
type of tyranny. As is known, this happened after Stalin
became the head of the Bolshevik party.[22]

Needless to say, such judgements on the dismal historical record of
Soviet-type regimes could not be voiced in the official media of any
other communist country. Real difficulties arise for Yugoslav
Marxist theorists when they try to transcend the frontiers of

criticism promulgated by the party and dare to broach the issues of power distribution in their own society. The trial of a group of dissidents in 1985 highlighted the regime's failure to come to grips with internal opposition.[23]

Post-Tito Yugoslavia is beset with widespread malaise, seething discontent, and pandemic cynicism. It is a country haunted by unassumed memories of tragic feuds and bloody revenges. Even more perhaps than in other communist countries, Marxism in Yugoslavia sounds infinitely hollow and stupendously irrelevant. Its narcissistic agony, cloaked in the jargon of bureaucratic optimism, cannot arouse but ironical grins. Conceived as a philosophy of salvation, Marxism in Soviet-type regimes is certainly the last resource one would take into account for redeeming purposes. Its obsolescence, unconvincingly denied by official clerks, is the direct result of its failure to advance more than utopian blueprints and exalt white elephants. Ironically, both Stalinism and Titoism look now terribly out-of-step with modern times, withered pictures from the family album of a ruined left.

Notes

1. See Héléne Carrère d'Encausse, *Ni paix, ni guerre*, and Mikhail Voslensky, *Nomenklatura*, pp. 319–55.
2. See Tamas Aczel and Tibor Meray, *The revolt of the mind* (New York: Praeger, 1959), pp. 428–9.
3. See Max Hayward, *Writers in Russia* (New York: Harcourt Brace Jovanovich, 1983), p. 203.
4. See L. Labez (ed.), *Revisionism*, p. 18.
5. See Adam Michnik, *Letters from prison*, p. 135.
6. See Vladimir Tismaneanu, 'Critical Marxism and Eastern Europe', *Praxis International*, vol. 3, no. 3, October 1983, pp. 248–61.
7. See Adam Michnik, pp. 326–8.
8. See Dorin Tudoran, 'De la condition de l'intellectual roumain', *L'Alternative*, nos. 29 and 30, September–October and November–December 1984.
9. See Adam Ulam, *Titoism and the Cominform* (Cambridge, Mass.: Harvard University Press, 1952), pp. 148–98 (the chapter 'Crisis in the Polish Communist Party').
10. See Vladimir Tismaneanu, 'The ambiguity of Romanian national communism', *Telos*, no. 60, Summer 1984, pp. 65–79.
11. See Ernst Halperin, *The triumphant heretic. Tito's struggle against Stalin* (London: Heinemann, 1958).
12. See Nora Beloff, *Tito's flawed legacy* (Boulder, Co.: Westview Press, 1986).
13. For Tito's relations with Stalin, see Vladimir Dedijer, *The battle*

Stalin lost (New York: The Viking Press, 1971).

14. See Gerson Sher, *Praxis*; Oskar Grunwald, *The Yugoslav search for man* (South Hadley, Mass.: Bergin & Garvey, 1983).

15. Quoted by Sher, p. 222.

16. See François Fejtö, *A history of the people's democracies* (New York: Praeger, 1971), pp. 83–98 (the chapter is tellingly entitled 'A holy alliance against revisionism and national communism').

17. For the role of the 'revisionist debate' in the intensifcation of the Sino–Soviet dispute, see Donald S. Zagoria, *The Sino–Soviet conflict, 1956–1961* (Princeton University Press, 1962), pp. 176–87 and 363–4; Robert H. McNeal (ed.), *International relations among communists* (Englewood Cliffs: Prentice Hall, 1967), pp. 98–112; Zbigniew K. Brzezinski, *The Soviet bloc*, pp. 309–37; William E. Griffith, *Albania and the Sino–Soviet rift* (Cambridge, Mass. and London: MIT Press, 1963).

18. See Pedro Ramet, 'Apocalypse culture and social change in Yugoslavia' in Pedro Ramet (ed.), *Yugoslavia in the 1980s* (Boulder and London: Westview, 1985), pp. 19–20.

19. Ibid. p. 20.

20. See Aleksa Djilas, 'Yugoslav self-management: a cause of crisis', *Soviet Analyst*, vol. 15, no. 20, 8 October 1986, p. 4.

21. See Slobodan Stankovic, 'Theorists offer radically unorthodox views', Radio Free Europe, Yugoslav SR, 16 May 1986, p. 19.

22. Ibid., p. 20.

23. See Henry Kamm, 'Trial of dissidents in Yugoslavia seems to have split communists', *New York Times*, 19 November 1985.

6

Reconstruction or Disintegration?

. . . the system created a psychology characteristic of communities subjugated by Communism. Long periods of apathy and depoliticization were interrupted by sudden political earthquakes. These, however, were not followed by programs of reform or alternative political plans. They were only protests, not reform movements.

Adam Michnik (1982)

A prominent leader of Polish non-violent resistance and an insightful political thinker, Adam Michnik nourishes no illusions about the real nature of communism: 'There is no such thing as a nontotalitarian ruling Communism. It either becomes totalitarian or ceases to be Communism.'[1] This is basically true, but it is difficult to deny the differences in vision, methods, and consequences between various communist regimes. In other words, not all totalitarian regimes are equally repressive. János Kádár's Hungary or Wojciech Jaruzelski's Poland are certainly non-democratic countries. There are however elements of the civil society, including the existence of democratic oppositional movements, that make those two regimes different from others in East and Central Europe. Pluralist trends are not encouraged by the ruling elites, but they subsist and develop in spite of government harrassment. At the opposite pole, the case of Romania is eloquent in many respects: since the non-communist leftist experience in that country was particularly anaemic, the ideological commissars could pursue their plans with no concerns about potential criticism from related quarters. Paradoxically, it was precisely the existence of anti-authoritarian socialist traditions that prevented in Poland, Hungary, Czechoslovakia and East Germany the most intemperate anti-cultural excesses.

During the Stalinist years, after World War II, specious values became the base of socialisation in Romania; national pride was methodically disregarded and derided. Intellectual traditions, including rationalism, were held in deep contempt. The new ideology was implemented by an overly zealous and uncompromising ideological apparatus. As soon as the Romanian Communist Party was granted legal existence in August 1944, the Agitprop (Russian abbreviation for agitation and propaganda) department came into being as a major institution to guide and supervise the crystallisation and inculcation of values associated with the interests of the Soviet Union. For this very reason, it is almost impossible to distinguish between the Stalinisation and the Sovietisation of Romanian culture. The former process aimed to establish undisputed party control over the cultural sphere, whereas the latter was supposed to eliminate the lingering forms of national identity and synchronise Romanian culture with the Soviet realm of socialist realism.

All spiritual sanctuaries had to be purged, old symbols to be supplanted by new symbols, and the low intellectual standards of Stalinism prescribed as an unquestionable dogma. Language and literature were imbued with mystical incantations of revolutionary romanticism. All cultural institutions were purged in the name of class criteria, recalcitrant writers and thinkers were mercilessly treated as ideological enemies and subsequently persecuted. In a country with a strong anti-Russian and anti-Soviet tradition, Russian and Soviet values were acclaimed as the quintessence of modern culture.

Totalitarianism is inherently axiophobic, allergic to the very principle of free competition of values. A hierarchy of merits was thus replaced by one of sycophancy, of mental conformity and mechanical enthusiasm. On the other hand, the more strident the adherence to the ruling dogmas, the greater the chances to acceed to the top of the pyramid.

Within such a system, the mind was muzzled and constantly insulted. Lying was institutionalised and provided with a definite social function. Deprived of its mendacious foundations, the system would inexorably fall apart:

> Totalitarianism implies the complete control by the state of all areas of life and the unlimited power of an artificial state ideology over minds; thus it can achieve fulfilment only if it

succeeds in eliminating the resistance of both natural and mental reality, i.e. in cancelling reality altogether. Therefore, when we speak of totalitarian regimes we have in mind not systems that have reached perfection, but rather those which are driven by a never-ending *effort* to reach it, to swallow all channels of human communication, and to eradicate all spontaneously emerging social life forms.[2]

Ironically, it was a primitive, cantankerous materialism supposedly celebrating 'objective reality' that served to create this pseudo-reality which is the substance of the ideological system. The more the Leninist preachers were chanting the virtues of a putatively scientific philosophy, the more they became prisoners of a superstitious jargon with no relation whatsoever to reality.

It goes without saying that what has postured as Marxism in Romania — and in all the other countries of the bloc, with differences rather in quantity than in quality — is light years away from any sophisticated Hegelian historicism. It is rather a half-baked combination of verbal stereotypes and stimulated faith, the outcome of deliberate ignorance of basic intellectual standards. In more recent years, sham nationalism was discovered as another ideological vehicle bound to foster the increasingly dwindling authority of ruling elites in East-Central Europe.

As mentioned, the Romanian cultural dictators during the heyday of Stalinism were Leonte Rautu and Iosif Chisinevschi, both endowed with impeccable credentials from the Soviet perspective. Rautu's biography is suggestive of a certain category in the moral typology of Stalinism. Born to a well-off Jewish-Bessarabian family, Rautu joined the clandestine Romanian Communist Party (RCP) as a student. In the 1930s he visited for the first time the Soviet Union for which he seemed to harbour an indefectible attachment. After a short enrolment in the Leninist School — an indispensable stage for propaganda apparatchiks in the Comintern — he returned to Romania and became a member of the underground nucleus in charge of cultural and theoretical matters. Later, Rautu was appointed chief-editor of *Scinteia*, the press organ of the RCP. When, as a result of the secret agreements between Stalin and Hitler, Bessarabia was annexed by the USSR (June 1940), Rautu decided to 'repatriate' and went to Moscow where he became the editor-in-chief of Radio Moscow's Romanian section. Incidentally, an equivalent position was held by Imre Nagy in the Hungarian section. Rudolf Slánský, the future

General Secretary of the Communist Part of Czechoslovakia, who was to perish in 1952 being accused by his comrades of having organised a 'subversive Zionist–Titoist center', was the chief of the Central European department of Radio Moscow. Rautu returned to Romania in 1945 and enthusiastically contributed to the implementation of the Stalinist scenario for that country.

In his essay on Solzhenitsyn, Georg Lukács said that the great realist literature dealing with the Stalinist epoch should focus on the psychological make-up of Stalinist ideological dictators. Thus, it would highlight the secret motivations of those 'aesthetes' of totalitarianism like Lukács's former pupil József Révai in Hungary, Leonte Rautu in Romania, or Jakub Berman in Poland who, while culturally prepared to analyse the aberrant nature of the system, had still underwritten and enhanced it. During the Stalinist 'great purge' (1936–9), Révai had been in charge of the Hungarian Communist Party at the Central European Secretariat of the Comintern. In this capacity, he witnesed the massacre of the Comintern main cadres by the NKVD, including the extermination of the ruling elite of his own party, among whom was Bela Kun, the former leader of the Hungarian Soviet Republic in 1919. Later, Révai was to preside over the asphyxiation of Hungarian culture under Rakosism and devise the most infamous Stalinist frame-ups as a member of the ruling quartet of Hungarian communism (in the company of Mátyas Rákosi, Ernö Gerö, and Mihály Farkas). After the Hungarian revolution, during which he took refuge in the USSR, Révai returned to Hungary in 1957 and published in *Nepszabadsag* (the official party organ) a vitriolic attack against Imre Nagy whom he described as 'the precursor and real political chief of the October counter-revolution'.[3] As for Rudolf Slánský, suffice it to note that he headed his party's delegation to the 1947 founding conference of the Cominform, to the 1948 conference when Tito was excommunicated, and to the last conference of the Informative Bureau in November 1949. As already mentioned, accused of being a 'traitor, saboteur, spy, and Zionist', Rudolf Slánský was tried in November 1952, declared guilty of conspiracy and espionage, and hanged shortly afterward.[4]

The mental chemistry of those Stalinist zealots remains a fascinating problem both for political science and for literature. They were perfectly equipped to understand the duplicity of the system and thus turn into its most ardent critics. At the same time, they were emotionally involved in the adventure of power and could not find the moral resources to break with the mesmerising ideological totems. Isaac Deutscher tackled these puzzling forms of behaviour in his splendid essay 'The tragic life of a Polrugarian minister':

> How much is there in common between the young man who once set out with Promethean ardour to conquer history's insanity as it manifested itself in capitalism and the middle-aged Cabinet Minister who vaguely feels that history's irrational forces have overpowered the camp of the revolution, too, and incidentally driven him into a trap? He does his best to bolster his own self-respect and to persuade himself that as statesman, dignitary, and leader he is still the same he was when he championed the cause of the oppressed and suffered for it in the prisons of his native land. But sometimes, while he solemnly receives delegations of peasants or salutes a colourful parade, a familiar sharp pain pierces his heart; and suddenly he feels that he is merely a pathetic wreck, a sub-polar beast of burden.[5]

Vincent Adriano, the hero of Deutscher's 1950 essay, was still committed to revolutionary values and therefore could hardly put up with all the twists and turns of the party line. His soul was divided and so was his mind:

> There are two Vincent Adrianos now. One seems never to have known a moment of doubt or hesitation. His Stalinist orthodoxy has never been questioned, his devotion to the party has never flagged, and his virtues as leader and statesman are held to be unsurpassed. The other Adriano is almost constantly tormented by this communist conscience, a prey to scruple and fear, to illusion and disillusionment. The former is expansive and eloquent, the latter broods in silence and hides from his oldest friends. The former acts, the latter never ceases to ponder.[6]

It is however necessary to amend Deutscher's portrayal of the Stalinist militant, at least with regard to the people like József Révai, Jakub Berman, or Leonte Rautu. The East European Zhdanovs were not prone to doubts and did not indulge in any form of self-questioning. They were professional survivors ready to carry out what they regarded as historical necessity. Stalin needed this human stuff to implement his designs for the cultural, economic, and political colonisation of Eastern Europe. Selfless agents of the Soviet interests, loyal perpetrators of Stalin's orders, they were convinced that history — certainly a history written in accordance with the party's directives — would vindicate their actions. In his interview with Teresa Toranska, the unrepentant Stalinist Jakub Berman candidly spelled out this boundless contempt for the rules of traditional democracy. Speaking in the early 1980s about pluralism, Berman proudly reiterated his old convictions:

> Who would need such a democracy? Even today, we cannot organize free elections. Now perhaps even less than ten or twenty years ago, because we would lose. There is no doubt about that. Then what would be the meaning of such elections? Unless we want to play the super-democrats, the gentlemen . . . One does not make politics for pleasure, to be understood or liked.[7]

Manipulated manipulators, East European Stalinists acted as masterful engineers of purges and repression. Leonte Rautu, for example, was perfectly aware of the devastating effects of his actions. The destruction of national values was in his case — as in Révai's — totally congruent with the plan to promote the cultural colonisation of Eastern Europe by the USSR. It should be noted that during the interwar period in Romania, culture had reached an unprecedented level of modernity and sophistication. Temerary avant-garde trends and an existential philosophy *avant la lettre* were the main ferments of this intellectual awakening. Mircea Eliade, E. M. Cioran, Eugène Ionesco, to mention some of the names now well-known in the West, were championing cultural debates in Bucharest, whilst *Korunk*, edited in Cluj by Gaal Gabor, was a cultural magazine of European reputation. The recent translation into French of Eugène Ionesco's volume *Non*, initially published in Romania in the early 1930s, compelled Jean-François Revel to write in deep melancholy:

> The reader of *Non* will feel the absurdity of the political division of Europe in 1945, the cruelty of the cultural *apartheid* embodied in the very expression 'Eastern Europe.' Pre-War Europe was neither Western or Eastern, but an intellectual and spiritual continuity, with a traffic of ideas, letters, arts and music in all directions. What we call 'Western culture'

reached out to or was born in Prague as in Paris, in Belgrade as in London, in Bucharest as in Warsaw.[8]

It was precisely this legacy that was to disappear under the heinous Stalinist administration of culture in East-Central Europe. Many intellectuals emigrated, others remained and experienced the ordeal of totalitarian de-enlightenment. Some perished in the labour camps, others survived and succumbed to the siren songs of the regime. Too few were those who had the stamina to oppose the regime against all odds.

Leonte Rautu was perhaps the most successful of Zhdanov's East European disciples. Romanian culture certainly survived, but the losses it underwent during the Stalinist cataclysm were incalculable. They are matched perhaps only by the damage provoked by Nicolae Ceausescu's 1971 'mini-cultural revolution', a grotesque caricature of the Maoist utopian experiment. Unlike other East European Stalinist ideological watchdogs, Rautu survived the 1956 political earthquake and remained one of Gheorghe Gheorghiu-Dej's closest advisors until the Romanian party leader's demise in March 1965. Indeed, he continued to be a member of the ruling team until the early 1980s. Ironically, Nicolae Ceausescu forced him into retirement after having publicly blamed him for 'educational errors' evinced by the decisions of members of his family to emigrate to the West. *Habent sua fata apparatchiki* . . .

The greater the ideological confusion, the more difficult it is for communist parties to keep society under strict control. No doubt, Marxism – Leninism is mistrusted and disdained, but the ideological cement is needed to prevent the resurrection of civil society and the breakdown of the precarious covenant — or new social contract, to think in Antonin Liehm's terms — that keeps together divergent social forces. In countries like Poland, Hungary, and Romania where, for quite different reasons, the authority of the party has been for years in marked decline, current evolutions were prepared by ideological erosion.

The loss of credibility of the ruling ideology, its flagrant failure to suggest answers and solutions to the agonising social problems, has further accelerated social crisis in Soviet-type regimes. There is indeed no 'big power' nationalism to be opposed to the critical claims, and the amalgam of socialism and 'Romanianism' — or 'Polishness', or, in East Germany, 'Prussianism' — could hardly provide the party with more than an updated and conceptually inconsistent version of the worst rhetorical excesses of the far-right.

Ideology in these 'mono-organizational systems' (T. H. Rigby) imposes and requires regimentation, either in the form of paternalism, or by making use of overt totalitarian techniques.[9] It has lost its enthralling force and relies primarily on residual apprehensions and semi-automatic reflexes. Ideology survives as a vestigial component of the superstructure, a lingering and unappealing memento of the once inspiring faith. In a discussion with the Belgrade magazine *Intervju*, Leszek Kolakowski linked the demise of the ideological chimeras to the collapse of Marxism as an appealing philosophy. Marxism has ceased to exert any impact on the minds of the citizens of the communist countries:

> Marxism both as an ideology and as a philosophy has become completely irrelevant . . . Even the rulers have largely abandoned this notion and even its phrases. They no longer use Marxist phraseology, not even the Communists. They use it at most in ceremonial cases. When the Polish government wants to enter into any sort of communication with the public, it no longer employs sweet phrases about the glorious future of communism or about Marxist–Leninist truths, because it knows that such phrases cannot excite anyone. They now refer instead to so-called geo-political arguments. This means that they want to persuade people that 'where we are now we cannot survive without the great Soviet Union, which is our brother; we cannot survive without the Soviet fraternal alliance and fraternal help, because we are surrounded by enemies' and the like.[10]

The intellectual sterility of official Marxism is a matter of evidence; it is amorphous and inchoate, and therefore it cannot energise or unify the body politic. Once tremendously powerful, Marxist ideology is nowadays a frozen artifact. The prophetical thrust, the chiliastic dimension, that was both the strength and the vulnerability of Marxism has faded away and has been replaced by a mere celebration of the *status quo*.

The unhappy consciousness, Hegel's metaphor for a spirit unreconciled with itself, has totally disappeared from the self-congratulatory discourse of institutional Marxism. It is obvious that such a rebellion against the very principle of universal domination would aim to subvert the basis of the communist confiscation of both temporary and spiritual powers. The phenomenology of dissent in Soviet-style societies entailed first the attempt to recuperate the negative-utopian strain of Marxism, then to restructure it in an emancipatory direction. Later, when disenchantment was all-embracing, it took the form of a counter-Marxism.

From the revisionism of the late 1950s and early 1960s to the sceptical treatment of Marxism in the writings of contemporary dissidents, there is a whole odyssey of ruined hopes and failed illusions. Instead of indulging in what Hegel called a 'litany of lamentations', serious dissident thinkers have tried to clarify the causes of this abortive denouement of the traditional idyll between Marxism and intellectuals. One of these determinations was the growing awareness of the inherent ambivalence of the Marxian message, in other words a discontent with pragmatic utopianism. Furthermore, it seems an inescapable conclusion that Marxism had been turned into an instrument in the hands of the powers that be, the main source of self-confidence for the rulers and an object of derogatory comments and aversion for the ruled. Revisionist intellectuals, and their partners in political coalitions, became increasingly convinced that violence and appeasement could not lead to palpable changes in the nature of the system. The mechanisms that had ensured the triumph of Stalinism over the critical intelligence were undermined by the official admission of crimes having been perpetrated in the name of socialism.

The foundations of 'Ketman' as a methodology of self-deceit, perceptively diagnosed by Czeslaw Milosz, crumbled during the years of the post-Stalin 'new course' and primarily during the months that followed the dissemination of Khrushchev's 'secret' speech. There was no doubt that the Stalinisation of Marxism had been both a historical and intellectual disaster. Isaac Deutscher summed up this painful sentiment in his analysis of the irrational mechanism of Stalinism, an astute effort to save whatever could be saved from Marxism and Leninism after the *Walpurgisnacht* of full-fledged totalitarianism:

> Marxism has its inner logic and consistency: and its logic is modern through and through. Primitive magic has its own integrity and its peculiar poetic beauty. But the combination of Marxism and primitive magic was bound to be as incoherent and incongruous as Stalinism itself. Stalin was exceptionally well equipped to embody that combination and to

reconcile to some degree the irreconcilables. But he did not himself create the combination. It was produced by the impact of a Marxist revolution upon a semi-Asiatic society and the impact of that society upon the Marxist revolution.[11]

The problem with Deutscher's line of reasoning is that it takes for granted the Marxist nature of the Russian revolution. It was precisely this incompatibility between the Marxist revolutionary idea and the strategy embraced by the Bolshevik party from its entrance on the historical scene that had indeed paved the way for the Stalinist foul play.

The 'secret speech' was the detonator of this tremendous search for the restoration of genuine Marxist values. Umberto Terracini, a veteran Italian communist leader, reacted angrily to the Soviet calls for moderation in the interpretation of Stalinism:

It is stated that things (in Moscow) have changed, but the truth is that the only thing that has changed is the men in the Kremlin . . . The truth of yesterday is not the truth of today. In this way many truths become doubtful and the responsibilities become collective.[12]

In his famous interview with *Nuovi Argomenti* ('9 Domande sullo Stalinismo', 16 June 1956), Palmiro Togliatti, the General Secretary of the Italian Communist Party and once a Comintern stalwart, pointed to some of the main flaws in Khrushchev's approach to Stalin and Stalinism:

. . . as long as we confine ourselves, in substance, to denouncing the personal faults of Stalin as the cause of everything we remain within the realm of the 'personality cult'. First, all that was good was attributed the superhuman, positive qualities of one man: now all that is evil is attributed to his equally exceptional and even astonishing faults. In the one case, as well as in the other, we are outside the criterion of judgement intrinsic in Marxism. The true problems are evaded, which are why and how Soviet society could reach and did reach certain forms alien to the democratic way and to the legality which it had set for itself, even to the point of degeneration.[13]

The Soviet leaders could not transgress certain mental and

sociological barriers and embark on a thorough-going investigation of the origins and significance of Stalinism. At the moment of his death, in the summer of 1964, Togliatti was writing his *Yalta memorandum*, a text openly critical of the Soviet inconsistent treatment of the Stalin question. The *Memorandum* was to become the theoretical basis of the Italian Eurocommunist approach.[14]

When the Soviet party itself acknowledged misdeeds that had been previously vehemently denied as vicious imperialist calumnies, communist intellectuals were overwhelmed with a deep sense of betrayal and desolation. Some of them clung to their original faith, others decided to put an end to moral double-dealing and embark on a real search for truth.

To his own misfortune, Nikita Khrushchev did not draw while in power the appropriate conclusions from the horrendous facts he had presented to the Twentieth Congress. Instinctively, he felt that Stalinism should be overcome. As an apparatchik, however, Khrushchev refused to preside over the dismantling of those institutions he identified with the very nature of communism. He actually opposed the calls for a reconsideration of the whole Soviet experience since Lenin's death in January 1924. On several occasions, Khrushchev branded anti-Stalinism as anti-communism. During the Sino–Soviet polemic after 1960, when Khrushchev postured as a reformer, Mao Zedong reminded the flamboyant Soviet first secretary of these statements and accused him of being the gravedigger of socialism. On the other hand, the Soviet party apparatus was increasingly irritated by Nikita Khrushchev's erratic behaviour. They resented the anti-Stalinist thrust of the resolutions adopted by the Twenty Second CPSU Congress in 1961. Khrushchev's ouster in October 1964 demonstrates that going half-way on the path of reforms cannot be a valid option for a communist leader who wants to stay in power. Khrushchevism was for all intents and purposes an attempt to square the circle and invent a more human face for a system that remains basically unchanged.

Disappointed by the hesitations and half-measures of Khrushchevism, critical intellectuals in Eastern Europe outran the official ideologues and ushered in a general operation of ethical reconstruction. They were convinced that Stalinist dictatorship could not rely on a real legitimacy in the traditional, pre-totalitarian sense. It was therefore necessary to comprehend the nature of the formation they had been living in, the mysteries of what Bertram Wolfe called 'the greatest power machine in all history'.[15] With an acute sense of historical irony, Wolfe put as motto of his critical exegesis of Khrushchev's secret report George Orwell's 1946 premonitory idea: 'In five years it may be as dangerous to praise Stalin as it was to attack him two years ago. But I should not regard this as an advance. Nothing is gained by teaching a parrot a new word.' In other words, the matter was to go beyond mere historical sermonising and try to expand the critique of Stalin as a bloodthirsty psychopath to that of the Stalinist system as the very opposite of what Hegel believed to be the reason in history: '. . . the development of the consciousness of Freedom on the part of the Spirit, and of the consequent realization of that Freedom'.[16]

Until it ended in the Soviet military attack on revolutionary Budapest and the subsequent massacre of the Hungarian insurgents, the first wave of de-Stalinisation could justifiably arouse enthusing dreams of reform. National communism was the means, not the final end. In the mind of the Hungarian revolutionaries it was vitally important to put an end to totalitarian despotism. François Fejtö is therefore right to regard the Hungarian social and political explosion as 'the first large-scale revolution under a communist regime, the first anti-totalitarian revolution'.[17] Hungarian intellectuals understood that freedom cannot be attained as long as totalitarian institutions continue to supervise social intercourse. The break with Stalinism involved more than a revision of certain dogmas; it was indeed necessary to engage in a revolutionary action which would bring about a new social and political order. The outcome of the whole process would have been the emergence of a more humane space for the individual, a society where the mind would be free to decide over its needs and interests. The enslavement of spirit, carried to almost perfection under mature Stalinism, had to be overcome through a search for authenticity and a reconstruction of the civil society. The role of the Stalinist party in society had to be redefined in the sense of a drastic curtailment of its unwarranted privileges.

Notes

1. See Adam Michnik, *Letters from prison*, p. 47.
2. See Leszek Kolakowski, 'Totalitarianism and lie', *Commentary*, May 1983, p. 37.
3. See Branko Lazitch and Milorad Drachkovitch, *Biographical dictionary of the Comintern*, pp. 396 – 7; Ernst Fischer, *An opposing man*, pp. 284 – 5.
4. Ibid., p. 433; Eugen Loebl, *My mind on trial* (New York and London:

Harcourt Brace Jovanovich, 1976).

5. See Isaac Deutscher, *Heretics and renegades* (London: Hamish Hamilton, 1955), p. 34.

6. Ibid., p. 30.

7. See Teresa Toranska, *Oni* (Paris: Flammarion, 1986); for the American edition, see Teresa Toranska, *'Them': Stalin's Polish puppets* (New York: Harper and Row, 1987).

8. See Eugéne Ionesco, *Non* (Paris: Gallimard, 1986); Jean-François Revel, 'The young Ionesco', *Encounter*, February 1987, p. 36.

9. See T. H. Rigby, and Ferenc Fehér (eds), *Political legitimation in communist states* (New York: St. Martin's Press, 1982).

10. See Slobodan Stankovic, 'Marxism is dead forever, Kolakowski tells Yugoslav periodicals', RFE, Yugoslav SR, 7 March 1986, pp. 28–9.

11. See Isaac Deutscher, 'Marxism and primitive magic', in Tariq Ali, *The Stalinist legacy* (Middlesex: Penguin Books, 1984), p. 116.

12. *The New York Times*, 30 March 1956, cf. *The anti-Stalin campaign and international communism*, p. 98.

13. Ibid., p. 120.

14. See Franco Ferrarotti, 'Eurocommunism, Italian version' in George Schwab (ed.), *Eurocommunism. The ideological and political-theoretical foundations* (Westport, Conn.: Greenwood Press, 1981), pp. 157–85.

15. See Bertram Wolfe, *Khrushchev and Stalin's ghost* (New York: Praeger, 1957).

16. See G. W. F. Hegel, *The philosophy of history* (New York: Dover Publications, 1956), p. 63.

17. See François Fejtö, *Behind the rape of Hungary* (New York: David McKay, 1957), p. 309.

7

From Criticism to Apostasy

Powerful and daring minds are now beginning to struggle upright, to find their way out from under heaps of antiquated rubbish. But even they still bear all the cruel marks of the branding iron, they are still cramped by the shackles into which they were forced half-grown.

Aleksandr Solzhenitsyn

Revisionism, which is a term coined by neo-Stalinist orthodoxies to stigmatise critical currents of thought, has been the main adversary encountered by ruling party bureaucrats since the times of the factional struggles in the mid and late 1920s. The resurrection of the revisionist temptation was an exhilarating experience for those intellectuals who had been seduced by the morbid historical romanticism of Stalinism. This craving for a moral reform of communism was the main motivation of the neo-Marxist revivalism in Eastern Europe. Richard Löwenthal is right in explaining this orientation through a moral revulsion among the communist intelligentsia against injustice and lies: 'Communist writers and poets, in particular, realizing that their talents had been misused for years to justify crimes and mislead their people, passionately hoped to redeem themselves by telling the truth and by boldly defending humanistic values.'[1]

What really mattered was to demolish deeply entrenched taboos, to strengthen the cohesion of oppositional intellectuals and workers, and to develop a sense of common values and interests. To the fictitious unity preferred by the system, critical intellectuals should respond in a unified manner. The system can easily do away with spontaneous outbursts of discontent. On the contrary, it would be far more difficult for the despotic oligarchy to stamp out

121

co-ordinated oppositional action.

It can be assumed that in February 1956, when Khrushchev delivered his 'secret' report, the Soviet leader was far from anticipating the long-term impact of his inconoclastic action. The whole history of world communism could now be reassessed. No wonder therefore that historical debates in Poland and Hungary dealt with burning issues concerning the nature of domestic communism and its links with the Muscovite centre. Recapturing the past meant dispelling the prevailing myths about the history of the ruling communist formations and their relations with the Moscow centre. One of the most inflamed debates organised by the Petöfi Circle in Budapest in the summer of 1956 was unleashed by Georg Lukács's presentation of some controversial issues in the history of the Hungarian Communist Party. It was obvious that these historical questions had vital implications for the destiny of Hungarian Stalinism. A quest for political autonomy was synonymous with an overall criticism of the Soviet model, and the local Stalinist leaders (Rákosi, Gerö, Farkas, in Hungary, and the Natolin faction in Poland) were not mistaken in regarding this critical direction as an attempt to bring about a different political order.[2] In other words, what was happening was a showdown between partisans of the Stalinist *ancien régime* and proponents of radical reforms.

The chances of the revisionist groups were enhanced by the aggravation of rivalries and political infighting at the top of the Soviet hierarchy. For the Soviet leaders, the only crucial thing was not to lose any of the satellite countries. All the rest could be negotiable, or at least that was what they wanted East European reformists to believe. Even a diehard Stalinist like Mikhail Suslov was at pains, in 1956, to defend the recently denounced Stalinist methods. At the Twentieth Congress, on the contrary, he had deplored the routinisation of party propaganda and called for a creative approach to Marxism-Leninism. Another Soviet leader, Anastas Mikoyan, was trying to cajole East European leaders with promises of equality in mutual trade.

Soviet politics towards Poland and Hungary, marked by confusion and oscillations, were actually a combination of stick and carrot tactics. Not that the Soviet party bureaucrats would have upheld the revisionist approach, but at that historical juncture they were stripped of a reasonable alternative to it. The Stalinist elites in Europe had been irredeemably compromised in countless atrocities and their popular support was practically nil. Under such conditions, the Soviet leaders decided to woo those open-minded communists who, they assumed, would be ready to come to terms with a somewhat subdued external domination. In Hungary, Imre Nagy was, in Soviet eyes, the prototype of such a manipulable personage.[3] His past was overwhelmingly linked to the Soviet Union and, though personally affable and warm-hearted, he was nevertheless the exponent of the political formation that any revolutionary movement would have wished to overthrow. To his everlasting honour, Nagy found the inner ethical resources to become the leader of the first anti-totalitarian revolution, a world-historical event that changed all the data of the power relations within the Soviet empire.

Reflecting on the Hungarian tragedy and its protagonists, Ferenc Fehér and Agnes Heller rightly consider that it expressed crystal-clearly the agony of Leninism and the début of a crucially different form of radicalism:

> . . . we can say that the Hungarian drama between 1953 and 1956 became a *representative drama of the inner disintegration of Bolshevism*, and that it produced, with many transitory types, *three representative figures*. The first was Kádár, the model type of the *Khrushchevite*, with his 'Khrushchevite Hungary' of the 1960s. The second was Lukács, the *inconsistent Bolshevik*; the man with the sincere conviction of being 'the authentic Bolshevik', and who, precisely because of this inconsistency, could become the defender of the revolution of 1956 — an indefensible cause when viewed from strictly Bolshevik premises. The third figure was Nagy. This man, through his inner torments, through that struggle between anxieties that is indeed dependent upon great moral qualities, had transcended Bolshevism. He merits a great place in the history of radical movements.[4]

To transcend the Bolshevik mystification and the system based on it, this was the dream of the revisionist, anti-authoritarian movement of 1956.

In order to have a right perception of the tremendous impact of Khrushchev's secret speech, one has to recall the religious nature of Stalin's cult. It was not a perfunctory adulation of a feared despot, but a deliberate experience of perpetual ecstasy. To put an end to this delusion, to call a spade a spade and a criminal a criminal, was more than self-serving rhetoric. Kolakowski captures the whole significance of that moment when he describes how

> Nikita Khrushchev announced to the Soviet Communist
> party, and soon to the whole world, that he who had been the
> leader of progressive humanity, the inspiration of the world,
> the father of the Soviet people, the master of science and
> learning, the supreme military genius, and altogether the
> greatest genius in history was in reality a paranoiac torturer, a
> mass murderer, and a military ignoramus who had brought
> the Soviet state to the verge of disaster.[5]

The suffocating monopoly of truth exerted by Stalin and the
horde of his sycophants was now open to question. All suppressed
intellectual currents within Marxism could resurface after long
decades of forced silence. Rediscovering the category of the individual, insisting on the dignity of particularity and difference,
reinstating the rights of alterity usurped by an all-absorbing
universality, these were the somewhat Aesopic formulations for
concrete political demands.[6] Regardless of its outrageous
omissions — Trotsky, Bukharin, Radek, Pyatakov, Zinoviev,
Kamenev and other victims of the show-trials did not fit
Khrushchev's image of the martyr, neither did the so-called
'kulaks', and the millions of non-party victims — the 'secret'
speech violated the conspiracy of silence fomented by the
nomenklatura. It was Vyacheslav Molotov who embodied the alternative to this opening, presumably the truly Bolshevik approach,
and later the Albanian and Chinese leaders were to follow in his
footsteps. But Molotov, Malenkov, Kaganovich, and the other top
Stalinists did indeed voice the apprehensions of the party rank-
and-file, the fears of those whose careers had been prompted by
Stalin's technology of terror. The main flaw of the Khrushchevite
analysis of Stalinism lies in the attempt to separate system and
leader: while lambasting the latter, Khrushchev went out of his
way to whitewash the former. With its inherent contradictions and
inconsistencies, Khrushchev's approach to Stalinism did not
prevent the regrouping of a conservative coalition which would
eventually succeed in demoting him in October 1964. Significantly, the *éminence grise*, the mastermind of the coup against
Khrushchev, was no one else but Mikhail Suslov, the party's top
ideologist. He accused Khrushchev of political adventurism and
ideological laxity. For Suslov, any manifestation of tolerance in the
cultural field would risk creating anarchy and disorder. Among

other sins, Khrushchev was reproached by his Politburo colleagues for approving the publication of Solzhenitsyn's masterpiece *One day in the life of Ivan Denisovich*. Neo-Stalinist bureaucrats cannot stand political and cultural spontaneity (*stihiinost*); when confronted with such phenomena their reactions are violent and abusive.

In their struggle against the ideological apparatus, it was important for revisionist thinkers to avoid dogmatic anti-Stalinism. The point was not to replace a form of dogmatism through another one. What really mattered was to spell out the roots of the atrocities, to endow criticism with a real *esprit de sérieux*. In other words, revisionism implied a renewal of the Marxist experience, a rehabilitation of the repressed legacy of Hegelian-Marxism, and the vindication of the upsurge against mechanicism (or determinism) so characteristic of leftist heresies of the 1920s.

Philosophically, revisionism could not formulate more than an alternative Marxism. It was caught in the obsolete paradigm of right versus left ideologies and could not therefore address the basic issues of a radical rethinking of the communist experience. To be sure, revisionist authors loathed the Stalinist nightmare, but they were still prisoners of the Marxist dream. Their disquisitions were written under the sway of utopia and they relished the condition of true spokesmen for the genuine doctrine. They blamed the ruling oligarchs for having betrayed and/or confiscated the Marxist ideal. In their researches, revisionists took Marxism for granted as a philosophy of freedom; the root of the evil was Lenin's Russianisation of historical materialism. In practical terms, the revisionists were driven to discover the risks of opposition and the inevitability of factionalism. They were not prepared for this form of resistance and it took years until they admitted that the solution for the authentic democratisation of Soviet-type regimes lay outside the ruling parties.

The more thorough their investigation of political authority and domination, the more compelling became the urge to dissociate themselves from the discourse of those in power. Writing about the revisionist experience in Poland, Adam Michnik indicates the refusal of a resolute and articulate break with the system as one of the causes of its marginalisation and final dissolution as an independent current:

> . . . the revisionists' greatest sin lay not in their defeat in the intraparty struggle for power (where they could not win) but

125

in the character of that defeat. It was the defeat of individuals being eliminated from positions of power and influence, not a setback for a broadly based leftist and democratic political platform. The revisionists never created such a platform.[7]

The main revisionist contribution was thus placed in the field of a generous *Aufklärung*, an enlightening movement meant to dissipate the mystical aura of totalitarian power. Their work catalysed the awakening of the civic sense among members of the intelligentsia and instituted an embarrassing challenge for the prevailing ideology.

The bold proclamations of 1956 were easily muted, the intransigence of many critical authors turned into pessimism and despair, but the seeds of resistance were to blossom in the Prague Spring and the Polish permanent boycott of the system. Revisionism expedited the decomposition of the sham legitimacy of Soviet-type societies: contested from within, Marxist–Leninist dictatorship could not but resort to naked repression. It was a protracted conflict, with no positive outcome within the existing political boundaries.

The disintegration of the Stalinist gnosis as a self-sufficient system of authoritarian norms and quasi-mystical precepts impelled the revisionist intellectuals towards the construction of what Kolakowski called an agnostic Marxism, actually a quixotic attempt to salvage the humanistic kernel of the doctrine lest the whole Marxist utopia fall apart. Less idealistic than their unorthodox adversaries, the ideological supervisors knew better. Committed to a cynical *Realpolitik*, they saw no reason to let the genie out of the bottle. Reified in the figure of ideological power, Marxism was doomed to survive as an empty symbolic ceremonial. Trying to secularise it, as the revisionist thinkers did, amounted eventually to intellectual self-eroticism. The point was not to recapture a presumed original libertarian thrust, but to formulate the actual conditions for the invention of a liberated social space. Some Western philosophers — primarily Cornelius Castoriadis and Claude Lefort — were perfectly aware of this task. Unlike many East European thinkers, predisposed to the traditional reformist illusions, they understood that, in order to gain credibility, the discourse of the opposition had to be de-Marxised. Dialectical trump-cards had to be debunked and taken for what they indeed were: convoluted justifications for the humiliation of the human being.

From the point of view of the opposition of Soviet-type regimes, the issue of human rights was certainly more than philanthropical rhetoric, since it touched their main vulnerability, the frail status of the human condition in a society pretending to represent the maximum of humanism. In their uninhibited analyses, dissidents expose the political, social, and cultural substratum of bureaucratic domination. Their mindset includes values rejected by official standards of social success. According to George Konrád and Ivan Szelenyi, marginal intellectuals in Eastern Europe, i.e., those who do not partake in the game of power, are divided into two basic categories. The first group is made up of the teleological critics of the system, and critical Marxists certainly fit into this category. They deeply resent the bureaucratic matrix of domination, but would not buttress the shift of the balance of power to the advantage of the technocracy. Their discourse is imbued with the themes of humanism and emancipation. Neo-Marxists favour a predominantly axiological approach to contemporary socialism:

> Stressing the historical role of man as a subjective agent realising himself by choosing among alternatives, and rejecting any kind of economic and sociological reductionism, they place the category of goal-oriented human totality in the center of their thought, and trace the contours of a Marxist phenomenology.[8]

The risk involved in this orientation is the possible co-optation of critical ideas by the ruling elite, precisely in the name of the values apparently shared with the opposition. Leszek Kolakowski pointed to the possibility of 'counter-reformation' as a technique to assimilate and thereby to defuse major critical themes. Drawing from Kolakowski's interpretation, in a recent essay on Gorbachev's campaign for *glasnost*, Adam Michnik scrutinised this strategy of communist elites:

> A counter-reformation is therefore not a restoration of the pre-reformist order, but rather an attempt to transform the institutions from within. It is a self-critical show of strength with the aim of incorporating those values created against the will of and outside the social institutions in order to stop them becoming antagonistic and subversive.[9]

As a response to this ominous possibility, critical Marxists have

127

deliberately enveloped their analyses in a speculative form, which could serve as a shelter against bureaucratic usurpation of their themes. The other side of the coin was that their message was too cryptical, too esoterical to be understood by people unskilled in the sophistries of Marxist (or Hegelian) dialectics. On the other hand, Konrád and Szelenyi tend to underrate the awareness of these limits on the part of at least some revisionist thinkers. Both Leszek Kolakowski and the members of the Budapest School went beyond 'philosophical resignation' and, in their latest works, critically (and self-critically) tackled the most sensitive issues of contemporary left-wing radicalism. As for the other category, the empirical revisionists, they have offered a critique situated beyond the Marxist values and contributed to the des-ideologisation of the oppositional stances. In countries like Poland, Hungary, and Czechoslovakia, empirical sociology and social psychology analysed the status of the working class and other social groups without paying more than lip service to the official dogmas. Even in Romania, at least between 1966 and 1974, sociology enjoyed a relatively autonomous status and could deal with some of the most disquieting social issues, including growing social stratification, the crisis in political and cultural communication, the contradictions of the educational system, etc.

The chances for renewal in Eastern Europe cannot be comprehended without taking into account the dissident subculture, constituted as a result of this common rejection of the techno-bureaucratic consensus:

> A common repression unites the marginal intellectuals, irrespective of their differences of opinion. They come to feel a solidarity with one another because of the similarity in the circumstances of their daily lives, including the difficulties of making a living and the periodic police harassment; and so they become more alike in their manner of living and values. They develop a special subculture of marginality, their own gallows humour, mutual tolerance, respect for one another's autonomy, a certain conspiratorial discipline even, and an antipathy to all official authority, whether embodied in the elite's political police or in the life-style of the technocracy.[10]

With all its shortcomings and vacillations, revisionism has decisively contributed to the breakdown of the established ideological concensus and heralded the beginning of a more resolute strategy of opposition to the system:

> By appealing, in its attack on Stalinism to the stereotypes of
> the same doctrinal tradition, it contributed to the internal cor-
> rosion of Communist ideology and initiated a movement that
> would in time cause its collapse. Certainly the revisionist
> movement, which found a large number of adherents within
> the ranks of the party intelligentsia, could not last very long.
> As it turned out, it was eventually compelled — as a result
> both of its own logic and of historical events — to reject
> Communism entirely.[11]

At the moment when in Poland the possibility of a vital coalition
was looming, manichean concepts like 'left' and 'right' looked
totally devoid of sense and therefore obsolete:

> . . . these labels had lost all recognizable meaning. All of the
> opposition groups stressed their commitment to democratic
> values and to the cause of Poland's sovereignty. The differ-
> ences among the various political currents were not focused
> on the validity of these general ideas.[12]

The historical compromise that led to the alliance between
radical intellectuals, the Church, and the workers, modified the
whole political spectrum in Poland. The idiom of power has been
deprived of its *ouvrierist* undertones, and the social demagogy of the
regime looks blatantly unappealing. It is thus comical to see the
leaders of Polish communism pretending to embody the willingness and interests of the working class while at the same time out-
lawing the independent Solidarity union with its 10 million
members. When confronted with a really organised proletariat,
the bureaucrats are panic-ridden and resort to undisguised
violence. This is true for Poland, but also for a country like
Yugoslavia where the ruling party publicly menaced the strikers in
March 1987 with repression undertaken by the military. As
Kolakowski put it:

> Communism in Poland has thus been reduced to a reliance on
> guns, and there is something quite natural in this culmination
> of its history . . . Polish culture and, indeed, Polish society
> will continue to live and to survive in a long struggle against
> the entire political structure, now stripped of all ideological

adornments and compelled to appear for what it is: naked coercion.[13]

In other words, it is now obvious where the real source of the evil lies: in the unlimited power monopoly of the Communist party, which has always been the most jealously guarded dogma of the Marxist – Leninist sects. Once Stalin's cult was exposed, the myth of the party was reasserted as an ersatz ideological ingredient. Stalin's purported omniscience was replaced through a shapeless entity baptised the 'collective wisdom' of the party. When all is said and done, one should admit that revisionism had a pioneering role in the toppling of the self-satisfied hegemony exerted by the Stalinist apparatus. It legitimised the idea of revolt and advocated the right to difference. It stripped the prevailing orthodoxy of the nimbus of infallibility and dissipated the simulacrum of irrefragable unity professed by the official doctrine. Short-lived and often self-contradictory, fragile and fatally narcissistic, revisionism was nonetheless infinitely more fruitful than the dogmas it opposed. Were it for nothing but its liberating effects on successive generations of critical intellectuals in Poland, Hungary, East Germany, and Czechoslovakia, it will still be remembered as a major moral and political catalyst, a confirmation of the possibility to overcome totalitarian conformity.

As mentioned, revisionism was tragically powerless precisely because of its obstinacy in observing the rules of the game imposed by the ruling power in spite of the incontrovertible evidence that such a tactic was eventually suicidal. For many years, revisionist intellectuals stuck to their Marxist pipedreams and stoically accepted the verdicts of the party tribunals. It took them decades to shred the mythological fabric of their beliefs and engage in a new experience of radical separation from the powers that be. The Marxist universalist arrogance had to be abandoned on behalf of a regained and redeeming sense of humility. The avatars of the East-Central European revisionist intellectuals form one of the most instructive and fascinating chapters in the history of contemporary Western civilisation. They had been prepared and conditioned to become the mandarins of the new ideological empire and their revolt indicated the weaknesses of a dictatorship with universal ambitions.

It is the curse of Soviet-type regimes that they cannot do without intellectuals. All the strategies of co-optation and integration, effective as they may have initially appeared, turned out to be deceptive for both agent and patient. The sacrifice of the intellect cannot be prolonged *ad infinitum*, though the advantages drawn from opportunism and conformity cannot be easily neglected. The controversy between Piotr Wierzbicki and Adam Michnik on the most suitable behaviour under a totalitarian regime suggests the moral difficulties encountered by oppositional activists. In his *Treatise on ticks*, Wierzbicki described the various forms of rationalisation of conduct normally regarded as cowardice. The psychology of the tick is the base for the regime's success in marginalising the dissident counterculture:

> Ticks congregate in coffeehouses, inciting people against the system, rooting for enemies of the people and intriguers. They read the opposition press, but still, they will never sign any protest letters, never write an antistate text, and never meddle in anything that might cost them their job.[14]

The tick is an expert in finding arguments against any form of radical action. He will not sign a protest letter, since he has a duty to the family: 'Protest letters are alright for bachelors and unmarried women, and also for basically irresponsible people. His hands are tied.'[15] The tick knows that nothing can ever happen without permission from the police, and in accordance with this logic, he dismisses all oppositional actions as provocations:

> How does the tick know these are all provocations? Why, because if the security police did not have a hand in it, no one would have taken to the streets, no one would have protested against anything, no one would have been able to found anything. The very success of the action is evidence of its provocative character. The security police don't let anything happen without their approval.[16]

The *Treatise on ticks* is not necessarily a normativist critique of political behaviour. It is rather a *cri de coeur*, an ethical warning, and an attempt to unmask the philosophy of conformity. This is what the author suggests when he addresses the cumbersome issue of who is entitled to write about ticks:

> The answer seems simple — the nonticks should write about ticks. But the answer is simple only on the surface; who can say of himself with a clear conscience that he is not a tick?

Who, indeed? It is the tragedy of the Polish intelligentsia, Polish culture, and simply Poland, and the reason that this study has been written, that all or almost all of us are, in whole or in part, or have been to a certain degree, ticks.[17]

In his turn, Adam Michnik rejects rigid distinctions between ticks and angels and questions the 'aesthetic cult of "clean hands"'. Michnik is worried about the danger of sweeping generalisations and reminds his readers about the quiet forms of resistance, particularly those unspectacular but still immensely important efforts to preserve the cultural values:

I really do understand Wierzbicki's anger and his opposition to the process that Milosz, some years ago, called 'moral decay' and 'Pétainism'. I understand too, however, the bitterness of people who, through all this, often clenching their teeth and enduring humiliations, created a morsel of our own mental reality, preserved and restored old values, and built up new ones, and now, today, are called 'ticks'.[18]

Soviet-type regimes are established on the basis of ideology and are therefore compelled to periodically reaffirm their ideological legitimacy. To do that, they need the assistance of a social caste whose main task is precisely the symbolic reproduction of the system. Ironically, it is from this ideological elite that the most outspoken critics of those regimes are recruited. Pertaining to a social group, as the sociology of knowledge from Mannheim to Gouldner has demonstrated, does not imply automatic solidarity with the group's behaviour, and alienation from that group is often conducive to a radical break with its professed values. The schism between apparatchiks and revisionists in Soviet-type societies, a conflict primarily characteristic of the Khrushchev years, was only a tardy epilogue to Marx's (or Lenin's, or Lukács's) repudiation of his class's views and values.

After the tragic events in 1956, traditional concepts like reform, revolution, masses, leaders, party, democracy, pluralism, had to be reappraised. The idea of change entered the realm of political discourse and the 'cold ideology' was publicly exposed as a fraud. The Marxist–Leninist cult of power was defied in the name of the powerless. The upheavals in 1956, and later the Czechoslovak Reform Movement, questioned not only the Stalinist model of socialism, but also the Soviet pretence to theoretical and political hegemony. The Czech reformers understood that political pluralism should be rooted in a pluralistic ownership of property. To quote Antonin Liehm:

> The Prague Reform Movement challenged the ownership-role of the Communist party. It did not challenge it immediately. In the early stages of the Movement the idea was to change the Party, and through the Party the system. 'Democratisation of the Communist Party' was the slogan when the wagon started rolling, and this was followed by calls for the democratisation of the press, culture, the judiciary, and so on . . . Eventually the call came for what I regard as the key element in the whole Reform Movement — the call for the *expropriation of the State*.[19]

The problem with the communist reformers was that they seemed to believe that the alternative to the bankrupt Stalinist institutions would be the internal democratisation of the Communist party. The leitmotif of the Prague reformers was that an end should be put to the politics 'behind closed doors' and that the party (one party, to be sure!) had to consult democratically with the masses. Alexander Dubček and his supporters seemed to believe that the main problem with a Leninist-type regime resided in the style of leadership and that once a new, more democratic, or simply democratic style was introduced, things would improve. Socialism would thus become an attractive political and social programme to be spontaneously embraced by the masses. These were the illusions that were shared by leading Czechoslovak intellectuals and by the political luminaries of the Prague Spring:

> Stalinism, to tell the truth, was not a deformation of socialism, but its downright corruption. Stalin's misuse of language was the grossest confidence trick yet practised on the citizen by any modern political system . . . What *we* tried to do in Czechoslovakia in 1968 was to inject genuinely democratic content into these atrophied and defunct institutions, starting with the democratisation of the nerve of it all: the Communist Party.[20]

Actually, the very structure of any Communist party is inherently opposed to democracy. For a Leninist party to embark on genuine reforms and admit the validity of pluralism would mean to overcome the sectarian assumptions that led to its creation as a political formation totally different from social-democracy and thereby to deny its very *raison d'être*. In this respect, the goals and achievements of the Hungarian Revolution were more ambitious and less self-restrained than those of the Prague reformers. A revolution against the faked revolution, this was a most unexpected and unthinkable event for the petrified minds of the apparatchiks.

All the tantalising efforts of the communist regimes to revamp their ideological facade cannot conceal one basic truth: the system has not been radically transformed since Stalin's days, the ideological underpinnings have not been reassessed, and the individual is still held prisoner of the statist-bureaucratic mechanism. The goal is the same as under mature Stalinism: the formation of the 'new man', and the totalitarian institutions bound to carry out its implementation have not been altered by alleged steps toward democratisation. Political police resort now to therapeutic rather than to prophylactic terror to propitiate 'recalcitrant elements', and ideological surveillance channels function as pivotal elements of the existing order.

Reforms, when attempted, are launched by the party and it is always the party that indicates their scope and limits. Even in a country like Hungary, with its New Economic Mechanism and the relative autonomy granted to small-size private initiative, the party continues to enjoy discretionary power over society. The appartments of leading dissidents are periodically ransacked by the police, visas for trips abroad are frequently denied to opposition authors, and the current social truce is often regarded as a provisional arrangement that could be easily repealed by the regime. Without overlooking the salient distinctions between contemporary Soviet-style regimes, it would be difficult not to underwrite Kolakowski's pessimistic view of the reality of communism:

> The only Communist regimes in the world are of Leninist–Stalinist pattern. On Stalin's death the Soviet system changed from a personal tyranny to that of an oligarchy. From the point of view of state omnipotence this is a less effective system; it does not, however, amount to de-Stalinization but only to an ailing form of Stalinism.[21]

Genuine de-Stalinisation would involve the introduction of constitutional provisions for a pluralist political order, an uninhibited approach to the past, including an unequivocal condemnation of dictatorship as a form of government and free access to the archives for all those interested, renunciation of repression as a main mechanism of social conservation, abolition of censorship, unrestricted freedom to travel, and other measures meant to ensure the revival of civil society.

It was indeed a most fateful illusion for non-Machiavellian reformers that a Leninist system could be reconstructed and renovated. They were convinced that Stalinism was primarily associated with the Soviet experience and believed therefore that a less brutal version of socialism ought to be imagined. It took them a long time to become aware of the real nature of the system they aimed to reform and most of them came out of that experience incurably disgruntled and embittered. 'National communism' and 'humanist Marxism' have remained utopian desiderata and Stalinism turned out to be more stubborn and resistant than most revisionist thinkers would have believed. All things considered, the fiasco of revisionism demonstrated the intrinsic non-reformability of institutional Marxism, its adversity to any critical trends and primarily to those rooted in the socialist creed.

The basic demands of heretical Marxism bore upon the democratisation of the body politic. The return to the original dialectical wellspring favoured a reappraisal of the whole dogmatic conception of the party as a privileged (chosen) group, endowed with a superior sense of historical necessity and objectively upholding the interests of the working class. This new approach to the issue of intra-party democracy was accompanied by an unavowed hostility to Soviet hegemonism. Revisionists were disgusted with the Soviet appropriation of Marxist truth. They considered this situation outrageously abnormal, but did not dare to question the ultimate relevance of Leninism. Their criticism was subsequently incomplete and their possible audience could not exceed the party's membership and sympathisers. Moreover, they favoured the thesis of continuity within socialist praxis and could not envision a meta- or even anti-Marxist oppositional platform, grouping social actors with no attachments to the leftist symbolic heritage. As mentioned already, the impasse of revisionism was fatal in the absence of a divorce from the language and values of domination.

The dynamics of critical Marxism forced the leading ideological apparatus to regroup and try to articulate a response to this challenge from within. Witch-hunts were organised against intellectual troublemakers and Soviet Marxism was once again congealed in a corpus of insipid platitudes and hypocritical sermons. What counts for ruling ideocrats is to keep a simulacrum of faith alive, regardless of the growing evidence of its complete irrelevance. Marxism in Soviet-type societies is nothing more than a doctrinary skeleton, a lamentable vestige of its past splendour. Any attempt to refurbish it, as Karl Korsch showed more than four decades ago, is essentially a reactionary undertaking. It is indeed an effort to deny reality, to oppugn evidence and defy common sense in the name of an abusive mystique. The lofty ideals of early Marxism, cynically perverted by Lenin and exploited by the Stalinist and neo-Stalinist bureaucracies, are now extinct as a source of inspiration for those who oppose the system.

The ethos of critical Marxism

'Marxism has been the greatest fantasy of our century.'[22] Thus Leszek Kolakowski characterised the mythical ambivalence of historical materialism, its intrinsic utopian dimension and longing for a new foundation of reality. Unlike other theologies, Marxism was able to deter for many decades the emergence of a sense of critical questioning, and to nourish passionate, even fanatical, attachments on the part of normally sceptical western intellectuals.

Contemporary Marxism presents a bewildering proliferation of neo-Marxist, critical, or even post-critical schools, many of them unequivocally opposed to authoritarian regimes of the Soviet type. Praxis — the process by which, according to Hegelian–Marxist dialectics, the subject and object of history are supposed to become one — has regained its abstract and speculative content. In this setting, the Budapest School audaciously defied the hypocrisy of Hungary party chief János Kádár's 'repressive tolerance' and inaugurated a far-reaching *démarche* whose basic aim has been to demythologise the ideology of 'really existing socialism' and to dispel illusions about its nature. In *Dictatorship over needs*, leading members of the Budapest School bear witness to the possibility of developing an uninhibited outlook capable of breaking through the veil of Marxist false consciousness. Nevertheless, these one-time pupils of Georg Lukács continue to insist on the relevance of the Marxian paradigm for the comprehension of authoritarian-bureaucratic systems. They persevere in investing their emotional capital in the humanist potential of the Marxist dialectic, although they are perfectly well aware that Stalinist and neo-Stalinist appropriation of historical materialism cannot but frustrate and severely compromose their own endeavour. The political-philosophical discourse of the Budapest School remains rooted in a certain type of existential Marxism. In other words, the authors base themselves on a Fichtean revolt against reality and claim, in good Hegelian tradition, that they would attain some 'truer' reality beyond the present, spurious one.

The members of the Budapest School reject any pose of neutrality and raise their voices on behalf of the beleaguered 'unhappy consciousness'. Abiding by a Blochian rather than a Lukácsian tradition, this school rebukes what Hegel called 'reconciliation with reality' and is deeply suspicious of the propensity of the radical-utopian left in the West to dismiss the long-term implications that the failure of Marxism in Eastern Europe has for the nature of revolutionary thought itself. The case of the Budapest School of thinkers is symptomatic for a group of distinguished intellectuals caught in a political and theoretical deadlock: they continue to practice a *sui generis* variety of Marxism, something that one could call anti-totalitarian Marxism, but which is nonetheless anchored in the same intellectual matrix they wish to overcome. They seem incapable of scrutinising the immanent pathology of historical materialism, of questioning its humanist pretensions, of introducing the criterion of praxis into their assessment of its contemporary hypostases. Yet, genuine post-Marxist critical philosophy — of which the Budapest School is in some sense a harbinger — must elaborate theses directly refuting the frozen axioms of historical materialism. One of their most recent volumes suggests that such a conceptual reconstruction is seen by Fehér and Heller as a main imperative.[23] In an ironic twist, these disciples of Max Weber's once most promising disciple — Lukács — have come to rediscover the tension between reason and unreason and embark on a thorough-going critique of political *ratio* itself.

The Budapest School views 'dictatorship over needs' as a consistent Stalinist socio-political system that is central to Eastern Europe's Soviet-type regimes. It begins with the assumption 'that the subjection of the 'rebellious' and 'individualistic' private person to a 'superior wisdom' has to be started at the level of his need system'.[24] 'Dictatorship over needs' is thus a key concept that grasps the inner logic of the East-Central European regimes — the persistence of latent Stalinism in them. It suggests the dissolution of the autonomous individual within the all-devouring framework of totalitarian controls. Furthermore, this concept helps us to understand the disastrous politicisation of the psyche, the unscrupled manipulation of the subjective field, the attempt to do away with the sphere of privacy as an ultimate sanctuary of the ego.

Despite certain 'liberalising' measures, the totalitarian order remains structurally unchanged, characterised by oppression *in actu* and *in potentia*, exercised in varying degrees according to the prevailing interests of the bureaucratic elite. The strategy of mass repression has been abandoned not because of a purported modification in the morality of the 'nomenklatura', but as a result of the growing awareness that it was politically and economically counter-productive. The mobilisational techniques of mature Stalinism could not serve the purposes of the ruling techno-bureaucracy in the attempt to modernise economy and convince the West about its good-will in the politics of 'peaceful co-existence', or, to use Brezhnev's terminology, 'détente'. It goes without saying, the ideological apparatus has taken great care to underscore the idea that political coexistence means indeed competition, perpetual rivalry, and that ideological vigilance should not be subdued. It is interesting to note that the exhausted Soviet ideological machine is still extremely active on the international arena, with consistent efforts to infiltrate peace-oriented, environmentalist, and other concerned groups in the West.

In evaluating Eastern Europe's Soviet-style regimes, the Hungarians see no principle of moderation, no democratic rationality underlying the functioning of the social organisation. On the contrary, the recourse to violence is always possible, should the *nomenklatura* (the self-perpetuating political elite) feel its hegemony jeopardised. One is tempted to make use here of the concept of structural violence, the basic political strategy developed by a frightened elite whose incorrigible debility originates in the never-solved complex of legitimacy issues. For communist bureaucracies there is no basis of legitimacy other than sheer power, no authentic meritocratic competition, no reasonable hierarchy of values. This is particularly conspicuous in the case of self-contained hyper-personalised — one might say pharaonic — regimes, such as the late Enver Hoxha's in Albania, Kim Il-song's in North Korea, and Nicolae Ceausescu's in Romania. At the same time it is obvious that the open and/or covert symbolic violence, to make use of a term coined by French sociologist Pierre Bourdieu, lies deep in the heart of the post-totalitarian order even in countries

138

where the regimes display less grotesque features than in Romania, Cuba, or North Korea. In his already classical essay 'The power of the powerless', Václav Havel explores this mechanism of internalisation of the reproductive, autogenerative symbols of the system:

> Part of the essence of the post-totalitarian system is that it draws everyone into its sphere of power, not so that they may realize themselves as human beings, but so that they may surrender their human identity in favour of the identity of the system, that is, so that they may become agents of the system's general automatism and servants of its self-determined goals, so they may participate in the common responsibility for it, so they may be pulled into and ensnared by it, like Faust with Mephistopheles.[25]

As a result of this general corruption, the individual becomes both a slave and a supporter of the system. The possibility of a different order of things, the image of historical transcendance, is systematically obliterated, and the system acquires the appearance of unalterability. Hopelessness is all-pervasive precisely because it is almost impossible to resist it in the name of a totally different principle of reality. The individual has been insidiously absorbed into this elusive dialectic, the result of which is the impossibility of drawing a clearcut line of distinction between *them* and *us*. It is true that most of the people are both 'ticks' and 'angels', but the very existence of dissident communities tends to bear out that a break with this ensnaring system is not out of the question. They are, however, besieged minorities and the conduct of the average person entitles Havel to consider that the system's quite successful strategy consists of blurring the visible opposition between rulers and ruled:

> Here . . . is one of the most important differences between the post-totalitarian system and classical dictatorships, in which this line of conflict can still be drawn according to social class. In the post-totalitarian system, this line runs *de facto* through each person, for everyone in his or her own way is both victim and a supporter of the system. What we understand by the system is not, therefore, a social order imposed by one group upon another, but rather something which permeates the entire society and is a factor in shaping it,

something that may seem impossible to grasp or define (for it is in the nature of a mere principle), but which is expressed by the entire society as an important feature of its life.[26]

Yet the communist regimes are not actually as solid and immobile as they appear to be. Examples like the Budapest School and the Democratic Opposition in Hungary, Charter 77 in Czechoslovakia, or the Committee for Workers' Self Defence (KOR) in Poland, refute the image of these regimes' total manipulation of and control over their societies. To take the case of the Budapest School: Kádár's ideological guardians had to put up with these intellectual rebels for many years before hitting upon the optimal bureaucratic solution of banishment. The KOR's public activities, the constitution of the workers-intellectuals coalition, and the emergence of Solidarity in Poland were, of course, another powerful argument against an outlook that would grant these systems an aura of immunity and infallibility.

There is a negative principle working at the core of these regimes, despite the apparently smooth functioning of their repressive institutions. The logic of domination cannot ultimately prevail over the counter-logic of emancipation. The problem is whether a culture of resistance should include Marxism among its main components or should jettison it as a key feature of the execrated autocracy that is being resisted. To be sure, Marxism, as a *Weltanschauung*, cannot be reduced to the verbal ritual practised by the servants of the 'dictatorship over needs'. But this political metaphysics cannot escape responsibility for the ruin of so many altruistic promises and the triumph of one of the most despicable forms of tyranny in history. For most East European intellectuals, Marxism cannot be separated from the political system established in its name. Furthermore, what is increasingly realised, even by once ardent advocates of its renewal, is that Marxism, with its emphasis on the traditional class paradigm and an anachronistic definition of politics, actually obstructs the configuration of a programme for the future and prevents the elimination of false divisions and discords within the opposition.

To go beyond myth and utopia, it is essential to discard the obsolete tenets and archaic symbols of Marxism, to transcend the 'previous philosophical consciousness'. Yet, unlike Kolakowski, the Budapest School is loath to commit intellectual parricide and remains sentimentally attached to the cultural-political horizon of historical materialism. These philosophers are obviously oriented

140

towards a desirable, but according to them non-existent, order of democracy and social justice. (Once again the real alternatives seem subordinated to ultimate metaphysical archetypes.) And if, as they argue, 'the world needs more, not less, socialism than it has today',[27] one should perhaps question Marx's ghost regarding the tragic fate of political idealism and historical romanticism when converted into revolutionary praxis.

Unlike the historical school of Isaac Deutscher, the Hungarian critical Marxists refuse to subscribe to the theory of the objective necessity of Stalinism. What has happened in the Soviet Union and in the other countries of the bloc should not be viewed as the awful 'price of historical progress', but rather as the consequence of the Marxist historicist hubris in which the myth of progress functions as a counterpart to what Hegel called the 'cunning of reason'. It is thus all the more urgent that these thinkers unify the theory of 'dictatorship over needs' with a comprehensive interpretation of Marxism as an instrument of intellectual and political subjugation.

The members of the Budapest School, despite their disaffection with Soviet-type regimes, still seem convinced that a dialogue is possible with certain enlightened West European Communist parties. It is for these writers a matter of intellectual honour to persuade Western Marxists that 'dictatorship over needs' is actually the opposite of any kind of humanist philosophy, including historical materialism. They therefore attempt to offer 'an elementary model of the functioning of the Soviet social systems'.[28]

Those regimes, artificial as they were at the outset, invented their own mechanisms of internalisation and succeeded in becoming a reference point, a second nature for various strata of the population. The main achievement of the system would be, eventually, to cauterise any sense of historical transcendence, to preclude the genesis of independent nuclei of thought and action — i.e. to effect a complete *Gleichschaltung* (regimentation). Totalitarian systems aim to suppress the very notion of individual autonomy.

The Budapest School authors correctly excoriate the immoral escapism of the western left in its attempt surreptitiously to dissociate the 'innocent' theory from the abominable praxis, and they remind the reader that 'these societies, however tragic this may be, do belong to the international history of that social and intellectual movement that bears the name of socialism.'[29]

The Hungarian philosophers' expectation (inspired by the experience of Solidarity in Poland) of the emergence of 'self-created organs of a counter-power'[30] seems an abstract and overly optimistic appraisal of the window of tolerance currently granted by the system. Is this anything more than another utopian blueprint, rooted in sublimated despair and embarrassed feelings of defeat? As the authors themselves have to admit, such pluralistic forms of self-organisation of various social groups can exist and survive only through violence, and, unfortunately, spontaneous oppositional violence in a police state is more often than not doomed to failure. Totalitarianism is totalitarianism precisely because it succeeds in combating and eradicating areas of spontaneity and informal centres of communication. This conclusion certainly applies to the post-totalitarian regimes, where repression has become more refined, less obvious, but by no means less effective. The recent crackdown on the Hungarian Democratic Opposition and the hardening of the Kádár regime's attitude toward its internal critics, including attempts to topple the democratically elected leadership of the Writers' Union, bode ill for the future of these independent networks of resistance.[31] These remarks should not be misconstrued as an attempt to invalidate the current heroic strategy of dissident resistance in East-Central Europe, including the gradual organisation of the counter-society (the only real one) in a daily confrontation with a bureaucratic Leviathan ready to make use of any means to suppress its adversary. Non-violence is, under the present circumstances, the only rational option for the opposition in Soviet-type regimes. All the obstacles notwithstanding, it seems possible to think of the coagulation of an oppositional avant-garde, a coalition based on a common repudiation of the system and a shared image of the anti-totalitarian struggle:

In a bureaucratic dictatorship, therefore, the revolutionary avantgarde of society is located in the independent alternative associations, in their national and international associations, in their improvement and expansion, in their rapid proliferation, and in their impact on the society as a whole.[32]

The matter is then how to outmanoeuvre bureaucratic manipulation and reinvent politics beyond the frontiers dictated by the system. In a recent essay, Hungarian dissident writer and social critic George Konrád addressed these issues of capital significance.

Writing from Budapest, Konrád states: 'To this day I maintain that a democratic revolution is needed in this city. This regime, which originated from the suppression of 1956, will come to an end sooner or later.'[33] In Konrád's inspired formulation, dissidents 'live in the Soviet empire as the Jews might well have lived in the Roman empire'. The programme of the opposition should avoid moralistic pontifications and sectarian excommunications:

> Working in the community, united with those who work for freedom at home and abroad, with the critics of censorship, the defenders of human rights, we are the carriers of that hidden, subconscious, underground-but-always-resurfacing, nowhere entirely defeated, never-tiring democratic process. We make no secret of being conspirators who want to loosen up these stiff muscles, knowing that defeated, anxious men assume cramped postures.[34]

Dissident groups are permanently harrassed by the repressive apparatus, but they are not ephemeral and will resist the new onslaught of obscurantism: 'We have come to know the mountain air; we cannot return to the stuffy house. We do not long for the scheming aesthetics of circumlocution.'[35] In an essay written in the spring of 1982, Hungarian dissident János Kis pointed to the need for the opposition to put together its views in the form of a coherent ideological programme: '. . . in order to formulate political alternatives and to assess various possibilities, we have to clarify our ideals and explain why we find them so important; we have to evince the institutional solution we imagine to reach those ideals.'[36]

'Dictatorship over needs' represents an updated version of Stalinist totalitarianism. Yet, although overt terrorism was replaced after Stalin's death with a more moderate dictatorial formula, the system has undergone no fundamental transformations that would warrant a different assessment of its essence. Stalin's successors generally get by without using horrid methods, but they have preserved the entire infrastructure, perpetuating the risk or even the likelihood of a tragic return to terrorism. One shares the pessimistic views of Albert Camus in *The plague*, for whom the pestilent rats, despite a temporary retreat, never totally surrender.

A principal function of communist bureaucracy is to exert dictatorship over ideas as well as over needs, to inculcate in its subjects its own image of the future, and to tame any form of resistance. The communist bureaucratic ethos involves a redoubtable *esprit de corps*, a solidarity developed through common existential experience, continued paternalistic behaviour and a jealously guarded monopoly of power.

The dissolution of the civil society and the maintenance of an atomised social space, the *sine qua non* of the 'dictatorship over needs', have engendered widespread moral indifference and intellectual corruption in Soviet-type societies. The individual is compelled to pay lip service to the values enshrined in the official ideology, while he or she perfectly well knows that no one takes them seriously. Duplicitous behaviour is the logical effect of this socially induced division of the self. Many heroes in Milan Kundera's novels do not despise the system more than they disdain themselves. In Soviet-type regimes, societal degradation and self-abasement are thoroughly interwoven and determine each other.

The 'magic' principle of *partiynost* replaces the obligation to search for truth which, according to one of the few Gramscian theses actually accepted and quoted by Marxist – Leninist missionaries, is supposed to be revolutionary. The Budapest philosophers aptly describe this enthrallment: 'The ways of the Party are enigmatic, indeed it is Kierkegaard's God that is embodied in it; no one can ever be in the right against it.'[37]

The hidden rationale for the soporific, wooden jargon of official sermons and simulated pathos remains the exercise of domination by the party bureaucracy. The language of Bolshevism has been the movement's most effective contribution to the desecration of humanist culture in the 20th century, and the source of its victory over competing totalitarian doctrines. This smothering rhetoric has imbued millions of books, booklets, and journals, and even a new species of human being, allergic to any sign of linguistic, let alone intellectual, spontaneity. The effects of this semantic purge were impressively described by Ludvik Vaculik:

> The languages people speak today are seen as embodying the evolution of human knowledge . . . The men I talk to, by contrast, act and speak as if they had been excluded from this evolution, as if nothing had existed before them, as if we had been waiting for them to come, to offer us everything that exists, and above all to keep it under surveillance.[38]

Converted into a state religion, Marxism – Leninism became the language of total domination. Critical Marxists have illumined the resulting moral dereliction. In the building of the 'new human being', the ethics of responsibility — the basis of Western moral philosophy — were abrogated and replaced by a new moral code, the pseudo-ethics of subservience. The individual, Stalin's 'cog in the mechanism', was absolved of personal implication in his deeds, and the party became the absolute arbiter of good and truth. George Konrád poignantly expressed the result in his historical-metaphysical novel *The loser*. These are the thoughts of a disaffected former Communist leader, a member of the generation of true believers:

> It still didn't occur to me that my jokes could cost me my life. Communism for me was a metaphysical future, a second creation, the work of man replacing God, the axis of all known human values — the thing we would accomplish together, correcting our errors as we went along, an open alternative to familiar oppression. I felt that if this experiment turned out to be a mistake, the human race would have lost its reason for being. What's more, the world of Communism for me was not merely living proof of its dialectics, but the pledge of my own survival, a unified force battling fascism which must, lest it be crushed, suspend its inherent benevolence from time to time, and, adhering to the rules of war, become as ruthless as its foes.

In the process the individual found himself victimised in the name of his ultimate freedom: 'For the spectators the blood was tomato juice; for us the blood was our own.'[39] In its Stalinist version, barbarism annulled any ethical concerns forcing the individual to live in a moral (or better said amoral) no man's land. This type of social order, according to Ferenc Fehér, 'is a social constellation in which the permanent tension between the bestiarium and transcendence has collapsed and where there are no longer effective institutions, accepted customs, or regular collective human efforts aimed at the transcendence of the prevailing inhumanity'.[40]

No one has better expressed the moral wreckage of Soviet-type regimes than these critical Marxists, but still they waver about engaging in a definitive settlement of accounts with Marxism. To quote György Márkus:

> While I actually doubt the survival of a 'critical' Marxism as

part of the counterculture in East European circumstances (at least in the more quasi-liberal environments and for the time being — and essentially not for intellectual reasons) I further think that — despite its most real crisis — this heritage represents in its totality the intellectually deepest and most synthetic attempt to deal with the crisis-phenomenon of modernity and as such both the theory and its crisis will stay with us for a long time.[41]

As such conceived, critical Marxism tends to become more of an exegetical (philological) exercise than a significant segment of the dissident counterculture. It takes note impotently of the abject degeneration of official Marxism into a pseudo-nationalistic ideology with a jingoistic flavour. In many cases (Jacek Kuron, Adam Michnik, Karol Modzelewski in Poland, György Bence and János Kis in Hungary, to some extent Karel Kosik and Mihály Vajda) former revisionist writers have come to embrace Kolakowski's conviction that Marxism has ceased to offer a critical ideology to explain the social structure and political conflicts in Soviet-style regimes. According to György Márkus, critical Marxism has remained a standpoint mostly among some Czech and Hungarian *emigrés*, albeit in many respects with a changed character. Summing up his intellectual trajectory, Márkus wrote to this author:

> . . . from the late sixties the emphasis was not on an essential counterposition of 'true' socialism to the 'existing' one, but an attempt to discover the oppressive logic of the system as a self-reproducing totality . . . The emphasis therefore shifted from early Marx to Marx's late critical analysis of total reproduction processes. It was also realized that the conceptual structure of this analysis cannot be taken over intact in view both of historical and theoretical developments. The slogan: 'return to Marx' was replaced by an attempt at his *critical* appropriation and transformation in face of these developments.[42]

The legacy of 1956

It is natural that the dissident counterculture is preoccupied with the Hungarian revolution of 1956 and seeks to retrieve the spirit of that magnificent experience and to find in it political symbols and moral archetypes that can nourish contemporary anti-totalitarian praxis. On 23 October 1986, a joint statement of 122 leading figures of the democratic opposition in Hungary, Czechoslovakia, the GDR, and Poland was issued to commemorate the 30th anniversary of the Hungarian insurrection. This was a most significant step in the coagulation of an international coalition to promote the values of freedom and pluralism in the Soviet bloc. It is important to note that the statement was endorsed also by three Romanian dissidents, all members of the now outlawed National Peasant Party. The declaration of the 122 points out the enduring significance of the 1956 upheaval against the Stalinist dictatorship in Hungary:

> Thirty years ago, on 23 October 1956, workers, students, and soldiers launched an attack on the Budapest radio station building because they had had enough of official lies and wanted to hear the truth and express their own demands. They destroyed the statue of Stalin and the credibility of a regime which claimed to represent the dictatorship of the proletariat and the people's republic. Their struggle showed clearly that what the Hungarian people really wanted was independence, democracy and neutrality. They wanted to live in peace in a decent and free society.

In order to point out the political genealogy of their action, the signatories of the memorable statement linked the Hungarian revolution to other attempts to overcome tyranny and establish democratic regimes in Eastern Europe: 'The Hungarian revolution as well as the Berlin uprising, the Prague Spring, and the social movement of the free trade union Solidarity in Poland were suppressed, either by Soviet intervention or by local armed intervention.' The dissidents acknowledged the internal developments in communist regimes, including a certain political relaxation and a loosening of the screws, provoked precisely by the ruling caste's endeavour to gain a modicum of legitimacy: 'During the past 30 years, life has become easier for many people, and some can express themselves without being thrown into prison.' It would be foolish however to take this apparent tolerance for more than a provisional concession on the part of those who still refuse to accept democratic control over the functioning of political institutions: '. . . the essential demands of the revolutionaries have not been satisfied'. This conclusion suggests the real programme of the opposition in the future, a political platform to inspire further social movements intent upon establishing a political order where the individual would be entitled to enjoy freedom and pursue his happiness:

> We proclaim our common determination to struggle for political democracy in our countries, for their independence, for pluralism founded on the principles of self-government, for the peaceful unification of a divided Europe and for its democratic integration, as well as for the rights of all national minorities. We emphasize our mutual reliance on the efforts of all of us to achieve, in our countries and in the whole world, a better life that is free and decent. The tradition and the experience of the Hungarian revolution of 1956 remain our common heritage and our inspiration.[43]

Ferenc Fehér and Agnes Heller wrote one of the most original analyses of the Hungarian revolution. Their book *Hungary 1956 revisited* is an invaluable introduction to one of the few world-historical events to occur in East-Central Europe in the aftermath of World War II and the Soviet occupation of the area. The Hungarian revolution marked the first time that Stalinist autocracy was challenged totally and uncompromisingly, not only at the level of foreign policy in the name of national autonomy, but at the fundamental one of the policical organisation of society. It engendered a new substantive principle, a new order of rationality that was the opposite of the mummified Stalinist technology of power — namely the emergence of the individual as the centre of the political discourse. It aimed to get rid of the Stalinist criminal system and achieve a real de-totalitarianisation of society.

The Hungarian revolution rehabilitated the concept and practice of human solidarity and thereby attacked one of the basic principles of totalitarianism — namely the artificially induced loneliness of the individual which, as Hannah Arendt showed, can turn into an all-destructive force:

> By destroying all space between men and pressing men against each other, even the productive potentialities of isolation are annihilated; by teaching and glorifying the logical reasoning of loneliness where man knows that he will be utterly lost if ever he lets go of the first premise from which

the whole process is being started, even the slim chances that loneliness may be transformed into solitude and logic into thought are obliterated. If this practice is compared to that of tyranny, it seems as if a way had been found to set the desert itself in motion, to let loose a sand storm that could cover all parts of the inhabited earth.[44]

Benefiting from their friendship with Georg Lukács and the opportunity to read some of the unpublished memoirs of Hungarian communist leaders, Fehér and Heller accomplished a praiseworthy task of moral, historical and political restitution. In the process, they demolished the fellow-traveller-style literature concerning Kádár's 'liberalism', and put forward a new reading of Eastern Europe's communist drama in this century, with all its internecine struggles, Freudian complexes, and Macbethian plots. Witness the assassination in Kadar's jail of Géza Losonczy, whose daughter, according to George Konrád, is still imploring her father's murderers to tell her where his grave is.[45] Losonczy, that irresistible, arresting intellectual who had been a hero of the anti-fascist underground and then, together with Kádár, a victim of the Rakosist terror, was Imre Nagy's most enthusiastic supporter.[46] During his last year, subjected to endless interrogations, he fell victim to a self-protective paranoia and confessed to a surrealistic chain of imaginary crimes:

> I confess to being a spy on the payroll of Josip Broz Tito and Eisenhower; I admit that I incited a fascist counter-revolution against my nation and against the army of the glorious Soviet Union, the fatherland of all workers.[47]

Losonczy, Nagy, József Szilágyi, Ferenc Donáth, Miklós Gimes, István Bibo, Lukács, Tamás Aczel, Gyula Hay, Pál Maléter — these people and their comrades epitomised the regained honour of Hungarian culture, its indomitable vitality. Of more global signifi-cance, they strove to establish a new body politic inspired by those values and principles that guarantee the treatment of the indivi-dual as an end in itself. The logic of heresy culminated in liberating apostasy. The dialectical celebration of wickedness, the unrestrained cult of sacrifice, and the mortification of the intellect through identification of truth with party, all those stifling rationalisations were finally exposed by the men of the Hungarian revolution. They succeeded thereby in breaking through the magic force of *History and class consciousness*, as young Lukács had entitled his noted contribution on the 'ineluctable' victory of universal categories over frail particularity.[48]

Quite justifiably, Fehér and Heller are interested in exploring the moral profile and the psychology of the post-Machiavellian politician. Their model is of course Imre Nagy, whom they regard as a novel type in political activity, radically different from the Leninist professional revolutionary or the Stalinist professional time-server. Furthermore, Nagy stands for them as an archetype of a new form of political praxis, structually different from traditional democratic systems to the extent that it unifies representation and participation in the process of a continual creation of the body politic.

This phenomenon is all the more exceptional because of the inexorable tendency of Leninist–Stalinist parties of beget whole cohorts of super-Machiavellians, from the Bolshevik Politburo to the inflexible champions of the Comintern (Georgi Dimitrov, Mátyás Rákosi, Walter Ulbricht, Josip Broz Tito, Palmiro Togliatti, to name but a few).

Although it would be hard to disagree with Fehér and Heller that Nagy incarnated 'the type of personality the anti-authoritarian revolution needed and will always need',[49] one still wonders how such a non-Stalinist activist (and he had been a true militant, in the Cominternist sense of the term) could put up for more than 30 years with the Bolshevik inquisition. Was he aware during the Moscow show-trials of that tortuous psychological mechanism Gramsci so aptly called 'the hypocrisy of self-criticism'? During his Moscow exile, did he experience — like Lukács — the pseudo-moral obligation to endorse, even if only by silence, the infamous sentences against the Old Bolsheviks? Was he convinced, like Ernst Fischer, by Vyshinskiy's devious *mise en scène*? Fischer, then a leading Austrian communist exiled in Moscow and working as an editor for the Comintern press, was, like the German writer Lion Feuchtwanger, a direct witness to the Stalinist show trial in 1937. This is the way he described his mental torments to grasp the hidden meaning of the Bolshevik exorcism:

> What misled me above all were not the interlocking confessions, or Radek's fitful flame, or Muralov's touching presence, but Pyatakov, the strongest personality in this dance of death, brave, intelligent, unemotional. From the way he stood there, more like a professor than a conspirator

with his reddish goatee, recounting in even tones the steps he had taken to organize sabotage in the industry of which he had been put in charge, . . . I believed I could perceive for the first time what the struggle for power really was.

Fischer was convinced that a historical battle was taking place among the Soviet elite, the result of which would decide the fate of mankind:

What was involved, we learned from Pyatakov, was a life-and-death struggle. He and his friends had regarded Stalin's policy as wrong. They had combated him openly and lost. Not being prepared to accept defeat they had continued the struggle, but with different weapons, had allied themselves with the devil. Now that they had lost this fight also, they would themselves suffer the fate they had intended to mete out to Stalin and his regime. In this attitude I detected the greatness of the fallen Lucifer, and my imagination was stirred.[50]

Was Imre Nagy's imagination also excited by those mindboggling bloody pageants? Or was he perhaps ready to follow Ernst Bloch and quote Socrates: 'What I have understood is excellent. From which I conclude that the rest which I have not understood is also excellent'? At any rate, for those idealistic communists who had faithfully obeyed Stalin, 1956 was a moral watershed. They had to choose between a past plagued with crimes, lies, and misdeeds, and a future of painstaking repentance. Unlike most of his comrades, Imre Nagy took the second path and thus became a genuinely revolutionary leader.

No one can question the sincerity of Nagy's commitment to the cause of the 1956 revolution, but it is still debatable whether he actually anticipated many of the crucial consequences of the historical decision to join the revolted masses instead of massacring them.

Nagy's last words suggest more than nausea and contempt for his former comrades who had endorsed the Soviet *diktat*, and the Hungarian writers are not mistaken in their conviction that these words, uttered in intimate closeness to a posterity already awaiting him, expressed more than a communist *querelle de famille*:

In this trial, in this tissue of hate and lies, I have to sacrifice my life for my ideas. I willingly sacrifice it. After what you have done to these ideas, my life has no value any longer. I am certain that history will condemn my murderers. One thing alone would repulse me: to be rehabilitated by those who will murder me.[51]

Nagy's 'last words' belong to the oral tradition of the radical practice in this century. György Krasso, a Hungarian intellectual who is among the most knowledgeable persons regarding the 1956 revolution, offered the following information in an interview published in a Hungarian *samizdat* periodical *A Hirmondo* (The Messenger), no. 2, December 1983:

What became known was what he (Imre Nagy) did *not* say. The official press and the official white book on the case obviously contained nothing on the subject. But almost every publication issued in the West contained the text of a dramatic declaration. According to this version, Imre Nagy, availing himself of the right to speak his last words, is reported to have said that he had twice tried to save the honour of socialism in the valley of the Danube, but that in both cases he had been prevented in doing so . . . And that he was afraid of only one thing — that his murderers would be among those commemorating him . . . A similar version of this last speech can also be found in (Sándor) Kopácsi's book (*In the name of the working class*, London, 1979). Kopácsi was, of course, present at the trial, but even so, it seems that these words were in fact never pronounced. According to a version which would seem more accurate, Imre Nagy did not avail himself of the right to speak his last words; he said that the circumstances of the trial proved there was no point in saying anything. However, later, when the death sentence had been passed, and the judge, in accordance with the rules of the judicial proceedings, asked him whether he wanted to appeal for pardon, he replied that he was not going to; he said he would be rehabilitated by the international labour movement. Now, taking into consideration Imre Nagy's character, I think this version — so far unpublished — is more likely than the other one.[52]

The result is that both versions, i.e. that mentioned by Fehér and Heller and the one defended by Krasso, converge on the most significant point: Imre Nagy's enduring commitment to the cause of democratic socialism, which for him was something absolutely different from, or opposite to, the lurid logic of bureaucratic domination. He went beyond the limited register of Khrushchevism, which was nothing but a desperate attempt to get rid of the most embarrassing and terrifying features of mature (read paranoid) Stalinism. Imre Nagy's political writings in 1955 and 1956, as well as his practical decisions as head of the Revolutionary Hungarian Government were thus primarily inspired by concern for the future of democracy in a really reconstructed and emancipated social space. Such a project may have been doomed to failure, given the global geopolitical arrangements, but it was nevertheless harboured by the noblest motivations.

As for the straitjacket imposed on historical research by Kadarism, it is significant that the records of the Nagy affair, including the interrogations and trial, have not been published in Budapest. This is perhaps an indirect avowal of the regime's failure to face its apocryphal legitimacy, or better said, to admit that its birth certificate was signed in blood. The Hungarian society has paid a terrible price for the relative stability and prosperity guaranteed by Kadarism:

> It was paid not just in having to live through the destruction of their aspirations immediately after 1956, but in accepting the Kádár dispensation as something beyond criticism. The complete depoliticisation of Hungarian political life, where even the vocabulary in which political questions can be raised has been falling into oblivion, is perhaps the most enduring monument built by Kadarism.[53]

Is anti-politics possible?

Dissident East-Central European intellectuals, with their outspoken discourse and refusal to acquiesce in the pragmatic imperatives of superpower politics, perceive Yalta as the starting-point of a calamitous evolution, of a pattern of cynical treatment of nations and countries, and as the climax of short-sighted *Realpolitik* guided by ill-conceived Machiavellian assumptions. George Konrád's *Antipolitics* expresses the growing malaise of those immediately subject to the long-term effects of the 'Yalta logic', a revolt against the iniquitous international order imposed, in his view, by a collusion of contemporary empires.[54]

It is one of the characteristics of Eastern Europe's post-World War II culture that literature and political sociology are inextricably linked, with literature being the main vehicle for conveying actual or potential dissenting views. As in pre-revolutionary Russia, so in Soviet-type regimes in Eastern Europe, literature is charged with a subversive content, with that dimension of disaffection with reality that is not permitted expression in political-philosophical works. This is, of course, true only for certain areas of the literary field, where censorship has somewhat subsided; it certainly does not apply to pseudo-artistic celebrations of the communist *status quo*. This commitment of literature to fundamental human values was best expressed by Jaroslav Seifert, the Czech Nobel Prize-winning poet, when he declared in 1956: 'If an ordinary person is silent about the truth, it may be a tactical maneuver. If a writer is silent, he is lying.'[55]

In the 1970s, Konrád co-authored (with Ivan Szelenyi) the already mentioned polemical interpretation of the status of the intelligentsia in the societies of 'really existing socialism'.[56] In certain points, the study anticipated many of the audacious hypotheses more recently advanced by the Hungarian writer in his unorthodox introduction to *Antipolitics*, including the 'emancipatory' mission assigned to a transnational intellectual elite. Echoing Karl Mannheim's theory of the free-floating intellectuals, an unbound social stratum able to transcend all class and group biases, Konrád suggests the guidelines for an alternative to the present political boundaries in Europe.

Unlike the East German Rudolf Bahro, Konrád nourishes no illusions with respect to the nature of the system functioning in East-Central Europe. Far from considering it the result of a 'revolution betrayed', he, like the members of the Budapest School, seems to view the prevailing system as an autonomous social formation, intrinsically hostile to the uninhibited development of the human personality. Yet he suggests that 'the nations of Eastern Europe have chosen a road that leads toward gradual and peaceful recovery of independence'.[57] Although Konrád concedes that 'what *Realpolitik* seems to be telling us, from both East and West, is that we can loosen our bonds only to the extent that the Soviet Union can accept some gentle relation without suffering injury to its prestige',[58] his hypothesis of marginal autonomy contains a good deal of wishful thinking. He overlooks possible Soviet reactions to any of the practical initiatives he is calling for, particularly the suggestion of a neutral Eastern Europe, which runs diametrically counter to the Leninist–Stalinist expansionist programme. It is, of course, little wonder that utopian proposals like this appeal to East European intellectuals, who desire to escape the tragic quandary of having to choose between the Scylla of resigned compliance with the Prince — i.e. more or less honourable capitulation — and the Charybdis of quixotic rebellion.

However noble Konrád's aspiration for the creation of an autonomous and neutral Europe, his proposal smacks of the suicidal self-delusive conciliatory tendencies found in the West, that state of voluntary blindness Norman Podhoretz described as 'the spirit of appeasement'.[59] Like pacifists and isolationists in the West, Konrád seeks to escape from the neo-Cold War rhetoric and find new paths toward dialogue and mutual comprehension. Specifically, he calls for abrogation of the Yalta agreements and the withdrawal of all foreign military forces, Soviet and American, from Europe. 'The key to peace,' he argues, 'is not disarmament but the mutual withdrawal of military forces.'[60] However, it is highly doubtful that any such Soviet withdrawal, unlikely in any event, would automatically result in the kind of East-Central European neutrality that the Hungarian writer is aiming at. On the contrary, the most probable consequence of such an occurrence would be a mood of perpetual anxiety on the part of the Soviet leaders, manifested in strengthened censorship and ruthless suppression of dissent. There are no Soviet military forces stationed in Romania or Yugoslavia, but the 'dictatorship over needs' keeps going there (with different degrees of repression and effectiveness). As Irving Kristol emphasised, 'it is a fact, not to be forgotten, that the Soviet Union has never reconciled itself to the dissolution of a Communist regime, anywhere, anytime'.[61]

One could further argue with Konrád's self-styled Central European Gaullism, evident in the suggestion that Europe become 'an independent agent in the debate between America and the Soviet Union.'[62] Commendable *in abstracto*, such a stance ignores the fundamental political values underlying the Atlantic Alliance, the fact that inasmuch as the West is confronted with an ideological imperialism — and I would doubt Konrád would disagree with this description of the USSR — it is of supreme importance for the Western democracies to overcome temporary conflicts of interests and nationalistic allergies. Only in the non-real world of antipolitics can Europe be a neutral partner to superpower dialogue. In our real and much too imperfect world, Western Europe remains a natural and willing ally of the United States in the unremitting struggle for the preservation of those very values that are imperilled by Soviet expansionism.

Getting rid of Yalta amounts to eliminating the causes of the Cold War, and Konrád cannot be so gullible as to think, together with the American revisionist school, that the United States provoked the peace-loving Soviet Union into this confrontation.

Konrád knows too well that communists — committed to the principle of totalitarian conditioning and domination — cannot accept democracy. Even the most intelligent of Western Marxists, Antonio Gramsci, was committed to the same ideal and praxis — the seizure and preservation of power, even if he talked to hegemony rather than monopoly with regard to political-cultural power. The Soviets are in Eastern Europe not for reasons of security, but primarily because they have to safeguard a myth, to prevent internal anarchy and the collapse of the system. They are there to forestall the denouement of what Adam Michnik calls 'the barren twilight of the old totalitarian dictatorship'.[63]

Antipolitics is a manifesto for 'the serpentine strategy of East European liberation'.[64] For Konrád, to foster anti-politics is to avoid millenarian temptations, to temper the ideological *ivresse*, to assuage visceral outbursts, and to encourage 'a healthy pagan cynicism toward dedicated fanatics'.[65] Antipolitics would eventually amount to rediscovering the heuristic value of memory, enjoying the 'dialogue rationality', and turning down the specious determinism of Soviet ideology. According to Konrád, a second culture would establish the authority of intellectual creativity over matters of the spirit by annulling, through cathartic irony and a new sense of objectivity, the hypnotism of ritualised cliches. In a word, the power of the spirit would undermine the power of the state. Antipolitics becomes thus another way of rejecting the senselessness of contemporary ideological battles and asserting the supremacy of eternal transpolitical values.

Prisoners of such insoluble dilemmas, swinging between utopia and despair, East European dissident intellectuals have acquired a sense of surreal political sociology unknown to their peers in the West. They are inheritors of that culture of apocalyptical irony symbolised by names like Franz Kafka, Robert Musil, Karl Kraus, Arthur Koestler, or Elias Canetti, a world where dreams and politics were mysteriously intertwined in a foreboding allegorical texture. How else could we read this aphorism of ultimate despair, Konrád's cryptical homage to all the failed hopes and neurotic anguishes of his intellectual forerunners: 'Our great dream: what would it be like if the Russian politburo were like the English queen?'[66]

Notes

1. See Richard Löwenthal, *World communism. The disintegration of a secular faith* (New York: Oxford University Press, 1964), p. 47.
2. See Zbigniew Brzezinski, *The Soviet bloc*, pp. 210–78; Ference Vali, *Rift and revolt in Hungary* (Cambridge, Mass.: Harvard University Press, 1961).
3. See Charles Gati, *Hungary and the Soviet bloc*, pp. 127–55.
4. See Ferenc Fehér and Agnes Heller, *Hungary 1956 revisited* (London: George Allen & Unwin, 1983), p. 118.
5. See Leszek Kolakowski, *Main currents*, p. 450.
6. See, as emblematic for this orientation: Adam Schaff, *Marxism and the human individual* (New York: McGraw Hill, 1970); Karl Kosik, *Dialectic of the concrete* (Dordrecht: Reidel, 1976); Leszek Kolakowski, *Toward a Marxist humanism* (New York: Grove Press, 1968): Robert Havemann, *Dialektik ohne dogma* (Hamburg: Rowohlts, 1964).
7. See Adam Michnik, *Letters from prison*, p. 137.
8. See George Konrád and Ivan Szelenyi, *The intellectuals on the road to class power* (New York: Harcourt Brace Jovanovich, 1979), p. 242.
9. See Adam Michnik, 'The great counter-reformer' in *Labour focus on Eastern Europe*, vol. 9, no. 2, July–October 1987, pp. 22–3.
10. See Konrád and Szelenyi, *The intellectuals on the road to class power*, pp. 246–7; see also Václav Havel (ed.), *The power of the powerless* (London: Hutchinson, 1985).
11. See Leszek Kolakowski, 'The Intelligentsia' in Abraham Brumberg (ed.), *Poland. The genesis of a revolution* (New York: Vintage Books, 1983), p. 60.
12. Ibid., p. 64.
13. Ibid., pp. 66–7.
14. See Piotr Wierzbicki, 'A treatise on ticks' in A. Brumberg, *Poland*, pp. 206–7.
15. Ibid., p. 207.
16. Ibid., p. 208.
17. Ibid., p. 211.
18. See Adam Michnik, 'Ticks and angels' in Brumberg, p. 215.
19. 'Eurocommunism and the Prague Spring' (an interview with Antonin Liehm), in G. R. Urban (ed.), *Communist reformation* (New York: St. Martin's Press, 1979), p. 103.
20. See 'Kafka returns to Prague' (an interview with Eduard Gold-stucker, former Chairman of the Czechoslovak Writers' Union during the Prague Spring), in Urban, *Communist reformation*, p. 43.
21. See Leszek Kolakowski, *Main currents*, p. 456.
22. See Leszek Kolakowski, 'Marxism. A summing up', *Survey*, Summer 1977–8, p. 165.

23. See Fehér and Heller, *Eastern left*.

24. See Fehér, Heller, Markus, *Dictatorship over needs*, pp. 227–8.

25. See Havel, *The power of the powerless*, pp. 36–7.

26. Ibid., p. 37.

27. See Fehér, Heller, Markus, *Dictatorship*, p. XIII.

28. Ibid., p. 40.

29. Ibid., p. 43.

30. Ibid., p. 297.

31. See Piroska Farkas, 'The writers and the party', *Frankfurter Allgemeine Zeitung*, 22 January 1987, (English version, FBIS, Eastern Europe, 10 February 1987, p. F1).

32. See Peter Uhl, 'The alternative community as revolutionary avant-garde' in Havel (ed.), *The power of the powerless*, p. 197.

33. See George Konrád, 'Informing on ourselves', *The Nation*, 28 February 1987, p. 254.

34. Ibid.

35. Ibid., p. 256.

36. See János Kis, 'Quelques idées pour l'opposition hongroise', *Esprit*, no. 74, February 1983, p. 57.

37. Fehér, Heller, Markus, *Dictatorship*, p. 191.

38. See Ludvik Vaculik, 'Thus spake Schweik', *The New York Review of Books*, 21 July 1983.

39. See George Konrád, *The loser* (New York: Harcourt Brace Jovanovich, 1982), pp. 138, 206.

40. See Fehér and Heller, *Eastern left*, p. 261.

41. Personal correspondence with this author by György Márkus from the University of Sydney, Australia, 29 March 1983.

42. Ibid., 2 July 1983.

43. For the text of the statement, see *Le Monde*, 22 October 1986. For interpretations of this document, see Vladimir V. Kusin, 'East European dissidents' appeal on Hungarian Revolution anniversary', RFE, RAD Background Report/151, 28 October 1986; Michael T. Kaufman, '122 in East Europe proclaim praise of Hungarian uprising', *New York Times*, 19 October 1986; for the trend towards a joint, cross frontier dissident approach to issues of vital interest (peace, environmental protection, reforms, human rights), see Michael T. Kaufman, 'East Europe moving to organize dissidence', *New York Times*, 4 January 1987.

44. See Hannah Arendt, *The origins of totalitarianism*, p. 478.

45. Reconfirmed in a conversation with George Konrád in New York on 19 January 1986; with respect to Kádár's regime refusal to mark the graves of the 280 revolutionaries (students, workers, and political figures) who were hanged for their participation in the insurrection, see Michael T. Kaufman, 'Section 301, where Hungary's past is buried', *New York Times*, 23 June 1986.

46. On Geza Losonczy's biography, see *The truth about the Nagy affair: facts, documents, comments* (London: Secker & Warburg, and New York: Praeger, published by the Congress for Cultural Freedom, 1959), pp. 122–3.

47. Fehér and Heller, *Hungary 1956 revisited*, p. 165.

48. Franz Borkenau insisted on Lukács's responsibility for the

crystallisation of the 'secret doctrine of wickedness', as an esoteric counterpart to the official theory which postulated identity between truth and the class consciousness of the proletariat. See Borkenau, *World communism*, pp. 172–3.

49. Fehér and Heller, *Hungary*, p. 128 (emphasis in the original);
50. See Ernst Fischer, *An opposing man*, pp. 308–9.
51. Fehér and Heller, *Hungary*, p. 136.
52. See 'The memory of the dead', an interview with György Krasso, *Survey*, Summer 1984, p. 144.
53. See George Schöpflin, 'The Hungarian revolution: 30 years on', *Soviet Analyst*, vol. 15, no. 21, 22 Oct. 1986, p. 3.
54. See George Konrád, *Antipolitics* (New York and London: Harcourt Brace Jovanovich, 1984).
55. See Michael T. Kaufman, 'Czech government eulogizes maverick poet', *The New York Times*, 22 January 1986.
56. Konrád and Szelenyi, *The intellectuals*.
57. Konrád, *Antipolitics*, p. 26.
58. Ibid., p. 27.
59. See Norman Podhoretz, 'Appeasement by any other name', *Commentary*, July 1983; also Walter Laqueur, 'The psychology of appeasement', ibid., October 1978.
60. Konrád, *Antipolitics*, p. 30.
61. See Irving Kristol, 'Let Europe be Europe', *The New York Times Book Review*, 10 June 1984, p. 15. The same point was made by Cornelius Castoriadis in 'Defending the West', *Partisan Review*, no. 3, 1984, pp. 375–9.
62. Konrád, *Antipolitics*, p. 33.
63. Michnik, *Letters*, p. 99.
64. Konrád, *Antipolitics*, p. 123.
65. Ibid., p. 172.
66. Ibid., p. 75.

8

Peace, Human Rights, Dissent

. . . one could safely say that no inhabitant in any of these countries who is not incorporated in the power apparatus, regards the United States as an enemy.

Ferenc Fehér and Agnes Heller

The discourse of contemporary Western peace groups is more often than not confusing. Justifiably concerned with the threat of a nuclear holocaust, their rhetoric is vituperative and comminatory, saturated with apocalyptic images and terrifying prophecies. They act as self-appointed guardians of human civilisation, but their political judgements are sometimes naïve and inconsistent. Until recently, their calls for the democratisation of international relations were accompanied by an inclination to single out the United States as the chief responsible for the maddening arms race. NATO and not the Warsaw Pact was the main threat of global stability. To take only the case of West German pacifist groups: the 'moralization of politics', to use a characterisation advanced by David Gress, has led to widespread anti-American sentiments and an adversarial attitude on the part of prominent West German intellectuals toward their own political system. Radical Social-Democrats and Green militants partake in this hostility toward a regime the leftist pundits regard as structurally dominated by the United States:

> Böll, Günther Grass, Siegfried Lenz, Martin Walser, and virtually all other prominent writers in West Germany, with only few exceptions, such as Peter Schneider and the East German refugee Reiner Kunze, support the peace movement

and deny the legitimacy of the authority, the institutions, and the democratic political order in West Germany.[1]

According to the Green influential leader Petra Kelly:

> As long as we keep Poseidon, Polaris, Trident, and the rest, we cannot tell the Russians to simply take all their medium-range weapons; we must start first, as we have far more in terms of quality . . . What we demand, first and foremost, is the removal of the Pershing II cruise missiles from Europe. They are first-strike weapons, which change the so-called balance qualitatively and strategically.[2]

The proponents of the Green 'alternative ideology' abhor the dissolution of the individual in the mass society and accuse the democratic system of having forgotten (or even stifled) the emotional life of the human being. Western values are derided as mere camouflage for the American colonisation of the Federal Republic. Many peace activists perceive Soviet policy as a defensive reaction to the Western, read American, aggressiveness.[3] This is not to say that all Western peace activists are blind to the dangers created by Soviet expansionism. They tend however to consider both superpowers equally guilty for the worsening of the international situation. The main problem with many Western pacifists is that they regard the USSR as a country like any other one and subsequently disregard opposite interpretations — those who emphasise the totalitarian nature of the Soviet regime — as vestiges of the Cold War mentality. Their criticism of the Soviet Union is always counter-balanced by negative references to American adventurism.

This ambivalent nature of Western pacifism is strikingly revealed by the difficulty of articulating its objectives with those of East European oppositional movements. A mutual suspicion seems to govern the dialogue between Western peaceniks and East European dissidents. Western peace activists tend to suspect East European dissidents of malevolent attitudes not only towards the communist authoritarian bureaucracies, but also against the very idea of socialism. Dissidents in Soviet-type regimes are seen to subliminally admire capitalist societies. All the claims to the contrary notwithstanding, dissidents are regarded as shortsighted persons, out of touch with the real global issues. Certainly, they deserve utmost respect for their behaviour, but their political views are often neglected by Western peace activists. Since dissidents are opposed to the official peace ideology proclaimed by the regimes they criticise, their conduct objectively serves the interests of the adversary camp. Unlike East European dissidents, some Western peace activists favour a manichean worldview. Because of their hostility to Western military and political establishments, they tend to play down the implications of Soviet international aggressiveness. As Jürgen Fuchs, the exiled East German dissident writer has emphasised, this attitude is particularly widespread among West German peace activists.[4]

What makes these two movements remarkably dissimilar is the larger environment of their activities. Western peace groups engineer their campaigns in a political context where free speech and freedom of information are universally shared values. They are beneficiaries of a political system they often depict as subjugated by a mythological 'military-industrial complex'. They are free to travel, to demonstrate and to proselytise. With no inhibitions or compunctions, they make extensive use of these basic freedoms. Western peaceniks abhor the military commitments of their countries and crusade against American bases in Europe. Private foundations and other sources, including the Socialist International, compete in sponsoring their relentless militantism. Their antagonism to the establishment does not lead them to jail or mental asylum. Some of their discourses are coloured with references to the issues of universal respect for human rights, but in practice they tend to disassociate the topic of political freedom in the Soviet bloc from that of global survival.

This phenomenon of discrepancy in both political conscience and practical purposes between independent peace groups in the Soviet bloc and peace movements in the West is described by Fehér and Heller as a form of communication disturbance, a conflict of visions and a different scale of priorities: 'Even where we are speaking of militants with genuine intentions of combining political freedom and survival, we must recognize that, in East and West, we are speaking of people who have experienced their political socialization in radically different social climates.' Western peace activists speak the language of insecurity, which has conveniently replaced the once fashionable lexicon of alienation. They are genuinely committed to the survival of civilisation, but at the same time they indulge in neo-romantic posturing and apocalyptical speculations. The other group, the East European dissident pacifist movement, is worried about the dangers to peace created by the totalitarian system. They know from within that the Soviet-type regimes cannot be trusted and that official peace campaigns are nothing but attempts to morally disarm their Western opponents. Unlike Western peace activists, who find democracy and industrial civilisation internally sick, dissidents in the communist countries do not think affluence is the root of the evil. Western peaceniks are terrified by the threat of a nuclear holocaust. Dissidents are horrified by the image of eternity projected by the system they live in:

> As a result, the mythology is different as well. 'Darkness at noon' is still a relevant symbol here but it means now the darkness of the tunnel that never ends. If there seems to be a light at the end of the tunnel, it is only a will-o'-the-wisp, a promise that never comes true. This is a world in which the myth of the eternal repetition prevails, the myth of disillusionment, where everything always starts anew only in order to end in the same, humiliating and frustrating way.[5]

As mentioned, anti-Americanism is a main emotional ingredient of West European pacifism. On the other hand, a nebulously conceived neutralism is the most the peace groups can offer as an articulate political programme. In their intentions and motivations, Western peace groups are indeed emotional rather than ideological phenomena. Their commitment to peace is genuine but, quite often, they fail to point out the correlation between peace and freedom.

Among the doctrinaires of Western pacifist movements are many former activists of the rebellious student groups of the 1970s. In these new movements they have found a golden opportunity to resume past political adventures. Romantic dreams of social upheaval have been replaced by the ideal of a neutralised, nuclear-free Europe. They tend to ignore the disturbing implications of the Soviet presence in that area: what they are mostly concerned with is the alleged American willingness to turn Western Europe into a testing ground for the most sophisticated weapons. For many members of the West German nationalist left, issues like human rights in communist countries, the expansionist nature of the Soviet empire or the preservation of the Stalinist legacy in the Soviet political culture are simply irrelevant. Their project consists of the phantasy of an alliance between a reformed Soviet Union and a unified and neutral Germany. Ferenc Fehér and Agnes

Heller do not exaggerate when they think that the perspective of a
new Rapallo is implicit in many statements of West German anti-
nuclear activists.[6] Their slogan is 'peace now', at any cost, against
all odds, regardless of the tribute to be paid in terms of freedom
and dignity. As Hannah Arendt has demonstrated in her classical
essay *On revolution*, the issue of freedom cannot be ruled out from
the discourse on war and peace. This postulate is condescendingly
glossed over by many Western pacifists.

At the other pole, East European dissident groups are beleaguered minorities, harrassed by the secret police, besmirched
by the corrupt official media, isolated from the larger community.
They are stripped of any form of institutional communication with
their fellow countrymen. Dissidents are sceptical of Western
peaceniks' unilateralist statements and sometimes dare to
challenge such questionable stances.

For many Western peaceniks, dissidents indulge in a kind of
moral arrogance. They act as troublemakers, their views are irretrievably biased, marked off by their experiences (admittedly
unpleasant) with the repressive communist apparatus. To be sure,
many Western peaceniks would agree, dissidents in Eastern
Europe are honourable people, their deeds are praiseworthy, but
they can barely be trusted when it comes to the real issue, namely
that of peace. Oppressed by the totalitarian regimes, dissidents
cannot transcend their limited horizon and perceive the crucial
issues that are at stake. Furthermore, obsessed as they are with the
evils perpetrated by the USSR, they fail to grasp the vicious nature
of American imperialism. The doctrine of moral equivalence of
the superpowers is hence the main ideological assumption underlying the rhetoric of Western pacifism. E. P. Thompson, for
example, writes of 'the tendency for both military alliances —
NATO and the Warsaw Pact — to become instruments of superpower political control, reducing the lesser states to abject cliency.
This is as true in the West as in the East of Europe'. Timothy
Garton Ash offers a suggestive analysis of the 'equilateralist' synd-
rome: 'Equilateralism is a *Weltanschauung* — a way of visualizing
or imagining the world. Its central image is a simple and extremely
powerful one: rational, civilised man or woman — a European —
stuck between two irrational, uncivilised giants — Gog and
Magog, United States and Soviet Union.'[7] In one of his recent
books, French political philosopher Régis Debray calls for the
'desideologisation' of our image of the Soviet Union which is,
according to him far more vulnerable and preoccupied with

domestic issues than the prevailing Kremlinological orthodoxy would have it. Debray's thesis can be reduced to the following axiom: 'Eastern Europe will not be de-Sovietized without des-Americanizing Western Europe.'[8] Now, the problem with this perspective is that it glosses over the main differences between Soviet-type regimes and Western democracies, and primarily the issue of political freedom. Authors like Régis Debray or Günter Grass do not risk anything when they proclaim their anti-American beliefs. This is not the case in Eastern Europe, where opposition to the existing military alliance (the Warsaw Pact) is considered a major criminal offence. This is why Jean-François Revel is not mistaken when he writes that all campaigns 'in favour of peace' aim at disarming the West and the West alone:

> Democrats cannot do this to their adversaries. They cannot plead their cause in totalitarian countries, organize groups of supporters, patiently knead the media and the public as if they were so much leavened dough ready to rise, or finance political parties . . . No mass movement originating in the West can be launched in the Soviet Union to persuade its government to experiment with unilateral disarmament to determine if the West will follow suit.[9]

For many Western pacifists, the main fault of East European dissidents is their naïve ignorance of the perverse strategic game fomented by the United States. Noble in their intentions, East European dissidents tend — according to such Western perceptions — to idealise Western societies. This picture of West European anti-nuclear groups would be distorted were one to overlook their recent opening toward dialogue with dissidents from the Soviet Union and East-Central Europe.

It is precisely to encourage communication with West European peace activists that Czech playwright and Charter 77 activist Václav Havel wrote a provocative and illuminating essay. *Reticence* is the central concept of his controversial text.[10] From the very outset, it seems clear to Havel that, for many Western peace groups, dissidents 'tend to appear as a fifth column of Western establishments east of the Yalta line'. But this is only one side of the coin. There is reticence among dissidents, too: they tend to beware of Western manifestos dealing with the issue of peace.

Who are these dissidents, much applauded in the West, but still much misunderstood and neglected? What do they stand for? In

Havel's poignant description, dissidents make up an enclave within the totalitarian universe, a 'minuscule and rather singular enclave'. They are a handful of righteous people who have chosen to defy the faked monolithical order, trying to dispel the illusion of unanimity and warn against the pervasive conformity and all-devouring cynicism: '. . . they speak their mind openly, heedless of the consequences'. They are different from their fellow citizens in terms of behaviour, not of opinions. Moreover, as it is well-known to students of Soviet affairs, dissidents tend to be supporters of reasonable, even self-restraining conduct whenever circumstances enable the masses to resort to direct action against the ruling caste. The case of Adam Michnik, a renowned Polish historian, a founding member of the Workers' Defence Committee (KOR) and an intellectual adviser to Solidarity, is illustrative in this respect. A main proponent of non-violence, Michnik was instrumental in persuading a raging crowd not to lynch some policemen during the hectic times of the independent union's legal existence. Michnik even evoked the accusations once proferred against him by the communist justice, reminding the mob that he was himself 'an anti-socialist force'. Imprisoned by those he certainly despises, but cannot come to hate, Michnik wrote in jail a letter to General Kiszczak, the Polish Minister of Internal Affairs. The conclusion of that letter, an outstanding synthesis of political intelligence and moral intransigence, is worth quoting:

> As for myself, I hope that when your life is in danger, I will be able to appear in time to help you as I did in Otwock when I helped to save the lives of those few of your subordinates, that I will be able to place myself once again on the side of the victims and not of the victimizers. Even if, afterward, you should once more wonder at my incorrigible stupidity and decide to lock me back in prison all over again.[11]

Now, dissidents may well be idealistic people, but they certainly know what it is all about in their countries. They have to invent strategies of gradual change precisely because they are too well aware of the potential terrorism of the system. Dissidents do not gloss over the axiomatic truth that communist regimes are rooted in resentment and hatred; hatred of the bourgeois elements, hatred of the kulaks, hatred of any form of distinction, hostility to any incarnation of alterity. The very principle of otherness is anathema to the communist mind. Dissidents create an alternative body

166

politic, fragile to be sure, but at the same time the only one to provide the individual with a value system worth living for. To the
deep moral crisis of communist regimes, dissidents oppose a
morally engaging alternative represented by the ideal of the
parallel *polis*, the network of independent groups, associations,
informal communities whose very existence is an argument that
the official lie can be defeated:

> These parallel structures, it may be said, represent the most
> articulated expressions so far of 'living within the truth'. One
> of the most important tasks the 'dissident movements' have
> set themselves is to support and develop them. Once again, it
> confirms the fact that all attempts by society to resist the pres-
> sure of the system have their essential beginnings in the pre-
> political area. For what else are parallel structures than an
> area where a different life can be lived, a life that is in
> harmony with its own aims and which in turn structures itself
> in harmony with those aims? . . . And does this tendency not
> confirm once more the principle of returning the focus to
> actual individuals? . . . In fact, all eventual changes in the
> system, changes we may observe here in their rudimentary
> forms, have come about as it were *de facto* from 'below',
> because life compelled them to, not because they came before
> life, somehow directing it or forcing some change on it.[12]

Critical intellectuals in Eastern Europe are perfectly conscious
of the cynical manipulation of peaceful slogans by communist
official institutions. They know that propaganda warfare is vitally
necessary for the survival of the established dictatorships. Dissidents are less amnesic than their Western interlocutors. They have
not forgotten the disgraceful times of the Stockholm Appeal concocted by Stalin at the height of the Cold War. It seems to them all
too obvious that totalitarian propaganda machines are most pro-
ficient in astute window-dressing concealing real expansionist
objectives. No one has ever outreached Stalin in statements of
good intentions and pledges to respect free elections and the
peoples' will. Furthermore, it should be born in mind that the
Cominform journal, *For a lasting peace, for people's democracy*, was
baptised by Stalin himself, presumably in an attempt to force
Western media to publicise Soviet peace slogans whenever referring to that source. Khrushchev enjoyed posturing as a champion
of peace, while Brezhnev's 'Peace Program' was lavishly praised

by communist propaganda. More recently, Gorbachev has gone out of his way to convince Western public opinion of his peaceful intentions; *Libération*, a French newspaper, made a pun speaking of Mr Gorbat-show, who is perhaps the first Soviet leader to master the art of public image.

The significance of such campaigns can hardly escape those who are not willingly or unwillingly benighted: they aim to divide the Western alliance, to cover the Soviet expansion in the Third World, and to disguise the attempt to change the global balance of power in favour of the USSR. In a recent book, French political scientist Hélène Carrère d'Encausse highlights the colossal political and military Soviet penetration of the Third World. Not unjustifiably, she speaks of the emergence of a 'second Soviet empire' englobing countries from Asia, Africa, and Latin America. As she puts it, the much contempted Brezhnev, the epitome of a declining gerontocracy, was actually a most successful architect of the Soviet imperialist policy. Taking into account the Soviet infiltration and expansion in Africa, it would be indeed appropriate to call the late General Secretary 'Brezhnev Africanus'.[13] Needless to add, this Soviet expansion coincided with the heyday of the politics of détente.

These are commonplaces for any informed denizen of the Soviet bloc. They are however brushed aside by some Western peace activists who conceive of their part of Europe as a privileged entity, a region purportedly immune to Soviet aggressive designs. First and foremost, it seems there is a semantic chasm between Western pacifists and East European dissidents. The former believe in a universal, almost Kantian concept of eternal peace, whereas the latter know how Soviet-type governments work and how their leaders think.

For East European dissidents, the sinuous ways of the Marxist dialectic are no longer a secret. It has been long since they have debunked the power's infinite capacity for semantic fraud. Theirs is perhaps the most sophisticated awareness of the arcane meanders of the Orwellian universe. Their expertise may sometimes be discarded by Western leftists, but it remains however a singularly illuminating source both on the ordeal of conscience under exceptionally inauspicious conditions and the means to thwart the system's symbolic and physical aggression.

No doubt, Havel is right when he states that in his part of the world, the word peace has lost any rational content. In the ritualised discourse of communist propaganda, peace has been perhaps the most frequently used and abused term. It has been deprived of any original sense and functions now as a mere means of symbolic justification for demagogic campaigns. Everything is portrayed as peaceful in a communist regime: 'our peaceful people', 'our party's generous commitment to peace', 'the CPSU general secretary's consistent peace initiatives'. For the people submitted to this ceaseless stream of nonsensical slogans, the word peace sounds strangely hollow. It is an exhausted symbol of a long-abandoned promise, no less fraudulently confiscated by communist doctrinaires than other lofty, altruistic ideals. People in those countries are suspicious of the pacifist rhetoric exploited by the official media.

The recent Copenhagen World Peace Congress (October 1986) is just another example to be added to the long list of communist methods to make use of pacifism as a successful device for the political anesthetisation of Western public opinion. Once again, peace advocates preached against those who indulge in a suicidal arms race only to increase 'their profits'. 'Imperialist warmongers' were consequently pilloried whereas Gorbachev, this archangel of peace, sent a message to the Congress reiterating well-known Soviet allegations. One *Pravda* reporter ironically referred to those participants who have tried 'again and again to propagandize the motheaten thesis of the "equal responsibility" of the United States and the USSR for the arms race'.[14]

In his 'Anatomy of reticence', Havel points precisely to the hypocrisy of the prevailing socialist ideology. Like so many other uplifting concepts, he says, peace has become a political tool for unscrupled timeservers: 'The word "peace" — much like the words "socialism", "homeland", and the "people" — has been reduced to serving both as one rung on the ladder up which clever individuals clamber and as a stick for beating those who stand aloof.' When turned into a ludicrous incantation, a hidebound catchword with no appeal whatsoever, is there any wonder that the word peace — but not peace as an ideal — is rather a matter of revulsion than the symbol of a cause worth fighting for? Even dissident statements on peace are regarded by the silent majority as an exercise in futility: 'A citizen of our country simply starts to yawn whenever he hears the word "peace".'[15]

Whenever confronted with independent peace groups in their countries, communist authorities do not hesitate to resort to authoritarian methods to dismantle them. The fate of the East German unofficial peace groups and associations, supported by

169

the Evangelical Church, is more than telling in this respect. They
have been stigmatised for having challenged state security. They
have been attacked for alleged attempts to undermine the country's
defence capability. The denunciation of the increasing militarisation of the East German regime is criticised by Honecker's spokesmen as 'prevention of state-controlled measures'. It is precisely
against this resurgence of a Junker mentality, the strange sym-
biosis of Bismarck and Marx in the East German militaristic
ideology, that such independent groups raise their voices. In an
appeal sent by East German to Western peace activists, it is
unequivocally stated: 'In the interest of peace we object to such
measures (militaristic decrees, including mandatory registration of
women for military service) and demand the demilitarization of
public life. This is an area where the GDR could carry out
unilateral disarmament without suddenly being defenceless.'[16]

The East German unofficial peace movement is rooted in a
resuscitated sense of Christian idealism. Since it bears upon the
individual's sphere of values, this movement is incongruent with
the communist requirement of ideological uniformity. As a result,
the communist leaders reacted nervously to the call of the Conference of the Governing Bodies of the Evangelical Church in the
GDR in 1982. How could communist zealots quietly behold the
coalescence of an articulate counter-ideology of peace? They cannot accept Biblical commandments as guidelines for human
conduct and could hardly tolerate the bishops' call for the fulfilment of the ancient behest: 'and they shall beat their swords into
ploughshares'. (Micah, 4,3) The originality of East German
unofficial pacifism has been to challenge communist authorities in
the name of ideals they pretend to serve or, in other words, the
movement revealed the flagrant failure of the regime to live up to
the values it claims to defend. When confronted with an alternative peace movement, official peace institutions have indulged
in tedious disquisitions on the class nature of the peace concept.
This is a clumsy, unconvincing tactic of the communist peace
bureaucracy to disguise its failure to gain genuine popular
support.

The devaluation of the peace concept under communist regimes
is even more conspicuous when one thinks that the only significant
military actions in Europe since the end of World War II were
undertaken by Warsaw Pact countries: the Soviet crushing of the
Hungarian Revolution in 1956, the invasion of Czechoslovakia in
August 1968, the military coup staged by General Jaruzelski in

December 1981. The spectre of the nuclear apocalypse is too abstract a scenario for those who have excruciatingly experienced the benefit of socialist 'fraternal help'. They tend to harbour a distaste for Western pacifist verbalism and look askance at the prophets of nuclear doomsday.

In his assessment of the meaning of pacifism, Havel highlights some of the mythological assumptions shared by Western peaceniks. It is, for example, their stubborn belief that East European peace groups should fight for the elimination of the Soviet missiles on their territories. Now, this is a magnificent dream, but it reveals nothing else but the tragically shortsighted perception, in the minds of Western activists, of how things really work in a totalitarian order. They ought to know that nothing is more jealously guarded by the *nomenklatura* than military secrets. Furthermore, there are draconian laws preventing any attempt to question the defence policy of the regime. There is no way of establishing parallels between conditions peace movements enjoy in the West and the climate of fear induced by a police state. As Havel aptly put it:

> To speak out against the rockets here means, in effect, to become a 'dissident'. Concretely, it means the complete transformation of one's life. It means the acceptance of a prison term as one's natural possibility. It means giving up at a stroke many of the few possibilities open to a citizen in our country. It means finding oneself, day after day, in a neurotic world of constant fear at the doorbell. It means becoming a member of that microscopic 'suicide pact' enclave surrounded, to be sure, by the unspoken good wishes of the public but at the same time by unspoken amazement that anyone would choose to risk so much for something as hopeless as seeking to change what cannot be changed.[17]

The fate of the Hungarian unofficial peace movement is another confirmation of the impossibility of organising a public debate on military issues in the Soviet bloc. The founding members of the *Dialogue* group assumed that their movement could work for the reorientation of the official peace movement and its transformation into an intermediary between the Soviet Union and the West. The March 1983 Resolution of the Politburo of the Central Committee of the Hungarian Socialist Workers Party labelled the movement as oppositional and unambiguously spelled out the regime's stance

on the future of unofficial pacifism: 'The Hungarian peace movement must be united and adhere to the guidance of the National
Peace Council; movements outside this framework may not be
legalized.' As Miklos Haraszti put it:

> The Government got over the fact of having flirted for a while
> with a new type of political formula, to return to the safe and
> traditional theory of a Communist structure of society: society
> must equal the state, and if society does not think so, then the
> police will help change its mind.[18]

Defying Soviet control over Eastern Europe amounts to a
quixotic, almost suicidal endeavour to bring down the *status quo*
and to invent a new principle of reality. It is precisely because of
their break with the prevailing shibboleths, with those daunting
taboos dictated by the system and systematically injected in the
collective mind, that dissidents have unleashed a Copernican
revolution in the history of self-proclaimed socialist regimes. If
communism, as a practical experience, is indeed a big insult to the
mind, as Czech writer Josef Skvorecký maintains,[19] then the
gesture of dissidents, who refuse to bow down before the overbearing orthodoxies, is really epoch-making. They may herald a
long-expected awakening of the masses in Eastern Europe, a
rebellion whose main thrust would not be, as in Ortega y Gasset's
gloomy prophecy, the triumph of the amorphous collectivity over
the individual, but quite the opposite: the resurrection of subjectivity in a universe plagued by fear and duplicity. When East
European dissidents talk about peace, they do it in the ominous
vicinity of labour camps and jails for conscientious objectors.
Theirs is ultimately an heroic behaviour, that follows the rules of
moral, rather than political, survival. Taking the issue of peace
seriously means, under East European circumstances, to reckon
with established customs and taboos. It entails the courage to risk
overwhelming solitude and state-induced vilification. In Havel's
words: 'The peace movement in the West has a real impact on the
dealings of parliaments and governments, without risking jail.
Here the risk of prison is real and, at least at this point, the impact
on government's decision-making is zero.' Most peaceniks in the
West tend to disregard the unfavourable conditions under which
East European dissidents live and act. They seem surprised that no
influential peace movements have emerged in the Soviet sphere of
influence. Abiding by enduring clichés, they cannot grasp the

crucial differences between their own political culture and the collectivist-authoritarian regimes: the result is therefore a persistent confusion, 'the wholly erroneous impression that only those weapons are dangerous which are surrounded by encampments of demonstrators'.[20]

The awareness of the Soviet danger, though verbally acknowledged, is automatically overshadowed by this concentration on the American threat to peace. Pretending to depoliticise the pacifist discourse, Western peaceniks do not ease the task of those who pursue similar goals in the other Europe. They minimise the predicament of East European citizens, the very fact that civil society has been dissolved, that the individual, according to the notorious Stalinist dictum, is nothing but a cog in the state machine. Pacifism is a form of political conscience and, under Soviet-type regimes, conscience as such has suffered a terrible erosion. Society is divided into 'them' and 'us'. The bureaucratic colossus is omnipotent, while the individual desperately seeks ways to salvage his dignity. Havel deems it appropriate to inform his Western readers about real life for the ordinary citizen in such a closed society:

> . . . 'they' can do everything they want — take away his passport, have him fired from his job, order him to move, send him to collect signatures against the Pershings, bar him from higher education, take away his driver's license, build a factory producing mostly acid fumes right under his windows, pollute his milk with chemicals to a degree beyond belief, arrest him simply because he attended a rock concert, raise prices arbitrarily, anytime and for any reason, turn down all his humble petitions without cause, prescribe what he must read before all else, what he must demonstrate for, what he must sign, how many square feet his apartment may have, whom he may meet and whom he must avoid.[21]

What the individual experiences under socialism is a tormenting sense of powerlessness, a painful rootlessness and, even more distressing, a total lack of perspective. Life flows mechanically, a chain of Pavlovian reflexes, without hope for real change in the foreseeable future. The human being is strenuously patronised, rewarded and castigated as a mindless child. The infantilisation of the whole society is the ultimate outcome of the Marxist-Leninist pedagogy. The sense of life has vanished in this atmosphere of corruption and mendacity. Can one then reasonably expect this individual to behave in a selfless manner, risking his ephemeral comfort and jeopardising his closest relatives? Unlike Kafka's Josef K., the human being under socialism knows too well who his judges are and what price he would have to pay for transgressing the customs of the city. Lawless as that society certainly is, it is nonetheless obsessed with rules and decrees. A huge police corps has no other job but deterring people from bypassing the officially sanctioned values. In such a rotten order, the moral self is emasculated. The ego, the reflexive self, celebrated by the whole Western philosophical tradition, is doomed to evaporate.

And here comes the Western pacifist, who cannot stand this political apathy, this universal indifference for matters he finds of stringent significance. He is irritated not only by the inertia of the East European masses but also, and perhaps even more, by the obstinacy of the dissidents who keep repeating the same leitmotifs about totalitarianism and tyranny. No doubt, these are important issues, but they pale when compared with the ultimate question, 'the fate of the Earth'. Let us try to go beyond limited topics and address the sole vital issue: the risk of an atomic cataclysm. To East European dissidents, and to the people they speak for, this discourse sounds dramatically alien, almost surrealistic. Their life experience has been marked off by countless catastrophes, but they fear their alleged friends in the West cannot empathise with them. For East European dissidents, the Western pacifist rhetoric is not only unilateral and therefore biased: it is irrelevant. Or, if we think of the frail East European independent peace groups, in East Germany, Poland, Czechoslovakia, or Hungary, it seems that it is only in that area that the real stakes are comprehensively conceived. Unlike Western pacifists, East European proponents of disarmament confront an armed-to-the-teeth bureaucratic machine whose unique goal is to inspire terror and project power. They are therefore driven into a political struggle with the powers that be, and in doing so they risk everything, including their lives.[22]

For the dissidents, it is of great importance to define peace as a political issue. In other words, it is necessary to deritualise the pacifist discourse, to rescue it from the shackles of pseudo-ethical considerations. When they express scepticism about the views held by Western peace activists, the dissidents spell out their bitter awareness of the system they are forced to live in. When everyday life is bedevilled by countless hardships, when winter comes and people do not know whether they are going to get enough heat to be able to survive, when, like in Poland, Romania, or the Soviet Union, they are forced to stay in line for hours for a bit of bread or meat, anti-war struggle seems an enormous joke. Right or wrong, these thoughts are nevertheless shared not only by dissidents but by all those who do not belong to the ruling caste. As for the rulers, they are indeed indifferent to pacifist ideas. What they are interested in is the continuation of their domination over society. Militarisation is an indispensable weapon to achieve this goal.

Dissidents in Eastern Europe have developed a consistent scepticism. They are distrustful of ingenious utopian projects of social engineering. They think that the onus of human existence is not lessened, but further increased by ideologies and political messianisms of all shades. This scepticism is rooted in Kafka's tragic sense of the senselessness of human fate, in Karl Kraus' comic, all-embracing irony, in Elias Cannetti's unmitigated nostalgia, in an unshakable conviction that all grandiose social designs are ultimately instruments of political domination. It is both melancholy and ironic, mordant and compassionate. It is instinctively inimical to pseudo-universal recipes of social happiness and scathingly critical of self-proclaimed prophetic healers. As Timothy Garton Ash has recently noticed, East-Central Europe is a place where traditional political games seem hopelessly superfluous. It may therefore become the birthplace for a new approach to political matters, the anti-politics as an attempt to reinvent the rules of an emancipated *polis*: 'To an imperial system whose main instruments of domination are lies, violence, the atomization of society and "divide and rule", the antipolitician responds with the imperatives of living in truth, nonviolence, the struggle for civil society — and the idea of Central Europe'.[23] In Havel's own formulation, this programme should help the opposition avoid being entrapped in the old political games. In a way, Havel's strategy meets Konrád's philosophy of anti-politics. They are both persuaded that a real revolution should begin at the level of the individual, through the instilment of a new sense of dignity, courage, and morality:

> . . . any existential revolution should provide hope of a moral reconstitution of society, which means a radical renewal of the relationship of human beings to what I have called the 'human order', which no political order can replace. A new experience of being, a renewed rootedness in the universe, a

175

newly grasped sense of 'higher responsibility', a new-found inner relationship to other people and to the human community — these factors clearly indicate the direction in which we must go.

The result of this existential revolution would be a reappraisal of the political vocation of the individual, an attempt to redefine the rules of social intercourse, and to restore the values of community through participation in self-organised structures: '. . . the systemic consequences of an "existential revolution" of this type go significantly beyond the framework of classical parliamentary democracy'. Having introduced the term 'post-totalitarian' for the purposes of this discussion, Havel refers to his 'anti-political' model as a 'post-democratic system'.[24] Conceived in this manner, the rebellious spirit of Central Europe belongs to a romantic tradition, one for which *Kultur* has no less dignity than *Zivilisation*. It may be argued whether this counter-utopianism does indeed announce a new formula for political life or is merely a spasmodic attempt to revive a spirit irrevocably repealed by the infectious doctrinairism of our century. Action, in such a view, is measured not by its immediate consequences, but by the depth of its spiritual intensity. It is tremendously important to seek: discovery as such is epiphenomenal.

One can perceive this Central European spirit in the writings of such authors as George Konrád, Milan Kundera, Adam Michnik, Pavel Kohout, and Zbigniew Herbert. One can detect it in Czeslaw Milosz's poems as well as in his unforgettable *Captive mind*. It permeates Arthur Koestler's memoirs and Manès Sperber's novels. It refuses to succumb to ideological siren songs and, through Karl Popper and Ernst Cassirer, it repudiates any tribalist temptation. It rejects political myth and is wary about such supra-individual entities like party, class, state, race, or nation. Free-wheeling without being frivolous, it is fascinated with syllogism and suspicious of utopian blueprints. Václav Havel gives a keen picture of this spirit:

> It is generally rather strange, a bit mysterious, a bit nostalgic, and at times even heroic, occasionally somewhat incomprehensible in its heavy handed way, in its caressing cruelty and its ability to turn a provincial phenomenon into a global anticipation of things to come. At times it gives the impression that people here are endowed with some inner radar

capable of recognizing an approaching danger long before it becomes visible and recognizable as a danger.[25]

Inheritors of this legacy, East European dissidents regard Western committed pacifists as proponent of another version of utopianism. Dissident intellectuals have had enough of ideological and political dichotomies. As Vladimir Bukovsky once put it, dissidents are neither from the left or the right camp, but from the concentration camp. The reality of universal censorship, both of ideas and sentiments, the dehumanisation of the individual in the name of a pseudo-humanistic utopia, have convinced East European intellectuals of the absurdity of any form of political intolerance. It is therefore urgent to transcend these frozen antinomies, ruinous political squabbles and polemics bequeathed by an age of fanaticism. In Havel's words:

> I can understand that in a world where political forces interact freely this might be to some extent unavoidable. Still, I wish it could be understood why for us, against the background of our experiences, under conditions in which ideology has utterly terrorised the truth, this all seems petty, erroneous, and far removed from what is actually at stake.

The 'glowing tomorrows' have long ceased to inspire other feelings but fear and disgust among denizens of the other Europe. Western preachers of the leftist gospel should therefore not be surprised when rebutted by critical intellectuals from the communist bloc: their rhetoric smacks of a too well-known and tantalising experience, a programmed mortification of the spirit one cannot — and should not — forget. Furthermore, as Fehér and Heller notice: 'In all the countries with a Soviet-type regime, the attempts at an East-West unity of the Left have been degraded into the not totally innocent farce of Western delegations banqueting with official Eastern peaceniks who take their instructions directly from Party and security organizations.'[26]

When really tackled, peace issues are regarded by dissidents as one component of the contemporary global dilemma. It is their belief that peace, however noble and worthy a cause it may be, is not to be treated as a separate issue. A peaceful life in a universal concentration camp is not the most encouraging perspective for these people. This is why they tend to react allergically to certain Western peace groups' over-statements.

Central European nostalgia

Recently, a kind of calibration between these movements in Eastern and Western Europe has become more likely than in the past. A memorandum addressed to 'citizens, social groups, and governments' was released in Vienna in November 1986. This document was signed by 200 people from 12 European countries: peace activists, environmentalists, and prominent intellectuals. What is particularly significant in this statement is the blending of Western utopian stances (the call for renouncing the doctrine of nuclear deterrence) and East European views on the necessity to link peace campaigns with the struggle for 'a thorough democratization of states and societies'. The memorandum openly rejects the communist interpretation of human rights: rights and liberties should be considered indivisible. Moreover, the authors came out against the militarisation of schools and universities, against paramilitary education, in favour of cuts in military service ('no longer than a year'), and against the persecution of conscientious objectors.[27] In the section on cultural co-operation, the memorandum upholds the idea of a European cultural identity based on a concept of civilisation which is 'inseparably wedded to the freedom of the individual and to the idea of a civil society that is independent of the state'. The thrust of this slightly veiled criticism of Soviet-type regimes is unmistakable. The very fact that Western peace activists accepted this formulation of a joint platform with East European dissidents is encouraging. It may accelerate a reappraisal of past options and prompt Western peaceniks to become more critical of Soviet solemn proclamations of peaceful intentions. On the other hand, Jacques Rupnik is right in pointing to the ambiguities involved in this association between Central European critical intellectuals and West European peace activists:

> . . . the Westerners' invitations to the Central Europeans — to attend peace conferences and sign joint declarations — are rarely perceived by Central Europeans for what they are: namely attempts by the Western peace movement to legitimize itself as the alleged equivalent or counterpart of the Central European dissident movement.[28]

It is perfectly understandable that intellectuals in that area yearn for the resurgence of an autonomous Central European political

identity, but it is debatable whether this reassertion does not entail
a degree of cultural arrogance toward other East European cul-
tures, namely those of the South-East European region, no less
affected by the Stalino-Sovietisation. In his 'Afterword' to *The book
of laughter and forgetting*, Milan Kundera gave a synthetical expression to this view:

> It was here, in Central Europe, that modern culture found its
> greatest impulses: psychoanalysis, structuralism, dodeca-
> phony, Bartok's music, Kafka's and Musil's new aesthetics of
> the novel. The postwar annexation of Central Europe (or at
> least its major part) by Russian civilization caused Western
> culture to lose its vital center of gravity. It is the most signi-
> ficant event in the history of the West in our century, and we
> cannot dismiss the possibility that the end of Central Europe
> marked the beginning of the end for Europe as a whole.[29]

The Spenglerian hyperbole aside, since it is more than questionable whether the Nazi catastrophe was less of a tragic milestone in
European history, one is puzzled by Kundera's barely sub-
stantiated preference for the identification of Central Europe as
the cultural heartland of the continent until the disaster of the
Soviet occupation. After all, one can easily counterpose to his list
the experiments in the novel undertaken by Proust or Joyce or
Thomas Mann and the avant-garde fermentation during the
Weimar Republic, or even another myth, namely Paris as the
cultural capital of Europe, and so on. Secondly, it was not simply a
Russian occupation of the area, but a *Soviet* one, and this fact
makes a tremendously important difference since it touches on the
issue of communist ideology and its role in the total subjugation of
the individual.

Those who now call for the renaissance of a Central European
identity do not always share the same political agenda and some of
their long-term objectives may be even opposed:

> . . . the Central European idea is not devoid of ambiguities
> and misunderstandings. In Central Europe it is primarily a
> way to assert an identity distinct from the one imposed by the
> Soviet overlord. In West Germany the new interest in
> Mitteleuropa is related to the search for the solution to the
> German question. This entails an assertion of greater distance
> *vis-à-vis* the West and the Atlantic community, and a degree

of understanding with Russia. As always, this is conceivable only over the heads of the Czechs, the Hungarians, and the Poles. The fact that these different concepts of Central Europe, east and west of the political divide, are rediscovered simultaneously does not imply that they are compatible, let alone desirable.[30]

European dissidents are instrumental in sensitising Western peace movements to the inherent expansionist, enslaving, and manipulative nature of the communist system. They justifiably point to the dangers of any politics of appeasement and warn against Soviet propagandistic peace crusades. It is in a sombre mood that Havel judges the fate of his country in this century:

> . . . the inability to risk, *in extremis*, even life itself to save what gives its meaning and a human dimension leads not only to the loss of meaning but finally and inevitably to the loss of life as well — and not only one life but thousands and millions of lives.[31]

For an East European politically-minded person, it is hard to contemplate the Western pacifist shows, where the United States is ceaselessly lambasted, whereas the perpetual Soviet aggressions are benignly ignored. The Soviet occupation of Afghanistan and the atrocious repression against resistance fighters in that country do not seem to be even a minor concern for those Western ideologues imbued with leftist sterotypes. Soviet imperialist policy is often ascribed to a paranoid reaction against alleged Western conspiracies to dismantle the communist system. Western peaceniks seem to be limitlessly biased in their arrogant Eurocentrism and dogmatic refusal to admit the ominous implications of Soviet Third World military adventurism. Furthermore, they should understand that peace is guaranteed by respect for mutually shared values. Among these, the most controversial now is the attitude toward individual rights. In Havel's words:

> Without free, self-respecting, and autonomous citizens there can be no free and independent nations. Without internal peace, that is, peace among citizens and between the citizens and the state, there can be no guarantee of external peace: a state that ignores the will and the rights of its citizens can offer no guarantee that it will respect the will and the rights of other peoples, nations, and states.[32]

The conclusion to all this, hard to be swallowed by dogged Western peaceniks, is that 'respect for human rights is the fundamental condition and the sole, genuine guarantee of true peace'. This view is held by all those who, in the Soviet-dominated area of Europe, keep on fighting and hoping against hope. Theirs is an unequal, and therefore all the more heroic, struggle with forces ostensibly interested in fostering a 'world peace', a frightening denouement that would actually amount to a global prison.

Notes

1. See David Gress, *Peace and survival. West Germany, the peace movement, and European security* (Stanford, Ca.: Hoover Institution Press, 1985), p. 136.
2. See Fritjof Capra and Charlene Spretnak, in collaboration with Rudiger Lutz, *Green politics* (New York: E. P. Dutton, 1984), p. 67.
3. See Elim Papadakis, *The green movement in West Germany* (New York: St. Martin's Press, London: Croom Helm, 1984), pp. 132–55.
4. See Jürgen Fuchs, *Einmischung in eigene Angelegenheiten* (Hamburg: Rowohlt Verlag, 1984).
5. See Fehér and Heller, *Eastern left*, pp. 184–6.
6. See Ferenc Fehér and Agnes Heller, 'Eastern Europe under the shadow of a new Rapallo' in *New German Critique*, no. 37, Winter 1986, pp. 7–57.
7. See Timothy Garton Ash, 'Equilateralism', *The New Republic*, 29 September 1986, p. 23; Melvin J. Lasky, 'The doctrine of moral equivalence — some causes and consequences,' *Historical Perspectives*, Winter 1986, pp. 33–40.
8. See Régis Debray, *Les empires contre l'Europe* (Paris: Gallimard, 1985), p. 323.
9. See Jean-François Revel, *How democracies perish* (Garden City, N.Y.: Doubleday, 1984), pp. 146–7.
10. See Václav Havel, 'An anatomy of reticence,' *Crosscurrents*, A Yearbook of Central European Culture, no. 5 (Ann Arbor: University of Michigan Press, 1986), pp. 1–23.
11. See Adam Michnik, *Letters*, p. 70.
12. See Václav Havel, 'The power of the powerless' in V. Havel (ed.), *The power of the powerless*, pp. 79–80.
13. See Hélène Carrère d'Encausse, *Ni paix, ni guerre*, pp. 17–145.
14. See M. Kostikov, 'Dialogue for peace,' *Pravda*, 19 October 1986, p. 5.
15. Havel, 'Anatomy', p. 3.
16. See Roger Woods, *Opposition in the GDR under Honecker* (New York: St. Martin's Press, 1986), p. 210.
17. Havel, 'Anatomy', pp. 20–1.
18. See Miklós Haraszti, 'The Hungarian independent peace movement', *Telos*, no. 61, Fall 1984, pp. 134–44.

19. See Josef Skvorecký, 'The big insult', *Crosscurrents*, no. 5, pp. 123–35.

20. See Havel, 'Anatomy', p. 5.

21. Ibid.

22. See 'The Moscow Helsinki monitors. Their vision. Their achievement. The price they paid', *A Helsinki watch report*, New York, 1986.

23. See Timothy Garton Ash, 'Does Central Europe exist?' *New York Review of Book*, 9 October 1986; George Konrád, 'Is the dream of Central Europe still alive', *Crosscurrents*, no. 5, pp. 109–21.

24. Havel, 'The power of the powerless' in Havel (ed.), *The power*, pp. 93–4.

25. Havel, 'Anatomy', p. 9.

26. Féher and Heller, *Eastern left*, p. 33.

27. See Vladimir V. Kusin, 'Eastern dissidents join Western groups in addressing Vienna Conference', RFE, RAD Background Report, 14 November 1986.

28. See Jacques Rupnik, 'Borders of the mind', *The New Republic*, 9 March, 1987, p. 19.

29. Quoted by Charles Molesworth, 'Kundera and *The book*: the unsaid and the unsayable', *Salmagundi*, no. 3, Winter 1987, p. 66; for the discussion on Central European cultural identity, see Czeslaw Milosz, 'Central European attitudes', *Crosscurrents*, pp. 101–8.

30. Rupnik, 'Borders', p. 18.

31. Havel, 'Anatomy', p. 15.

32. Ibid.

9
Neo-Stalinism and Reform Communism

And when the individual finally gains a place there and tries to make his or her will felt within it, that automatism, with its enormous inertia, will triumph sooner or later, and either the individual will be ejected by the power structure like a foreign organism, or he or she will be compelled to resign his or her individuality gradually, once again blending with the automatism and becoming its servant, almost indistinguishable from those who preceded him or her and those who will follow.

Václav Havel

For a long time the very idea of reform has been anathema to the Soviet political mind. It was Stalin's faithful underling, Vyacheslav Molotov, who, opposing Khrushchev's de-Stalinisation campaign, spelled out this aversion to any sweeping changes: 'There are reforming Communists, and then there are the real Communists.'[1] After the lethargy of Brezhnev's last years, and particularly after the short-lived and inconclusive Andropov and Chernenko interludes, Mikhail Gorbachev has risen to prominence as a dynamic leader, expected by both Soviet citizens and Western observers to reinvigorate an exhausted, hyper-routinised political system.[2] Legitimate questions have flooded specialised journals with regard to the personality of the new Soviet leader: Who is he and what political faction was instrumental in his election? What is his political background? What values, interests and opinions does he represent? Is he going to institute dramatic reforms or will he follow a more moderate path, trying to refurbish rusty dogmas and to restore old mobilisational techniques? In sum, and the answer to this question is still a matter of conjecture, is Gorbachev intent upon resuming Khrushchev's moderate de-Stalinisation or will he rather promote a kind of managerial effectiveness, with no concern for the basic issues of a genuine democratisation of the Soviet political system? Taking into account the urgency of an elite turnover, whom will he favour to replace the remnants of Brezhnev's gerontocracy?

There was an avalanche of speculation in the West regarding Gorbachev's open-mindedness, his alleged commitment to a radical transformation of the ossified structure of the Soviet command economy, and very few were those who bore in mind what should have been a minimal caveat: that the new Soviet general secretary had been selected by the Politburo precisely because he is the embodiment of the party apparatchik, the archetype of *homo sovieticus*. For him, as for so many other former luminaries of the Komsomol, Stalin's times were inherently associated with the tremendous victory against Germany as well as with the feelings of adour and excitement described by Aleksandr Zinoviev: '. . . Stalin's was a time of idealism, dedication, and even heroism. We had an aim and fought for it. It is not often in history that one can do that.'[3] It comes, therefore, as no surprise to read Gorbachev's outspoken praises of the Stakhanovite movement as well as his hesitating approach to the Stalin problem. It seems that for the putatively reform-minded general secretary, the issue was resolved at the Twentieth Congress in February 1956, and any further elaboration on this thorny topic — the 'dreadful and bloody wound' as Konstantin Simonov called it — is bound to undermine the prestige of the USSR. In Gorbachev's own formulation, Stalinism (referred to scornfully with quotation marks), is a notion 'thought up by the enemies of communism and widely used to discredit the Soviet Union and socialism as a whole'. In other words, Stalinism is a pseudo-problem, a propagandistic gimmick employed by sworn enemies of 'socialist humanism'. Furthermore, Gorbachev, paying lip service to the Twentieth Congress, concluded:

> It is thirty years since the 20th Party Congress raised the question of overcoming Stalin's personality cult and adopted the CPSU Central Committee resolution on this question. To put it bluntly, those were difficult decisions for our Party. They were a test of Party principledness and fidelity to Leninism. I think that we passed that test worthily and drew the proper conclusions from the past.[4]

Ironically, it was precisely on the eve of the thirtieth anniversary of Khrushchev's devastating attack on Stalin's myth that the CPSU official newspaper published a lavish eulogy of Andrei Zhdanov, Stalin's faithful lieutenant and the scourge of the Soviet intelligentsia.[5] More recently, in his campaign for political reforms in the USSR, Gorbachev has expressed support for the rehabilitation of Stalin's Bolshevik victims. This seems to be the result of the intense struggle for power in the Politburo: confronted with the conservatives, Gorbachev is compelled to resume Khrushchev's aborted de-Stalinisation. He is supported by a group of dynamic party intellectuals who have understood the need for a drastic modernisation of Soviet institutions.

The confines of criticism

An orthodox Marxist-Leninist, Gorbachev cannot conceive of independent centres of authority within Soviet society. The leading role of the party, the kernel of Soviet political ideology, remains sacrosanct, and most of the general secretary's initiatives are destined to enhance this overall control. Discussion of the power and privileges of the *nomenklatura* is no less taboo nowadays than under Brezhnev. Certainly, the campaign against Dinmukhamed Kunayev, a former Politburo member and the party boss in Kazakhstan during all of the Brezhnev era, has touched the issue of privileges enjoyed by top apparatchiks, but it seems that this is rather a settlement of accounts between two competing groups — Gorbachev's followers versus the nostalgics of Brezhnev's times — than a systematic attempt to reconsider the social status of the party bureaucracy. No breathtaking theoretical innovations were advanced in the Political Report to the Twenty-seventh Congress in February 1986, Gorbachev's main rhetorical performance until his dramatic January 1987 speech 'On restructuring and the party personnel policy'. Carefully avoiding antagonising veteran members of the party elite, Gorbachev has been adamant with regard to the observance of party discipline and no spontaneity coloured the speeches of those who took the floor during the congress. The tone was set by the general secretary himself whose criticism of the sluggishness and inertia, the main features of the late Brezhnev era, never went beyond the superficial:

For a number of years the practical actions of party and state

bodies tailed behind the needs of the times and life itself —
not only because of objective factors, but also for reasons
which are primarily subjective. The problems in the country's
development built up more rapidly than they were being
solved.[6]

The principal obstacles mentioned by Gorbachev were the inert-
ness and stiffness of the forms and methods of administration, the
decline of dynamism in the party's work, and an escalation of
bureaucracy. According to the Political Report, the situation has
reached a turning point, and decisive measures are required to
meet the challenges of the present day:

> The priority task is to overcome the negative factors in
> society's socioeconomic development as rapidly as possible, to
> impart to it the essential dynamism and acceleration, to draw
> to the maximum on the lessons of the past, so that the
> decisions we adopt for the future should be explicitly clear and
> responsible, and the concrete actions purposeful and
> effective.[7]

The call to reform sounds hollow and unconvincing as long as the
party elite clings to established bureaucratic patterns of leadership,
and criticism is restricted to euphemism and speculation. There
was nothing in Gorbachev's tedious speech to encourage resolute
denunciation of the dictatorship of the *nomenklatura*, no inspiring
agenda for the regeneration of the Soviet political system. Regardless of some perfunctory remarks about the threat of bureaucratic
asphyxiation, the general secretary carefully avoided offending his
older colleagues.

Unlike the ebullient and often unpredictable Khrushchev,
Mikhail Gorbachev is inclined to preserve the principle of continuity in the Soviet leadership and the Twenty-seventh Congress
cannot be described as a decisive break with the past. The limits of
change are still prescribed by the basic value of stability. It would,
of course, be unfair to minimise the scope of the changes in the
party's outlook on social and economic issues, but they are still a
matter of promise and exhortation rather than an articulate and
coherent reformist blueprint. The members of Gorbachev's
leadership team are seemingly convinced that repeated enthusiast
injunctions can overcome the pervasive apathy of the Soviet
population. The Soviet public has been too long subjected to

propagandistic self-serving operations engineered by the *nomenkla-tura* to readily grant a *carte blanche* to the new hegemonic team. An editorial in *Pravda* on 12 April 1986 denounced 'parasitic attitudes' obstructing the new line formulated by the Twenty-seventh Congress. Basically echoing Gorbachev's Political Report, *Pravda* deplored the passivity of Soviet officialdom, its reluctance to adopt the new orientation symbolised by the general secretary.[8] The main theme of Gorbachev's criticism of the past is contained in his recurrent call for *glasnost* (a notion which in Russian means frank-ness, to make public, to bring into the open), an invitation addressed to the party apparatus to acknowledge the basic short-comings of the Brezhnev era. There are few indications that the general secretary would welcome any thorough-going criticism of the basic mechanisms of the Soviet economy, in the sense of a new role for the market regulation of prices, or support determined steps toward a radical liberalisation of the political system. The Soviet elite, for whom Gorbachev is the legitimate spokesman, would hardly underwrite the conclusions of a widely circulated *samizdat* document:

> There is open distrust of all imaginative, critical, and active individuals. In this situation, conditions are created whereby advancement in one's career is not furthered by professional excellence or adherence to principle . . . Limitations on freedom of information not only make control of the leader-ship more difficult and undermine the initiative of the people, they also mean that authorities at intermediate levels are deprived of knowledge and thus transformed into bureaucra-tic functionaries, lacking any kind of independence. At the highest level, information is incomplete and predigested, which makes it impossible for the leadership to make effective use of its authority. . .[9]

There is certainly a struggle between conservatives and modern-isers in the Soviet highest echelons, but there is no evidence to portray the latter group as intrinsically anti-Stalinist. Writing in the early 1970s, at a time when Mikhail Gorbachev was the first secretary of the Stavropol *kraykom*, Roy A. Medvedev pointed to the strength of neo-Stalinism, an indispensable means of ideological legitimation for the party apparatus:

> It (neo-Stalinism) still is the prevailing ideology in a large

section of the party and state apparatus, particularly at the middle level — in the regional and city party committees and among functionaries concerned with ideology. There are also neo-Stalinist tendencies in the leadership of the party, as well as in the top ranks of the army, trade unions and youth organizations; they are a powerful influence in literature, art and the social sciences.[10]

It seems, thus, a matter of evidence that had Gorbachev nourished any heretical inclinations throughout the Brezhnev era, he efficiently concealed them and persuaded his protectors (Fyodor Kulakov, Mikhail Suslov, Yuriy Andropov) of his impeccable credentials as a loyal 'soldier of Lenin's party'. A disciplined apparatchik, Gorbachev skilfully cultivated those highly influential members of Brezhnev's Politburo who promoted his ascent not because of his frankness but as a reward for his obedience and readiness to carry out the party's decisions. No doubt, to become and remain a member of the Politburo one has to be an excellent actor, a virtuoso of dissimulation, and those who gain entry to the Soviet Olympus are far from being a collection of figureheads or simpletons:

On the contrary, they have to possess an extra qualification, that of being able to conceal their real political talents while not creating the impression of being incompetent or insufficiently qualified. Though all of them except the Secretary General seem colorless, the members of the Politburo and the Central Committee Secretariat are very astute politicians.[11]

It comes as no surprise, therefore, that Gorbachev has refrained from bold experimentation and truly innovative reforms. His political mind is indebted to the never abandoned Stalinist traditions of secrecy and opportunism that flourished under Brezhnev, and the only major effect of his calls for renewal has been a generational mutation in the elite. Gorbachev's self-styled reformism is rooted in the Stalinist legacy, in an emotional identification with the existing order as virtually the best of all possible worlds:

Gorbachev's reformism also stresses authoritarian rule, discipline, and predictable conformist behavior. Cultural experimentation, not to speak of expanded political rights, has no place in his world. To him, 'liberalism' suggests negative characteristics . . . Should Gorbachev prove successful in making the state more efficient, the extent of its oppressiveness will also increase.[12]

Discipline, order, effectiveness, and productivity appear to be the core values of Gorbachev's approach. In other words, the last thing he would readily promote would be a spectacular reconstruction of the Soviet political system along the lines of a truly pluralist evolution. Liberalism could bring about large-scale criticism, uninhibited assaults on the Stalinist heritage, questions about the relevance of Marxist – Leninist orthodoxy — all inextricably associated in the apparatchik's mind with the spectre of anarchy.

Confusing signals

The blend of authoritarian ideology and anti-bureaucratic stances was the hallmark of the 27th Congress. It seems that Gorbachev, though more assertive and apparently more self-confident than his predecessors, is still seeking the creation of a new consensus within the Soviet supreme hierarchy. He managed to replace some of Brezhnev's old cronies (Prime Minister Nikolay Tikhonov, Moscow First Secretary Viktor Grishin, Pyotr Demichev) with people who are presumably his allies (Nikolay Ryzhkov, Boris Yeltsin, Aleksandr Yakovlev), but enough representatives of the old guard remain in the decision-making bodies to deter the general secretary from embarking upon Khrushchev-style 'harebrained' reforms. To mention only one, Viktor Chebrikov, a full member of the Politburo and chairman of the KGB, a man who served for fifteen years under Andropov at the pinnacle of the political police. It was precisely at the much celebrated April 1985 Central Committee Plenum that Chebrikov was promoted from candidate to full membership in the Politburo. On 6 November 1985, Chebrikov delivered the October Revolution anniversary speech in the Kremlin.[13] In addressing the Twenty-seventh Congress and on other occasion, Chebrikov made clear that the new leadership had decided to consolidate the repressive institutions and to uproot all dissidence. The KGB boss is indisputably one of the strongest men in Gorbachev's Politburo, more influential than the defence minister, who is only a candidate member.

Chebrikov's hard-line approach has certainly tapped responsive chords among the members of the *nomenklatura*. This group can only look askance at any attempt to exceed moderate readjustments of the traditional Soviet institutions. The apparatchiks may pretend to be thrilled by Gorbachev's calls for renovation, but they are viscerally hostile to deep structural changes. This is a most conservative community, with special interests and characteristic values to defend. All the more astonishing, therefore, was Boris Yeltsin's speech to the Twenty-seventh Congress on 26 February 1986, an unequivocal indictment of old-fashioned bureaucratic methods and one of the very few recent Soviet statements reminiscent of the de-Stalinisation campaigns under Nikita Khrushchev. Without appararent fear of alienating the party bailiffs, the then first secretary of the Moscow *gorkom* (who was also a candidate member of the Politburo) vented long-pressed frustrations. He developed Gorbachev's onslaught on 'complacency, ostentation, and verbosity' and expressed discontent with the way the party central apparatus exerts its leading role. According to Yeltsin, the structure of the Central Committee's departments only duplicates the ministeries. At the same time, this presumed reformer deplored 'the weakening of party influence over literature and art', another indication of the ambivalence of the current reformist approach. The most exiting part of Yeltsin's speech was his all-out criticism of the Brezhnev leadership's failure to establish feedback with the masses:

> Why do we hear, at congress after congress, about exactly the same problems? Why has the alien word 'stagnation' turned up in our Party vocabulary? Why after so many years have we not been able to root our bureaucratism, social injustice, and abuse of power? Why is it that even now the demand for radical change gets bogged down in an inert layer of time-servers with Party cards?[15]

Yeltsin's address is one of very few official statements to broach the disquieting issue of personal responsibility and to urge the Soviet leaders to proceed to genuine self-criticism:

> Who was to blame? . . . How many times can the same old mistakes be committed with no account being taken of the lessons of history? . . . Delegates may ask why I did not say all this in my speech at the 26th Party Congress in 1981. So be it. I can answer, and answer frankly, that I clearly lacked

sufficient courage or political experience at that time.[16]

Confessions of personal lack of courage (a euphemism for cowardice) are quite infrequent among members of the *nomenklatura*, and some people should have felt anguish listening to Yeltsin's utterance. Later, commenting on the results of the Twenty-seventh Congress, the Moscow first secretary vigorously took to task those who refused to set their sails according to 'the fresh wind of change'. He admonished the party apparatchiks who had closed their eyes when faced with urgent social problems such as:

. . . extremely difficult working conditions (in some Moscow factories — V.T.), similar living conditions and problems that have gone unresolved for years, the total indifference of executives toward social questions, and behaviour just for appearance sake . . . Ambition, superficiality, and irresponsibility — these are the only ways to characterize such disregard for people.[17]

Virulent accusations were formulated not only against Sharaf Rashidov (who had been first secretary in Uzbekistan from March 1959 until his death on 31 October 1983), but also against the demoted Kirgiz first secretary, Turdakun Usubaliyev, who had 'encouraged servility and intriguing'.[18] Significantly, Vladimir Shcherbitskiy, the Ukrainian first secretary, managed to survive this first of the elite purge and was re-elected a member of the Politburo at the 27th Congress. Furthermore, despite Gorbachev's conspicuous displeasure in having to co-operate with the Ukrainian party leader, he could impose on the local Central Committee Shcherbitskiy's ouster (at least until the moment this analysis was written, i.e. November 1987). Another former republican first secretary directly associated with the Brezhnev leadership (Eduard Shevardnadze) seems now to be among Gorbachev's closest allies, and it is unlikely he is an ardent partisan of meaningful political and economic reforms.[19] Should Gorbachev pursue the strategy of renewal, these bureaucrats may easily discover the risks of such a precipitous approach and weigh the methods and chances of ridding themselves (and the Politburo) of a troublesome 'renovator'. This possibility of a preemptive strike by the apparatus's highest echelon is a most significant deterrent to be kept in mind by any real or would-be Kremlin reformer.

The April 1985 Plenum of the CPSU Central Committee is cele-brated by the Soviet media as a crucial turning-point. According to a *Pravda* editorial, a most important effect of the April Plenum and the subsequent period was 'the lesson of truth'. 'Truth' and 'frankness' have become the catchwords employed by party propagandists to emphasise the historical change brought about by Gorbachev's coming to power. The 'de-Brezhnevization', perhaps the most appropriate description of the current phase, is supposed to end the practice of half-measures: 'The party is stopping the practice of delays and procrastinations. The new rule is: ''Do not deviate from concrete actions, do not postpone things indefinitely''.'[20] The divorce from the old, compromised methods has to be translated in a new cadre policy, or at least this is what *Pravda* suggested:

> Reorientation must take place at every workplace — from the individual labor collective to the top organs of management and party committees. It is important clearly to see the distinction between those who have really begun to reorient themselves and care about the cause from those who are only bending to the new winds without changing anything in practice.[21]

It is only natural that the average Soviet citizen is eager to benefit from this quite partial 'thaw'. The campaign for truth, with all its inconsistencies and vacillations, can channel dissatisfaction with the most scandulous abuses of the *nomenklatura*. Whether Gorbachev is going to encourage further criticism of important Soviet officials is not certain, but there are signs that this drive toward controlled openness is directly buttressed by the general secretary. For example, in February 1986, *Pravda* published excerpts from letters addressed to the editor destined to endorse the line of the April 1985 Plenum. One reader, not a party member, referred to Lenin's bitter remarks about communists abusing their positions:

> Vladimir Ilyich had indignantly criticized the Moscow Party Committee, which in the spring of 1922 tried to protect officials who had committed abuses in the allocation of houses. Lenin regarded this as the virtual indulgence of 'Communist criminals' and emphasized that 'the courts are obliged to punish Communists more harshly than non-

Communists'. And he added angrily: It's the height of shame
and outrage when the Party power defends its "own"
scoundrels!!' I'm happy to see that now things are becoming
uncomfortable for the scoundrels in our life.[22]

Other letters reviled 'the poisonous roots of bureaucratism, abuse
of office, favouritism, and the ability to live "in high style" at the
state's expense'. Even more telling was a letter advocating a
drastic reshuffle of the party apparatus as the indispensable prerequisite for the success of the new line: '. . . between the Central
Committee and the working class there still hovers an immobile,
inert and viscous "Party-administrative stratum" that doesn't
much want radical changes. Some people merely carry Party cards
but have long since stopped being Communists.'[23]

These are the vicissitudes of the political struggle in the
Kremlin: in order to improve his image as a die-hard reformer,
Gorbachev spurred the publication of views so inimical to the
vested interests of the *nomenklatura* that one could easily take them
for documents of left-wing neo-Leninist dissidents.[24] The climax of
this wave of ostensibly spontaneous letters was reached with the
message sent by an old Bolshevik whose belief is that 'the law
stipulating periodic purges should be re-established in our Party'.
This was an unmistakable allusion to the other side of the coin:
Gorbachev the reformer could easily turn into Gorbachev the
purger. *Pravda* hastened to assuage any forebodings within the
party rank-and-file:

> The Party is now conducting a huge amount of work,
> including work to cleanse its ranks. It is not a purge that is
> under way but a cleansing. We abandoned mass purges long
> ago and for rather weighty reasons that were set forth in a
> resolution of the 18th Congress of the All-Union Communist
> Party (Bolsheviks) in March 1939. Back then, the need for a
> strictly individual approach to resolving the question of Party
> membership was recognized as completely justified and
> warranted. Such an approach is needed today as well.[25]

The make-up of the party bodies elected at the Twenty-seventh
Congress can barely justify unqualified optimism regarding
Gorbachev's reformist impetus. Not only was the general secretary
unable to articulate the guidelines of an effective campaign against
the party bureaucracy, but the people now deciding Soviet policy

(Gorbachev, Ryzhkov, Ligachev, Chebrikov, Zaykov, Gromyko, *et al.*) are logically and psychologically attached to the preservation and perpetuation of the existing order. Their mental horizon is determined by the prevailing political structure and they are not going to succumb to the euphoria of true reformist attempts. On the other hand, it is symptomatic that among those re-elected as members of the Central Committee are well-known dogmatics like former Premier Tikhonov (born 1905); former *Gosplan* Chairman Nikolay Baibakov (born 1911); sycophantic, ultra-conservative writer, chief editor of *Literaturnaya Gazeta* and reportedly the ghost-writer of Brezhnev's once celebrated memoirs, Aleksandr Chakovskiy (born 1913); former Ambassador to Czechoslovakia (during the 1968 invasion), later chief of the CC Department for Cadres Abroad, Stepan Chervonenko (born 1915); the champion of fossilised Marxism-Leninism, Pyotr Fedoseyev (born 1908); Brezhnev's first deputy in the Presidium of the Supreme Soviet and one of the main survivors of Stalin's apparatus, Vassiliy Kuznetsov (born 1901); former secretary in charge of international affairs and a last Comintern relic, Boris Ponomariov (born 1905); and many others belonging to the same family of spirits. Their re-election does not represent a challenge to the new team, but is rather the public confirmation of Gorbachev's pledge to abide by the principle of continuity of cadres. Stability is the golden rule, the sacred value of the *nomenklatura*, and Gorbachev chose to avoid useless definance of this norm. Those who expected a sensational reappraisal of the past found only an ironic consolation in the election of Nikolay Ivanovich Bukharin, a senior research associate from the Institute of Economics of the World Socialist System, to the Central Auditing Commission. This onomastic coincidence with the man who had personified the chances of a less inhuman model of socialism perfectly epitomises the nature of the current 'thaw'. Bukharinism has not been reconsidered, but there is now a Bukharin to sing praise to the general secretary's theoretical inventiveness.[26] As mentioned, Bukharin might be however the first member of Lenin's Politburo murdered by Stalin to be rehabilitated under Gorbachev.

The reformist temptation

Gorbachev is the exponent of *nomenklatura's* interests, but at the same time, like Khrushchev, he is concerned about the long-term prospects for the modernisation of Soviet society. He is not intent upon altering the existing matrix of domination and cannot be suspected of harbouring genuine revisionist convictions. The area of reform he can envision is quite limited, and it is not at all probable that the Soviet general secretary would be attracted to the reformist programme initiated by Alexander Dubček in Czechoslovakia after January 1968. Recent statements of the Czechoslovak leadership do not leave any doubt about the differences in approach between the Prague Reform Movement, which is still described as 'right-wing opportunistic', and the new Soviet line bound 'to foster the socialist institutions'. Even Gorbachev's strongest attack on the apparatus during the January 1987 Plenum of the Central Committee of the CPSU does not seem to have particularly disquieted the Prague conservative leadership. There is no organised intellectual opposition in the Soviet Union, and there are few indications that Gorbachev is interested in encouraging the radical consciousness of the intelligentsia. Revitalisation of Soviet society is certainly his goal, but he would not underwrite spontaneous expressions of discontent and criticism. Reforms in the USSR are determined by the willingness of the apparatus to accept a certain curtailment of its power monopoly.[27] To work against the long-term interests of this powerful group would mean political suicide for any communist leader. Gorbachev, therefore, must out-manoeuvre conservative critics and keep virtual centrifugal forces under strict control.

Under current Soviet conditions, genuine reforms would mean increased autonomy for the government, improvement of the economic performances in both industry and agriculture, limitations on the KGB, loosening the party stranglehold over the spiritual life, a new approach to the issues of legality and human rights, and cultural and ideological relaxation. These are not utopian requirements and do not entail a dramatic reconsideration of the dogmatic underpinnings of the Soviet system. It is signigicant, however, that Gorbachev has shown more interest in Honecker's 'technocratic socialism' than in Kádár's more market-oriented economic experiments. For fear of alienating his supporters in the highly centralised party apparatus, the Soviet leader may find it inconvenient to emulate the Hungarian model with its emphasis on a less authoritarian pattern of political leadership. It would, therefore be an unfounded assumption to credit him with having in mind a revision of the main functioning principles of the Soviet regime: the party is still there, ubiquitous and omnipotent, the hidebound Leninist ideology is still the fundamental reservoir of legitimacy, the society is still atomised, and no independent groups are allowed to coalesce in the USSR. Neo-Stalinism, or Soviet-style political conservatism, means precisely the commitment to this traditional pattern of leadership, the suppression of civil society and the exaltation of the party's dictatorship. Introducing radical reforms — human rights improvement, encouragement of private initiative, decentralisation — would mean jeopardising the fictitious ideological monolith and subverting the structure of the prevailing political authority.

This is the excruciating dilemma confronting the current Soviet leadership. As a result, one can barely expect Gorbachev to launch those broad reforms that, according to one sanguine observer of the Soviet scene, would lead to the 'revitalization of the Soviet political life'.[28] It would be more useful to admit that the most Gorbachev can imagine in terms of reforms is a reorientation of the economy toward the production of consumer goods, a less triumphalistic approach to economic issues, a loosening of censorship, and a less patronising attitude towards the intelligentsia. Being aware of the ill-fated historical experiences of reform communism, he will try to simulate innovative economic behaviour, while preserving those petrified political institutions and defending those musty values that justified Leonard Schapiro's 1970 description of the Soviety system as totalitarian:

> Everything points to the fact that the strings are still firmly held at the centre — in the Politburo, in the Secretariat, and its departments and in the instruments such as the security force, which all those bodies control . . . In this situation the party remains what it has been for many years: a powerful network of influence and control, but to a large extent atomized, and always dependent for its influence and authority on the personal links which its individual, leading officials or members can forge to the dominant wielders of influence at the top.[29]

Furthermore, the Soviet general secretary has to consider the possible disruptive effects of crucial reforms within both the USSR and the allied countries. A Dubček-style abrupt renewal would certainly result in the resurgence of revisionist tendencies in Eastern Europe, would help the crystallisation of autonomous centres of political and social initiative, and thus would endanger the future of the Warsaw Pact as a Soviet-dominated military-political alliance. The established bureaucracies in the countries of the 'socialist community' would leave the scene, and genuine reformers would come to power to resume the suppressed projects of nationalist communism. The *retour du refoulé* (return of the repressed) would become a practical historical opportunity. In other words, a probable effect of radical reforms in the USSR would be the revival of the now almost extinct revisionist neo-Marxist alternative to Stalinism and the emergence of pluralist institutions in East-Central Europe. That such an occurrence would not be welcome by Gorbachev and his peers was made perfectly clear in December 1985 when *Pravda* celebrated the fifteenth anniversary of Husak's ignominious 'theoretical' indictment of the Prague Spring.[30]

Gorbachev's 'imperial' mandate is to prevent the disintegration of the Soviet bloc, and his signals to East European leaders suggests that he is strongly committed to further enhancement of 'socialist integration'.[31] It may well be that Gorbachev is very much a child of the 20th Congress, an atypical, almost extraordinary apparatchik, but he is still the mouthpiece of a certain political group that deeply resented Khrushchev's tempestuous attack on Stalinism.[32] It is true, on the other hand, that some of the people recently appointed to supervise ideological and international affairs have been perceived if not as 'party democrats', at least as opposed to the rabid nationalism that blossomed under Brezhnev: Alexandr Yakovlev, a former ambassador to Canada, now a secretary in charge of propaganda and since June 1987 a member of the Politburo, is well known for his criticism of Russian chauvinism and 'national Bolshevism' and is largely credited with the ongoing cultural 'thaw'. It is symptomatic, however, that Yakovlev has to share responsibility over ideological and cultural affairs with Yegor Ligachev, the hard-nosed number two man in the Kremlin.[33]

Limited as they are in scope and ambitions, Gorbachev's reformist plans should rather be compared to Malenkov's smoothly introduced 'new course' than to Khrushchev's extravagant and capricious offensives.[34] They are designed to offer a more human image of the Soviet elite, less worried about its own privileges and more concerned about the fate of the population. Gorbachev is aware of the widening gap between rulers and ruled, and his public performances (visits to workers' apartments, conversations with people in the street), dutifully reported by the

Soviet media, are bound to consolidate his image as a popular, accessible leader. His objective is to be regarded as the protector of the average Soviet citizen, and not as a distant demigod dictating his will from a secret residence. This is another attempt to strengthen the institutionalised sources of authority of the Soviet leadership, with special emphasis on the rulers' populist, anti-elitist programmes and practices. Primarily pragmatists, Gorbachev and his colleagues make use of ideology mostly as a spiritual ingredient, with no particular concern for the appeals, mobilisational force, and uplifting potential of the party slogans. They are inheritors of, not believers in Leninism.

If neo-Stalinism primarily means conservation of the party's dictatorship and intensification of the repressive functions of the state apparatus, together with the increasing militarisation of the economy and an expansionist (imperial) foreign policy, what would be Gorbachev's tasks as a presumably anti-Stalinist reformer? Is he ready for a showdown with the most conservative forces? Would he accept the suppression of censorship and the free access of researchers, writers and journalists to the party and government archives and, even more, would he welcome the publication of their most revealing findings? What about the human rights and how does Gorbachev's image as a reformer fit with the new emigration law, which is even more intolerant and restrictive than the previous one? Are Ligachev, Zaykov, Ryzhkov, Chebrikov, Shevardnadze, and the other stalwarts of the current Soviet leadership team eager to endorse an authentic divorce from the past? Even Yakovlev, reportedly the most liberal member of Gorbachev's team, carefully avoids any revisionist statement. Prudence in expectation would, therefore, be the most appropriate attitude in order to avoid painful disappointments which inevitably result from such an overly optimistic historical forecast: 'Gorbachev will continue his efforts to push the more intransigent officials out of the key positions; and then, having constructed a broad constituency of his own, will launch a program of reforms.'[35] For the time being, what we are witnessing is a cascade of statements of good intentions, pathetic calls for 'restructuring', and very few tangible political changes. In his January 1987 Plenum speech, Gorbachev admitted that Soviet ideology has lost more of its inspiring power: 'Lenin's dictum that the value of a theory consists in its providing an exact picture "of all the contradictions that are present in reality" was often merely ignored. The theoretical concepts of socialism remained to a large extent at the level of the 1930s – 1940s.' In other words, Soviet Marxism has not surpassed the intellectual abyss of the *Short course*. In an oblique reference to Stalinism, Gorbachev acknowledged that:

The causes of the situation go back far into the past and are rooted in that specific historical situation in which by virtue of well-known circumstances vigorous debates and creative ideas disappeared from theory and social sciences while authoritarian evaluations and opinions became unquestionable truths, that could only be commented upon.

Along the same lines, Gorbachev deplored the consequences of Brezhnev's methods of government over the whole body politic:

Elements of social corrosion that emerged in the last few years had a negative effect on society's morale and inconspicuously eroded the lofty moral values which have always been characteristic of our people . . . As an inevitable consequence of all this, interest in the affairs of society slackened, manifestations of callousness and skepticism appeared and the role of moral incentives to work declined. The stratum of people, some of them young people, whose ultimate goal in life was material well-being and gain by any means, grew wider. Their cynical strand was acquiring more and more aggressive forms, poisoning the mentality of those around them and triggering a wave of consumerism. The spread of alcohol and drug abuse and a rise in crime became indicators of the decline of social mores.

And to make this grim picture even more impressive Gorbachev added:

Disregard for laws, report-padding, bribe-taking and encouragement of toadyism and adulation had a deleterious influence on the moral atmosphere in society. Real care for people, for the conditions of their life and work and for social well-being were often replaced with political flirtation — the mass distribution of awards, titles and prizes. An atmosphere of permissiveness was taking shape, and exactingness, discipline and responsibility were declining.[36]

Now, an elementary question to be raised is where was Gorbachev when all these nuisances developed? Why did he keep a low profile and not try to warn the Brezhnev leadership about the degradation of moral standards? The answer to this question is too obvious to need further elaboration: a member of the apparatus, he was no more and no less opportunistic than his peers, equally subservient and ready to bow before the then all-powerful ruler. Now he pretends to march in the avant-garde of the struggle for democratisation, but it is doubtful that this has always been his secret dream. As for the practical results of his impassionate plea for renewal, one should notice the reluctance of the Central Committee to endorse Gorbachev's convoluted proposals to organise secret party elections. This is not too discrete a warning not to underestimate the *esprit de corps* of the political body whose representative he is supposed to be.

The Soviet general secretary is certainly a wary politician, a man who has internalised the basic principles of the Leninist methodology of deception. His gradualist approach to the regeneration of the Soviet system has encouraged certain intellectuals to voice their discontent with the official falsification of history and the administrative tutelage of culture.[37] Truth and sincerity, Gorbachev's favourite slogans, were indeed the crux of Alexander Tvardovskiy's editorial statements in the liberal days of the journal *Noviy Mir*. On the other hand, despite such official or semi-official blaming of the past, there is no doubt that dissident views are still outlawed in the USSR while the party conveniently resorts, yet again, to 'literary Zubatovism'.[38] Among the cultural events permitted under Gorbachev is the performance of a play entitled *The silver anniversary*. Written by Alexandr Misharin, the play follows the return of a high official to the provincial town where he began his political career. There he learns about the misdeeds perpetrated by two of his local protégés. One journalist described his theatrical event as a synthesis of the exhilarating debates generated by Gorbachev's rejuvenation of the party elite and the elimination of the Brezhnevite ankylosed cadres: 'Conflicts of privilege and responsibility, corruption and integrity, old and new styles of leadership, central versus regional authority — even the anti-alcoholism campaign — emerge in an evening that begins with the celebration of a silver anniversary and ends with thunder, hysteria and tears.'[39]

Since Gorbachev is widely perceived as a less dogmatic, more innovative leader, it is perhaps useful to mention here some of the views expressed by a number of Italian Marxist ideologues. It is well known that relations between the CPSU and the Italian Communist Party (PCI) have been strained at least since the 1968 intervention in Czechoslovakia.[40] During a discussion organised by *Rinascita*, the theoretical publication of the PCI, one of the participants pointed precisely to the enduring conservative dimension of Soviet political culture:

> One should not underestimate the vested interests that are opposed to reforms and to mere adjustments. For one thing that needs to be said is that the present system enjoys a vast consensus of support in wide sectors of the population. One should not, furthermore, forget that as a superpower the USSR requires stability and patterns of continuity with regard to international questions such as security, its world image, etc. . . . . Finally, one element that traditionally weighs in favor of the stability of the Soviet system but that in certain conditions can become a potential factor of instability is the sheer size of the country and its multinational character.[41]

As for the theoretical perspective of the new version of the CPSU programme adopted at the Twenty-seventh Congress, it could scarcely be a source of inspiration for reform-minded communists. It is instead a collection of outworn clichés, run-of-the-mill slogans which cannot hide the extinction of theoretical imagination in the CPSU ideological headquarters.[42] Still confident in the vitality of Marxism, despite past disillusions, Zdenek Mlynař, a leading doctrinaire of the Prague Spring, interpreted this programme as the viewpoint of those conservative forces his one-time friend Mikhail Gorbachev supposedly stands against:

> In general, one can say that in both the old (1961 — V.T.) and the new versions of the program the world and the Soviet society are viewed through the same ideological spectacles that distort reality to suit the desires of the wearer. The capacity to analyze the past and the present in a critical manner is thus thoroughly reduced, to the point of disappearing.[43]

Zdenek Mlynař is one of those ex-communists who really should know what it is all about: a heretic rather than a renegade, to make use of Deutscher's typology, he is among the most trustworthy sources regarding the mentality and the general outlook of the highest Soviet elite. Moreover, he was one of the authors of the Action Programme of the Communist Party of Czechoslovakia, the charter of the Reform Movement quelled by Warsaw Pact tanks in August 1968.[44] Mlynař, a friend of Gorbachev when both attended Moscow University's Law School in the early 1950s, has issued some of the most influential statements concerning the Soviet general secretary's personality:

> He (Gorbachev — V.T.) is a man who attributes more importance to his own experience, lived and felt, than to what he has read. At the same time, he is capable of assessing his own experience with great rationality and of developing it with help from other sources. He is capable of acting in a pragmatic manner but also of theoretical reasoning. In his life permanent values have an importance beyond temporary successes, and he has enough confidence in himself to give up a course that he himself has not found to be correct.[45]

This hopeful encomium, read as an authoritative opinion on Gorbachev's temperament, should be judged in the light of Mlynař's bitter confession about his current pessimistic mood primarily caused by 'very ugly experiences' in Husak's Czechoslovakia. Mlynař's overly optimistic expectations with regard to a possible resumption of the Reform Movement in Czechoslovakia under the auspices of the Soviet campaign for renewal, were recently denounced as wishful thinking by no one else than Vasil Bilak, Husak's lieutenant in charge of ideological affairs. Asked by *Rude Pravo* to characterise the difference between the Soviet present objectives and the goals of the Czechoslovak 'right-wing opportunists', i.e. reformers, in the past, Bilak did not waver over his answer:

> Nothing is identical. The CPSU leadership is striving to strengthen socialism and the unity of the socialist community, whereas our 'fighters for socialism with a human face' strove in 1968 to dismantle socialism and to break up the socialist community . . . Certain posthumous children of right wing opportunists, who are striving to 'rehabilitate' those who were politically shipwrecked . . . are pursuing the same goal as in 1968 — to return Czechoslovakia to the lap of capitalism.[46]

There is a visible contrast between the Soviet general secretary's reformist exhortations and his unequivocal hard-line approach to liberal experiments in the East European empire. Gorbachev's speech to the Tenth Congress of the Polish Communists was conceived as an ultimatum addressed to those forces in Eastern Europe which might be tempted to interpret current Soviet self-criticism as an indication of weakness or declining willingness to dominate the empire. His statement can be considered an endorsement of the notorious Brezhnev Doctrine of limited sovereignty, an arrogant reassertion of Soviet pre-eminence within the bloc and an undisguised attack on would-be liberal forces. There was no sign in Gorbachev's Warsaw speech of any kind of sympathetic understanding for independent social movements. On the contrary, he chose to emphasise the dogmatic, neo-Stalinist view of international relations. According to Gorbachev, socialism appears now as 'an alliance of states closely linked by political, economic, cultural, and defence interests'. Furthermore, any attempt to question prevailing interstate relations is bound to engender a speedy Soviet reaction. National communism remains an unforgivable heresy and the Soviet Union will not allow any of its allies to indulge in such 'adventurous' experiments: 'To threaten the socialist order, try to undermine it from outside, and tear one country or another from the socialist community means encroachment not only on the will of the people but also on the entire postwar order and, in the final analysis, on peace.'[47]

One cannot come closer to the Soviet justification of the 1968 intervention in Czechoslovakia in the name of the defence of the 'international interests of the socialist community'! Hence, it is legitimate to wonder how long this disjunction between efforts to advance even a modest internal renewal and the drastic refusal to accept any form of liberalisation in East-Central Europe can last? The shock waves of the *glasnost* campaign are bound to contaminate East European political and intellectual elites who cannot be long denied the right to follow the pattern emphatically proclaimed by the Soviet general secretary. The 1953–6 'new course' resulted, among other things, in the limited de-Stalinisation carried out during Imre Nagy's first premiership (1953–5) and, more significantly, in the Polish crisis and in the Hungarian Revolution. The current campaign against red tape and dogmatism, which is directly linked to Gorbachev's coming to power, may sound like an invitation to a reassessment of the historical experience of communism in Eastern Europe and could provoke the revival of the critical consciousness among disenchanted circles of the intelligentsia both in the USSR and in East-Central Europe.

Gorbachev's main objective is apparently to restructure the party apparatus, though no meaningful changes have been undertaken that would decisively affect its deeply entrenched structure of privileges and interests. He has sharply criticised the 'blind faith in the omnipotence of the apparatus' and expressed discontent with excessive centralism. In order to increase the credibility of his repeated urges to a new approach to social and economic issues, Gorbachev will have to insist on developing internal party democracy and will probably increasingly rely on those groups interested in preventing the repetition of past crimes and abuses. He is, thus, a prisoner of the tormenting dilemma between loyalty to tradition and commitment to innovation, and most likely he is still looking for an appropriate tactic to deal with renewal without catalysing a major political crisis.

Cornelius Castoriadis has suggestively shown why the system cannot bring about a genuine reform movement:

> Firstly, a real self-reform would amount to the self-liquidation of an enormous part of the bureaucracy. Secondly, it would require *ideas*, the last thing that the party would be able to produce. Thirdly, it would need hundreds of thousands, or even millions, of new cadres who would be ready and capable to ceaselessly push forward the reformist measures . . . throughout the endless morass of bureaucratic Russia.[48]

For the time being, Gorbachev prefers to posture as the spokesman for 'truth', in this ongoing struggle against the conspiracy of illusions and self-delusions. Quoting Lenin's warning that 'illusions and self-deception are terrible', the Soviet general secretary has placed himself in the avant-garde of this alleged crusade against mendacity:

> The party and the people need the whole truth, in matters large or small. It is only truth that educates people with a developed sense of civic duty, while lies and half-truths deprave the conscience, deform the personality, and prevent the elaboration of realistic conclusions and evaluations, without which there can be no active party policy.[49]

One can only add that the party's truth is more often than not different from, if not the opposite of, historical truth, that, for the

Leninists, truth is pragmatically defined, and objective criteria for its determination are usually discarded as 'bourgeois ideological infiltrations'. Objectivity and party-mindedness (*partiynost*) are, for Soviet Marxism, synonymous. Gorbachev's advocacy of truth should thus be regarded as a temporary political device, an instrument in his struggle against real and potential opponents to his programme, and a way of reinforcing his public image as a restorer of party democracy and an unyielding foe of conservatism and stagnation. It was indeed this motivation which inspired Gorbachev's suggestions addressed to a group of leading Soviet writers during a meeting reportedly characterised by frankness and outspokenness:

> The word of the writer and the voice of the artist are especially important and especially influential. Literary people can play a considerable part in implementing the psychological and moral reshaping of life in the struggle against negative phenomena. And here it is clear that the artistic investigation of our time demands bold, unstereotyped thinking and an understanding of the deep phenomena and processes of life.[50]

Gorbachev's indications were eagerly followed by many Soviet writers during their recent congress. The general secretary's statements on behalf of truth in social life permitted such writers as Yevgeniy Yevtushenko, Andrey Voznesenskiy, Daniil Granin, Bulat Okudzhava, Grigoriy Baklanov, and Sergey Zalygin to spell out their worries about bureaucratic abuses in the field of culture, the impending ecological crisis in the USSR, the aberrant architectural policy, the degradation of human relations, and the devolution of ethical criteria. Certainly, there were no calls for the abolition of censorship and no one dared question the party's overall control of literature and the arts, but the very fact that the speeches were not checked beforehand by the cultural bureaucracy made this congress an unprecedented tribune for critical views. Voznesenskiy openly asked for the full-fledged rehabilitation of such 'pariah' writers as Zamyatin, Gumilev, and Khodasevich and requested complete editions of Anna Akhmatova and Boris Pasternak (including *Doctor Zhivago*), and recent developments in Moscow — including Pasternak's 'rehabilitation' and posthumous reinstatement as a member of the Writers' Union and the publication of Akhmatova's *Requiem* in the pages of the weekly *Ogonyiok* — indicate that his words did not fall on deaf ears. Voznesenskiy advocated the urgent need for sincerity, the unquenchable thirst for a moral reconstruction of society:

> Why do readers turn aside from certain books? There are many reasons. But the most important is that the people want openness. They know the truth about the monstrous forces of evil, lawlessness, corruption, extortion, deception, and duplicity . . . Alas, only an isolated few of us sounded the alarm about the monstruousness of these crimes. And now — the main enemy within our society is bureaucracy — which hampers restructuring, everything new; it is stagnation, the old way of thinking, which alas, has not surrendered.[51]

These are harsh words which have not been heard since the 1961–3 second 'thaw'. The same merciless denunciation of bureaucracy characterised Yuriy Bondarev's open call for a 'politics of consciousness':

> Criticism in life and literature must militate against fossilized tastes, vulgar habits, false group values, that is, it must militate against second rate ethics and perverted morality. At the same time, criticism, knowing well that it is the expression of national consciousness, cannot be a synonym for bad taste.[52]

Lately, Bondarev has become increasingly critical of the liberal writers and allied himself with the neo-Stalinist wing in the Writers' Union.

If nothing else, the Soviet Writers' Congress has confirmed the vitality of the moral commitment of the intelligentsia and offered enough elbow-room for those writers who think that reforms should be consistent, courageous and far-reaching indeed. The congress may have intrigued many members of Gorbachev's entourage, including the apparent second-in-command, Central Committee Secretary, Yegor Ligachev, whose views could hardly be considered convergent with those so candidly expressed by some of the leading Soviet writers. The long-term effects of this real milestone in the history of Soviet culture cannot be ignored both in terms of impact on the public and of further redistribution of alliances in the Kremlin. The triumphalist tone of socialist realism was vehemently excoriated at the congress, and it was precisely Yulian Semyonov who stigmatised certain officially sponsored sub-literary products:

Everyone knows how much pulp literature has to be published for every Akhmatova and Shukshin! But pulp goes on being published. This is yet another example of the opposition to new things that have been emerging in our country since the April plenum.[53]

No doubt, these writers really mean what they say and they seem deeply committed to fighting for an 'ecology of culture' — as Voznesenskiy put it — against the duplicity and the dictatorship of self-righteous half-truths.

At the same time, the party doctrinaires will closely follow the dynamics of cultural life and will curb any attempt to bypass the rules prescribed by the Politburo. Under Gorbachev, dissidence is likely to remain no less an offence than under his predecessors. The boundaries of criticism and the thrust of reforms are established by the same party bureaucracy which is now ostensibly under fire. Mikhail Gorbachev craves to consolidate both his power and authority and he may find it convenient to encourage certain critical or semi-critical intellectual groups. His power base, however, is the party apparatus and his main options and programmes are determined by the support this group is ready to bestow on him. Thus, it follows that the main obstacle to furthering truly innovative reform is precisely the *nomenklatura*, whom Gorbachev credits with a presumed willingness to partake in this search for renewal. Inasmuch as the current debate is maintained at a strictly theoretical level, inasmuch as it does not beget alternative platforms and genuine political controversies, the campaign against bureaucracy will be regarded suspiciously by the apparatus, but will not be combated as a mortal danger. The inner dynamics of change may, however, break up the current (apparent) concensus and precipitate the polarisation of forces in the Politburo and the Central Committee. Paradoxically, Mikhail Gorbachev, who rose to prominence as a faithful man of the apparatus, may have to confront the plots fomented by neo-Stalinist hierarchs, for whom another Khrushchevite experiment cannot be but ruinously counter-productive. It is certainly difficult to intimate the stakes and the implications of the current arguments in the Kremlin, but there is no scarcity of indications that Gorbachev is far from having acquired the status of an undisputed and unanimously followed leader. Neo-Stalinism is no less a temptation for the Soviet political mind than its counterpart, reform communism, and it will take patience, single-mindedness and special acumen for the general secretary to navigate the Kremlin's troubled waters.

The seventieth anniversary of the October Revolution could have been the best opportunity for Gorbachev to break with some of the most rudimentary views on Soviet history. Many in the West expected the general secretary to announce the political rehabilitation of Nikolay Bukharin and other Old Bolsheviks executed during the Stalinist terror. Instead, he preferred to postpone the analysis of the most controversial issues.

The Stalin question was broached by Gorbachev in a very ambiguous way: Stalin did indeed sin against the party, was guilty of the creation of a general climate of fear and conformism, but he was also the architect of the historically justified programme of industrialisation and collectivisation. Even more significant, Stalin was credited with a tremendous role in the victory against Nazi Germany. In other words, Gorbachev refuses to admit that Stalinism represented the very antithesis of the Marxist promise of human emancipation. The Soviet leader is still a prisoner of the Leninist mindset and cannot endorse any attempt to subvert the ideological underpinnings of his regime. This is why, despite his personal affinities, Gorbachev joined the neo-Stalinist hard-liners, headed by Yegor Ligachev, at the moment Boris Yeltsin criticised the slow pace of reforms during the October 1987 Plenum of the Central Committee. Yeltsin's chief fault was that he took *ad litteram* Gorbachev's calls for liberalisation. Too much radicalism does not pay off in Moscow nowdays. More than any other prominent member of Gorbachev's team, Yeltsin symbolised the new political style associated with *glasnost*. He was outspoken and ebullient, ready to lambast and confront the inertia of the party bureaucracy. For Moscow liberal intellectuals, Yeltsin appeared as a more enlightened party leader, whose protection assured the publication of long-banned books and manuscripts. More than any other Soviet city, Yeltsin's Moscow seemed infected with the new political values. Such a situation could not be tolerated by the Politburo's conservatives. On several occasions, Yeltsin complained about the activities of the anti-reformist group. His frustration with Ligachev's sabotaging of restructuring and *glasnost* exploded during the October Plenum when Yeltsin offered his resignation from both the Politburo and Moscow party committee's leadership. Surprisingly, the incident was announced by the official spokesman of the Central Committee. Later, on November 11, a plenary meeting of the Moscow City CPSU

Committee relieved Boris Yeltsin of his duties as first secretary and member of the Bureau of the Moscow City Party organisation 'for major shortcomings in his leadership of the Moscow City Party organisation'.[54] He was replaced by Lev Zaykov, a former leader of the Leningrad Regional CPSU Committee, widely regarded as a colourless apparatchik. The proceedings of the plenary session, which was attended by both Gorbachev and Ligachev, got extensive coverage in Soviet media. Symptomatically, Yeltsin was pilloried by all his former subordinates in speeches strikingly reminiscent of the Stalinist purges. Gorbachev himself delivered a confusing speech, accusing Yeltsin of demagogy and adventurism:

> Comrade Yeltsin placed his personal ambitions above the interests of the party. Incidentally, he had these manifestations pointed out to him by the Politburo, and he promised to draw the necessary lessons. But, as we can see, these promises were not worth very much. In the overall opinion of Central Committee members, the irresponsible and immoral actions of Comrade Yeltsin were damaging the thing we need most just now — the pooling of all forces and the mobilisation of all potential in order to resolve the major tasks of reconstructuring.[55]

Gorbachev's performance should be regarded in the light of his vital need to placate the fears of those who resent the new course. To defend his positions against the neo-Stalinists, Gorbachev had to distance himself from the intempestous Yeltsin. This tactic might be however counterproductive. Those who abhor the liberalisation will not limit themselves to mere procrastination. A political showdown between reformers and counter-reformers cannot be any longer avoided. The forthcoming CPSU national conference, planned to take place in the summer of 1988, will show how powerful the general secretary really is. For the time being, Stalin's heirs work hardly to deter Gorbachev from embarking on bolder political reforms. Approving of Yeltsin's purge, Gorbachev has disappointed many of his most enthusiastic supporters. As astute a manoeuvrer as he certainly is, the Soviet leader cannot afford to wage a war against the *nomenklatura* without the wholehearted assistance of those who think like Yeltsin. It is thus obvious that, with Yeltsin gone, Gorbachev's rear is unprotected: 'He is left as the man so many of his colleagues have mutteringly suspected him to be: the chief shaker and breaker of communist traditions and communist privileges.'[56]

Three decades after 1956, the year of the Twentieth Congress, of the Polish October, and of the ruthless crushing of the Hungarian Revolution, the Soviet Union seems to be ushering in a new era, when fresh ideas and daring solutions are ostensibly invoked as the main political desideratum. There is certainly something new — if not a wind of change, at least a breeze of innovation — associated with Gorbachev's coming to power. Whether the Soviet people, and the peoples of the Soviet-type regimes in East-Central Europe, will find this new climate more breathable is still an open question. A long-delayed elite replacement, the rise to power of a new generation, the heightening of the conflict between those with a stake in reforms and the partisans of the *status quo*, all these developments have to be cautiously pondered and dispassionately examined in order to acquire a balanced understanding of the current situation. To pin all hope on Gorbachev as a *deus ex machina*, a miraculous reformer, a born-again Leninist (or Bukharinist) with no Stalinist nostalgias, would amount to ignoring seven decades of Soviet history and taking mythological fallacies for historical evidence.

Notes

1. Quoted by Stephen Cohen, *Rethinking the Soviet experience* (New York: Oxford University Press, 1985), p. 131. Shortly before his death, this patriarch of the Stalinist tradition was reinstated in the party and offered the possibility of posturing as a respectable retired statesman. An interview with the 96-year old Molotov was published in *Moskovskiye Novosti* on 2 July 1986, where this unflinching Stalin loyalist gave vent to his presumably enthusiastic views on the current changes: 'I am up to date with all the events. I am inspired by the changes which are taking place in our life. It is a nuisance that age and health do not permit me to take an active part in it.' (See 'Moskovskiye Novosti interviews former leader Molotov', FBIS, *Soviet Union*, pp. R9–10; Serge Schmemann, 'Soviet paper depicts a "Happy Molotov" at 96', *New York Times*, 3 July 1986).

2. See William G. Hyland, 'The Gorbachev Succession', *Foreign Affairs*, Spring 1985, pp. 800–9.

3. See George Urban, 'A dissenter as a Soviet man. A conversation with Alexander Zinoviev', (II), *Encounter* (London), May 1984, p. 32.

4. See 'Otvety M. S. Gorbacheva na voprosy gazety *L'Humanité*', *Pravda*, 8 February 1986. Earlier, in his speech on 8 May 1985, Gorbachev emphasized the personal contribution to the victory of 'the head of the State Defense Committee, Iosif Vissarionovich Stalin'. (See Julia Wishnevsky, 'Treatment of Stalin in Soviet propaganda thirty years after

the Twentieth Congress', *Radio Liberty Research*, RL 70/86, 13 February 1986).

5. See V. Glagolev, 'Iz pokolenia bolshevikov', *Pravda*, 24 February 1986. For Zhdanov and Zhdanovism, see Gavriel D. Ra'anan, *International policy formation in the USSR. Factional 'debates' during the Zhdanovshchina* (Hamden: Archon Books, 1983). In an article published in *Pravda* (10 May 1986), Boris Ponomariov extolled the 'experience gained by the party during the country's industrialization'. Elaborating on the idea of the 'monolithic unity of the party', Ponomariov indulged in a full-fledged rehabilitation of the Stalinist elite: 'Lenin's comrades-in-arms and pupils, the entire iron cohort of Bolsheviks who played a decisive role in the implementation of these goals of socialist construction, serve as a model for the present and future generations of communists and all Soviet people.' (See 'Enduring relevance of Leninist principles viewed', FBIS, *Soviet Union*, 22 May 1986, p. R20.) It seems obvious that Ponomariov, the most prominent official authority on party history, has in mind people like Stalin, Molotov, Voroshilov, Kirov, Zhdanov, and many others whose careers were facilitated by the defeat of various oppositional factions. No wonder, therefore, that on the occasion of the 45th anniversary of the formation of the State Defence Committee, *Pravda* extolled the role of the CPSU leaders directly involved in the activity of this body: Stalin, Molotov, Voroshilov, Malenkov, Bulganin, Voznesenskiy, Kaganovich, Mikoyan. This is perhaps the first time that the names of the members of the 'anti-Party group' purged by Khrushchev in June 1957 were allowed to resurface from the memory hole of communist oblivion. Certainly, Beria's name was omitted, or better said, it was included in the category *et al.* See *Pravda*, 30 June 1986, p. 7.

6. See 'Political report of the CPSU Central Committee', delivered on 25 February 1986 by M .S. Gorbachev to the 27th CPSU Congress, FBIS, *Soviet Union* (National Affairs), 28 March 1986, p. 10.

7. Ibid. It is significant that Gorbachev shunned any consistent approach to the social origins of bureaucratic immobilism.

8. See Elizabeth Teague, '*Pravda* editorial testifies to strength of opposition to change', Radio Liberty Research, RL 192/86, 15 May, 1986.

9. See Roy A. Medvedev, *On socialist democracy* (New York: W. W. Norton, 1975), p. 37. The concept of *glasnost* was initially developed in the dissident Democratic Movement. See Irina Kirk, *Profiles in Russian resistance* (New York: Quadrangle, The New York Times Book Company, 1975).

10. Roy A. Medvedev, *On socialist democracy*, p. 53. For Gorbachev's political career, see Archie Brown, 'Gorbachev: new man in the Kremlin', *Problems of Communism*, May – June 1985, pp. 1 – 23; Zhores A. Medvedev, *Gorbachev* (New York: W. W. Norton, 1986); 'The man and the myths', *The Economist* (London), 29 March 1986, p. 77; Iain Eliott, 'The great reformer', *Survey* (London), Spring 1985, pp. 1 – 11; and Michel Heller, 'Gorbachev for beginners', ibid., pp. 12 – 18.

11. See Mikhail Voslensky, *Nomenklatura*, p. 264. For the way the CPSU apparatus works, see Seweryn Bialer's excellent books: *Stalin's successors* (New York: Cambridge University Press, 1980) and *The Soviet*

Paradox (New York: Knopf, 1986). The political mechanisms of the Brezhnev regime were convincingly analyzed by Harry Gelman in *The Brezhnev Politburo and the decline of détente* (Ithaca and London: Cornell University Press, 1984).

12. See Seweryn Bialer and Joan Afferica, 'The genesis of Gorbachev's world', *Foreign Affairs. America and the World 1985*, p. 620.

13. See *Pravda*, 7 November 1985, pp. 1–2; Amy Knight, 'The KGB under Gorbachev', Radio Liberty Research, RL 83/86, pp. 1–3.

14. See 'Secret policeman's ball', *The Economist*, 7 June 1986; Peter Kruzhin, 'Military representation in the leading organs of the CPSU following the 27th Congress', Radio Liberty Research, RL 139/86, 27 March 1986, pp. 1–9 (with an appendix listing the military officers elected to the party's ruling bodies).

15. See *Pravda*, 27 February 1986; Elizabeth Teague, 'Yeltsin's speech to the 27th Party Congress', Radio Liberty Research, 28 February 1986, RL 104/86, pp. 1–3.

16. Ibid.

17. See 'Concrete deeds are the measure of restructuring', *The Current Digest of the Soviet Press*, vol. XXXVIII, no. 5, p. 10.

18. See 'Kirgiz Party Congress hits Usubaliyev', ibid., p. 10.

19. Shevardnadze established excellent KGB connections in the past when he held responsible positions in that organisation in Georgia.

20. See 'Nachalo bolshoi raboty', *Pravda*, 24 April 1986, p. 1.

21. Ibid.

22. 'Party officials' "special privileges" decried', *The Current Digest of the Soviet Press*, vol. XXXVIII, no. 6, p. 1.

23. Ibid., p. 2.

24. See Rudolf L. Tökes (ed.), *Dissent in the USSR* (Baltimore and London: John Hopkins University Press, 1975); and Roy Medvedev, *On Soviet dissent. Interviews with Piero Ostellino* (New York: Columbia University Press, 1980).

25. See T. Samolis, 'Ochishchenie. Otkrovenyi razgovor', *Pravda*, 13 February 1986, p. 3. It is symptomatic that reference was made to the 18th Congress, which was the first to follow Stalin's great purge (1936–9), and not to the 20th or to the 22nd Congresses where Stalinist terrorist methods against party members were officially condemned. On the other hand, mention should be made of the veiled criticism of this *Pravda* collection of readers' views expressed by Yegor Ligachev, Gorbachev's main ideological watchdog and the second-in-command within the CPSU hierarchy in his speech at the 27th Congress. Ligachev warned against exaggerations in the ongoing campaign against bureaucratism and singled out *Pravda* for having sometimes overstepped the mark. See Archie Brown, 'Change in the USSR', *Foreign Affairs*, Summer 1986, p. 1054. For a penetrating analysis of Ligachev's role as an *éminence grise* in the present Soviet leadership team, see Michel Tatu, 'Les changements dans l'appareil', *Politique Etrangère* (Paris), no. 3/1985, pp. 603–9.

26. For the composition of the CPSU ruling bodies see *Pravda*, 7 March 1986; for Bukharinism and its appeal to Soviet neo-Marxist (or neo-Leninist) dissidents, see Roy A. Medvedev, *Nikolai Bukharin. The last years* (New York and London: W. W. Norton, 1980); Stephen Cohen,

Rethinking the Soviet experience, pp. 71–92; for a critical assessment of Cohen's views on Bukharin, see Richard Pipes, 'U.S. and them', *The New Republic*, 14 October 1985, pp. 32–4. More recently, in accordance with Gorbachev's calls for a 'recuperation of memory' Bukharin's name re-emerged in the Soviet media. It seems that he might be the first among Lenin's comrades killed by Stalin to be politically rehabilitated under Mikhail Gorbachev.

27. See Richard Pipes, *Survival is not enough* (New York: Simon and Schuster, 1984), pp. 199–208.

28. See Stephen F. Cohen, 'Sovieticus', *The Nation*, 18 January 1986, p. 40.

29. See Leonard Schapiro, *The Communist Party of the Soviet Union* (New York: Vintage Books, 1971), pp. 626–7.

30. See I. Biriukov, 'Vazhnyi politicheskii zavet', *Pravda*, 14 December 1985, p. 5.

31. See Bill Murphy and Vladimir Kusin, 'Is Gorbachev another Khrushchev?' Radio Free Europe Research, RAD Background Report/32, Eastern Europe, 4 March 1986, pp. 1–3; Seweryn Bialer, *The Soviet paradox*, pp. 191–212.

32. For Gorbachev's assessment as a maverick, relying primarily upon information provided by Zdenek Mlynař, the exiled former secretary in charge of ideology during the Prague Spring, see Jerry F. Hough, 'Gorbachev's strategy', *Foreign Affairs*, Fall 1985, pp. 32–55.

33. See Ann Sheehy, 'Gorbachev's new propaganda chief — a critic of Russian nationalists', Radio Liberty Research, RL 357/85, 31 October 1985, pp. 1–5; Julia Wishnevsky, 'Aleksandr Yakovlev and the cultural "thaw" ', Radio Liberty Research, RL 51/87, 5 February 1987, pp. 1–4.

34. See Zbigniew Brzezinski, *The Soviet bloc*, pp. 155–84; Abraham Brumberg (ed.), *Russia under Khrushchev. An anthology from Problems of Communism* (New York: Praeger, 1962); and Robert Conquest, *Russia after Khrushchev* (New York: Praeger, 1965).

35. See Peter Reddaway, 'Waiting for Gorbachev', *New York Review of Books*, 10 October 1985, p. 10.

36. See Mikhail Gorbachev, 'On reorganization and the party's personnel policy', FBIS, Soviet Union, 28 January 1987, p. R7.

37. See, especially the full text of Yevgeniy Yevtushenko's speech at the RSFSR Writers' Congress, *New York Times*, 18 December 1985; for the significance of the speech, see Julia Wishnevsky, 'Yevtushenko's speech at the RSFSR Writers' Congress', Radio Liberty Research, RL 10/86, 23 December 1985. A scathing critique of Yevtushenko's indulgence in half-truths came from Vassiliy Aksionov, 'A hard speech to stomach', *Harper's*, May 1986, pp. 58–61. An indication of the impending changes in the cultural field was the removal of Pyotr N. Demichev, minister of culture since 1974 and a symbol of the conservative approach to intellectual matters (June 1986).

38. Zubatov was a police officer in the early years of the century. With approval from his superiors he set up trade unions which tried to orient the workers' social claims toward mere economic objectives. This was an example of 'police socialism' which made the distinction between genuine

and 'police appointed' opponents of the system cloudy. For the concept of 'literary Zubatovism', see Max Haywards's illuminating essay 'Dissonant voices in Soviet literature' in his *Writers in Russia*, pp. 85–117.

39. See Serge Schmemann, 'Bold play (à la Gorbachev) makes audience gasp', *New York Times*, 8 January 1986. The ambiguity of the present political situation is noticed by Schmemann who mentions Yegor Ligachev's speech at a meeting of the party cell of the State Committee for Television and Radio Broadcasting. According to Ligachev, 'all television and radio programs should serve one aim — propaganda, the clarification and implementation of party policy'. Even such a hardened apparatchik as the committee's chairman, Sergei Lapin, found this statement unpalatable and expressed reservations regarding Ligachev's rigid views. As a blatant refutation of the alleged tolerant, dialogue-prone mood of the current Soviet leadership, Lapin was retired on 15 December 1985. However, the chances of the liberal forces in the cultural realm were again enhanced through the election of Elem Klimov, one of the most controversial movie directors, as first secretary of the Board of the USSR Cinema Workers Union. See *Pravda*, 17 May 1986; and Julia Wishnewsky, 'Former outcast elected head of Cinema Workers' Union', Radio Liberty Research, RL 200/86, 21 May 1986, pp. 1–5.

40. For a detailed examination of these relations, see Joan Barth Urban, *Moscow and the Italian Communist Party* (Ithaca and London: Cornell University Press, 1986). Gorbachev managed to establish warmer personal relations with Alessandro Natta, the PCI General Secretary, and Lev Zaykov led the CPSU delegation to the latest congress of Italian communists.

41. See Kevin Devlin, ' "The USSR under Gorbachev", *Rinascita* Round Table Takes Stock', Radio Free Europe Research, RAD Background Report/87 (World Communist Movement), 27 August 1985, p. 5.

42. For an extensive and well-documented analysis of the main directions within Soviet philosophical thought, see James P. Scanlan, *Marxism in the USSR* (Ithaca and London: Cornell University Press, 1985).

43. See Kevin Devlin, ' New Soviet program — old ideology", Mlynař Tells *Rinascita*', Radio Free Europe Research, RAD Background Report (World Communist Movement) 120, 5 February 1985, p. 2.

44. See 'The Action Program of the Communist Party of Czechoslovakia, adopted at the plenary session of the C.C. of the Communist Party of Czechoslovakia on April 5, 1968' in *Czechoslovakia's blueprint for 'freedom'* (Washington, D.C.: Acropolis Books, 1968), pp. 89–178 (introduction and analysis by Paul Ello).

45. See Kevin Devlin, 'Some views of the Gorbachev era', Radio Free Europe Research, RAD Background Report/57, 28 June 1985, p. 5.

46. See 'Bilak compares current restructuring to 1968', FBIS, Eastern Europe, 25 February 1987, pp. D3–4.

47. See Mikhail Gorbachev's speech to the Warsaw Congress on 30 June 1986, FBIS, *Soviet Union*, 1 July 1986, p. F3. According to Gorbachev, the Solidarity movement was manipulated by sworn enemies of socialism who managed to exploit the difficulties created by the 'subjectivist deviations' committed under the Gierek leadership: 'The Polish crisis . . . was not a protest by the workers against socialism. It was

above all disagreement with those distortions of socialism in practice that pained the working class. The enemies of socialist Poland within the country and outside its boundaries were able to make use of such disagreement for their own ends' (ibid.).

48. See Cornelius Castoriadis, *Domaines de l'homme* (Paris: Seuil, 1986), p. 212.

49. See Mikhail Gorbachev's Report to the June 1986 Plenum of the CPSU Central Committee, FBIS, *Soviet Union*, 18 June 1986, p. R5.

50. See *Pravda*, 22 June 1986, p. 1.

51. See *Literaturnaya Gazeta*, no. 27, 2 July 1986, p. 6 (emphasis added). For the English translation, see FBIS, *Soviet Union*, 31 July 1986, pp. R3–5.

52. See *Literaturnaya Gazeta*, p. 4.

53. Ibid., p. 9. One of the most successful Soviet authors, well connected with party and KGB officials, Semyonov has developed a literary genre which plays both on Russian nationalism and Westernising sympathies among certain sectors of the intelligentsia. In Walter Laqueur's apt description: 'In contrast to the sectarian, hard-line Leninist – Stalinist tradition, Semyonov seems to propagate some modified form of Kadarism: whoever is not against us is for us — at least a potential ally.' (See Walter Laqueur, 'Yulian Semyonov and the Soviet political novel', *Transaction/Society*, no. 5, July – August 1986, p. 79.)

54. *Pravda*, 12 November 1987.

55. *Pravda*. 13 November 1987.

56. 'Darkish at noon', editorial in *The Economist*, 21 November 1987, p. 14.

Epilogue

Only the future is interesting, the fullness of what is possible, not the straitjacket of what has already been, with its attempt to impose on us the illusion that, because things were thus and not otherwise, they belong to the realm of necessity.

Ernst Fischer

Philosophically, critical Marxism tried to transcend the ossified structure of *Diamat*. Lenin's theory of reflection was exposed as a vulgar reductionism, an attempt to get rid of the active side of consciousness. Lukács's early Marxism was rediscovered as an antidote to this primitive materialism. The infinite articulations of objectivity and subjectivity, the concept of *Vermittlung* (mediatisation) were invoked against the infantile shibboleths of Stalinist determinism. Later, it became clear that it was not possible to revive Lukács's messianic Marxism without risking reiterating his fateful pact with the party. Critical Marxists in Poland, Hungary, Czechoslovakia, and the GDR could not partake in his unreconstructed views about the indisputable superiority of any socialism over the liberal-democratic societies. Personalism, phenomenology, and existentialism were rehabilitated and many critical Marxists sought to establish a dialogue with currents once viciously besmirched.

Critical Marxism wanted to regenerate the moral dimension of political praxis. Revisionism pondered the relation between means and ends and arrived at the conclusion that no goal could justify the manipulation and degradation of the individual. Ethical relativism was exposed as a most harmful deception and moral values were again postulated as transcendent values, independent of contingent circumstances and selfish interests. Later, some critical Marxists went even further and called for a general demystification of the realm of politics. Kolakowski, for example, has raised his voice against the idolatry of politics associated with radical-utopian ideologies:

> . . . we try to survive in a world torn asunder by a conflict that cannot be seen simply as a competition between big powers vying with each other to enlarge their respective areas

216

of influence. It is a clash of civilisations, a clash that for the first time in history has assumed worldwide dimensions. However distasteful our civilisation might be in some of its vulgar aspects, however enfeebled by hedonistic indifference, greed, and the decline of civic virtues, however torn by struggles and teeming with social ills, the most powerful reason for its unconditional defense (and I am ready to emphasize this adjective) is provided by its alternative. It faces the totalitarian civilisation of Sovietism, and what is at stake is not only the destiny of one particular cultural form, but of humanity as we have known it . . .[1]

Human dignity has to be regarded as an ultimate value and all endeavours to deny or diminish it should be adamantly opposed. The Petöfi Circle in Hungary and the Polish revisionist current were the initial stage in the coalescence of a true counterculture of resistance. There was, unfortunately, no international co-ordination between these nuclei of critical thought and conduct. They were, however, opposed by a concerted ideological counter-offensive, engineered in Moscow and willingly supported by the communist parties all over the world. Heretics were ruthlessly purged, professors were deprived of their university chairs, journals were closed down, and the orthodoxy enjoyed its temporary triumph over neo-Marxist idealism. In Poland, Hungary, Czechoslovakia, and East Germany, the party doctrine survived only as a phantomatic echo of its past. In the Soviet Union the literary dissidents and the human rights movement merged after the Siniavskiy-Daniel affair in 1965-6. In Romania the official ideology was imbued with neo-feudal, xenophobic motifs, and Nicolae Ceausescu was proclaimed the greatest contemporary Marxist.

The revisionist onslaught on orthodoxy had subverted the very foundations of Marxist–Leninist mythical self-confidence. Later, criticism was developed beyond the confines of the Marxist discourse. The human being and his/her rights will become the centre of the oppositional stances, the counter-value opposed to the solemn and fatuous rituals of dogmatism.

There is no doubt that contemporary bureaucrats have lost any kind of sentimental relationship to the doctrine they pretend to venerate. The umbilical cord between the values of the fanatical generation and those cherished by present-day *nomenklaturas* has been irrevocably broken. Principles and ideas are nothing but a camouflage bound to cover an unquenchable greed for power for its own sake:

> Instead of people who, even if they had taken part in the atrocities of Stalinism, were in their way loyal Communists and attached to Communist ideals, the reins of power were now held by cynical disillusioned careerists who were perfectly aware of the emptiness of the Communist slogans they made use of. A bureaucracy of this kind was immune to ideological shocks.[2]

The bureaucratic mind is so inimical to sincerity that the official ideology is insufferably afflicted by a pseudo-gravity that makes any form of irony potentially disruptive. The role of the joke in communist systems is thus immensely enhanced by this artificial seriousness of the ruling ideology: 'Like a dotted line, the joke perforates our reality and galvanizes it. It not only recreates reality but actually restores it to us, and under its impact, reality begins at least to resemble something intelligible and real'.[3] Critical thinkers had thus to adopt the status of the jester, disparaging the specious consensus and reminding the bureaucrats of the possibility of an alternative to the current ethical quagmire. 'Living in truth' became the moral precept for all those who did not want to have their minds and souls sullied with the omnipresent lie:

> We are often accused in the West of being naively humanistic and utopian moralists, and in a sense this is true. But it must be understood that behind the utopian appearance of our movement lies, above all else, a need for information and truth. We need to live without falsehood — or, as the Socialist-Revolutionaries used to say at the beginning of the century: 'We are thirsty for justice.' In their quest for a truthful and just society, the dissidents are putting morality back into politics; they are the ones demanding freedom of speech and information, and fighting for human rights; it is they who ask that the economy become scientifically transparent and that society be organized in a transparent manner.[4]

It was vital for these writers to insert their discourse in the contemporary philosophical dialogue. Sectarianism could not be surpassed without an attempt to define Marxism as only one, and not necessarily the best, of the possible answers to contemporary dilemmas. Furthermore, this answer was plagued by logical inconsistencies and associated with abominable practices. The Marxian paradigm was thus perceived as a limit whose suppression would eventually release critical thought and allow it to address paramount human issues. Marxism could not pass the test of historical verification and has lost its once galvanising power.

Human rights were reappraised and a philosophy of natural law was adumbrated in the writings of post-critical Marxists. Opposition from within the system has to be superseded by a different orientation. Nowadays, in Eastern Europe, anything smacking of Marxism can only make the opposition suspect and ineffective. It matters therefore to reconstruct the idea of resistance, to elaborate the ethos and the strategy of a genuine counterculture. The more conservative and exclusive the official ideology, the more consistent has become the programme of the opposition in countries like Poland, Hungary, or Czechoslovakia. Since sham nationalism has increasingly permeated the idiom of power, the opposition had to reshape the grammar of a European consciousness. Ironically, the only internationalism now existing in the Soviet bloc is the moral prerogative of those who have repudiated the dogma of 'proletarian internationalism'. Theirs is a consciousness of the limits of all universalist dogmas and an increasing interest in the moral dimension of international relations. To many advocates of *Realpolitik*, both East and West, the discourse of the dissidents may sound disturbing and even discomforting.

Certainly, Marxism is dead as a convincing theoretical option in Eastern Europe. At the same time, the ruling caste cannot dispense with it without losing its last source of 'legitimacy'. The appearance of a consensus must be safeguarded, and the party's sole and unique requirement is not to touch its ideological monopoly. Its political mandate is actually derived from this ideology, countenanced by it, and the party cannot afford to acquiesce in its gradual attrition. It is precisely to shun the final eclipse of ideology that a whole superstructural system is kept in motion, from party academies to all the forms of Marxist adult education:

It follows that the ideology no longer needs to be believed, not even in the form of the false evidence and gnostic pseudo-empiricism under which it had earlier gripped revolutionary consciousness. It was fact: it was power. It did not thus need to be carried out. Since the ideology had foreseen democratic elections and the unanimity of the electors in favour of social-ism, all that was needed was to organise these elections care-fully, so as to consolidate the ideology not in its mode of belief but in its mode of power. It is the same with the huge army of propagandists and the printers where all books are printed, in editions of hundreds of millions: their aim is not to convince, but to make manifest the fact of the power of the ideology.[5]

Propaganda is the backbone of the ideology and a whole army is mobilised to inject the theses of the 'party documents' into the minds of the subjects of this operation. Repeated *ad nauseam*, these trite generalities are supposed to convince the rank-and-file about the 'correctness' of the party line.

The magnitude of the propaganda empire in the USSR and in other Soviet-type regimes is strikingly revealed by the following description of Mikhail Suslov's responsibilities, which are now the domain of Yegor Ligachev, Mikhail Gorbachev's second-in-command:

> As the Politburo member responsible for ideological issues, Suslov stood at the apex of a pyramid of institutions. In the Central Committee he supervised the sections dealing with culture, agitation, and propaganda, science, schools and institutions of higher education, two international sections, the political administration of the Soviet Army, the Central Committee's information department and its training com-mission, and the department dealing with the Komsomol (the Young Communist League) and social organizations. He also had overall control of, and supervised, the Ministry of Culture, the State Publishing Committee, the Cinemato-graphy Committee, television and radio, the entire press and censorship apparatus, the official news agency TASS, the Communist Party of the Soviet Union's links with other Communist Parties, and Soviet foreign policy.

Furthermore, he controlled the so-called creative unions, the theatres and music-halls, the system of party education, all social science institutes and state relations with religious bodies and church organisations: 'And even that is not a complete inventory of his responsibilities.'[6] The main function of the enormous apparatus is to carry out the ideological programme of the party, i.e. to perpetrate a relentless aggression against the human mind:

> Among the various infringements on the rights of thinking
> human beings that totalitarian dictatorships commit, the
> insult to the intellect is perhaps the gravest — if you agree,
> that is, that human essence is not in man's ability to work,
> drink, and make merry but in that unique activity of his brain
> which is detached from immediate concerns. The chimpan-
> zee, after some deliberation, can put two hollow sticks
> together and reach a banana that lies too far outside his cage.
> Man can immerse himself in a mental activity that provides
> him with no bananas but with the equation $E = mc^2$. The
> dogmatisation, tabooisation and ritualisation of the results of
> such mental activities, these three processes that inevitably set
> in under totalitarian rule, become the absolute insult to the
> capacity that distinguishes man from chimpanzee. They
> become the Big Insult.[7]

This remorseless rape of the mind is committed in cold blood,
like a well-planned robbery, and the people are expected, or better
said required, to slavishly obey party decisions:

> To my mind, this is the deepest insult to human intelligence.
> It negates what is best about the history of European thought
> and politics, as epitomised by Voltaire's 'Sir, I totally dis-
> agree with you, but to my last breath I shall defend your right
> to express your opinion!' It is a slap in the face of every
> intellectual.

As for those Western intellectuals who still endorse in one way or
another the totalitarian idea, Škvorecký rightly believes that they
are guilty of what Julien Benda once called 'the betrayal of the
intellectuals': 'As such, they are guilty of the gravest crime an
intellectual can commit.'[8] The irrational mechanism underlying
the recurrence of these radical socialist illusions was dissected by
Igor Shafarevich:

> All this shows that the force which manifests itself in socialism
> does not act through reason, but resembles an *instinct*. This
> accounts for the inability of socialist ideology to react to the
> results of experience . . . A spider, spinning its web, will
> complete all the six thousand four hundred movements

necessary if its glands have dried up in the heat and will produce no silk. How much more dramatic is the example of the socialists, with the same automatism constructing for the nth time their recipe for a society of equality and justice: it would seem that for them the numerous and varied precedents which have always led to one and the same result do not exist. The experience of many thousands of years is rejected and replaced by clichés from the realm of the irrational, such as the claim that all the different socialisms of today and yesterday or created in a different part of the globe were not the real thing, and that in the special conditions of 'our' socialism everything will be different . . .[9]

In Soviet-type regimes ideology has a fundamental apologetic role: all the aberrations created by the various turns in the party line have to be presented as a necessary result of insightful interpretation of the 'objective laws'. Catastrophes turn into earth-shattering triumphs as a result of the ideological miracle. Defeats become victories overnight, and a bankrupt economy is converted in a veritable cornucopia:

And so, as real socialism in theory denies its own, immanent interpretation of its own reality, and since in practice it deepens the contradictions between this reality and the permanent Communist programme, it makes up for it all in the sphere of ideology. In its entire spirit and thrust, real socialism is an ideology *als ob*, an ideology of *as if*: those who preach it behave *as if* the ideological kingdom of real socialism existed in 'what we have here now' *as if* they had, in all earnestness, convinced the nation of its existence; the nation behaves *as if* it believed it, *as if* it were convinced that it lived in accordance with this ideologically real socialism. This *as if* is a silent agreement between the two partners. Since one partner is powerful and the other powerless, both sides break the agreement whenever possible.[10]

This contract involves all the layers of the ideological apparatus and many medium-rank apparatchiks may even confess in private conversations their own doubts and discontent. They have to behave as if worshipping the Supreme Leader, as if being happy with the mockery of patriotism professed by the regime, as if not tormented by all too human passions and anguishes.

222

Epilogue

The fate of critical Marxism and of other dissenting orientations suggests that heresies are short-lived unless they turn into real social movements. No one can deny the fact that ideological opposition is of tremendous significance in those regimes. According to a group of prominent Soviet exiled intellectuals (Vassiliy Aksyonov, Vladimir Bukovsky, Eduard Kuznetsov, Yuri Lyubimov, Vladimir Maximov, Ernst Neizvestnyi, and Aleksandr Zinoviev), Gorbachev's *glasnost* campaign cannot be trusted inasmuch as it has not affected the ideological heart of the system: 'Ideology is that hard core of the Soviet system that does not allow the country to deviate too far for too long; unless the central ideological tenets were to be challenged, long-term Soviet strategy would remain imprisoned by its own assumptions.'[11] Systems established in accordance with Leninist norms are intrinsically hostile to any effort to reassess their ideological foundations. Allowing such myth-breaking research would eventually result in the denial of their claims to legitimacy and subsequently undermine their stability. Preservation and perpetuation of privileges in socialism require a conservative-bureaucratic ideology and those philosophers deluded by the promises of a 'critical and revolutionary dialectic' are victims of a tragic misperception of the world they would wish to change.

Marxism in Soviet-type societies has become outrageously anachronistic, a legacy of other times, with no word to say about contemporary issues. Its obsessions cannot be taken for scientific propositions. Instead of being the solution to social enigmas — as Karl Marx emphatically proclaimed — communism is nowadays itself an ultimate, most disconcerting, conundrum.

To reattain a respectable status, Marxism has to come to terms with its own past, to dispel convenient legends and conceive of itself as only one of the chapters, the most tragic rather than the most glorious, in the history of modern rationalism. It has to go beyond the utopian-prophetic dimension that has such a perversely addictive power:

> The prophetic element in Marx's creed was dominant in the minds of his followers. It swept everything else aside, banishing the power of cool and critical judgement and destroying the belief that by the use of reason we may change the world. All that remained of Marx's teaching was the oracular philosophy of Hegel, which in its Marxist trappings threatens to paralyse the struggle for the open society.[12]

As for the Marxist ethical rebellion, it has to be rescued and maintained as a form of permanent concern for justice, a protest against all iniquities, including those committed precisely in the name of the Marxist utopian ideals:

> It is this moral radicalism of Marx which explains his influence; and that is a hopeful fact in itself. This moral radicalism is still alive. It is our task to keep it alive, to prevent it from going the way which his political radicalism will have to go. 'Scientific Marxism' is dead. Its feeling of social responsibility and its love for freedom must survive.[13]

East European critical Marxism, in its most outspoken phase, has debunked the sclerotic logic and apocryphal legitimation of the existing regimes. Its moral-political message, which seems now almost extinct, functioned until the early 1970s as a ferment of radical opposition to the ruling bureaucracies, contributing to the breakdown of the official mythology and the development of the dissident counterculture. This process was accompanied, primarily in Poland, Hungary, and Yugoslavia, by a progressive disenchantment with the merely humanist (ethical) critique of the communist regimes. This awareness pointed to the necessity to turn dissidence into opposition and, as a logical inference, to abandon Marxism as an inaccurate and even misleading historical perspective. The only remaining possibility of defying the system and exposing its imposture is to rediscover the elementary virtue of truth and to act accordingly:

> Violence does not always necessarily take you physically by the throat and strangle you! More often it merely demands of its subjects that they declare allegiance to the lie, become accomplices to the lie. And the simple step of a simple, courageous man is not to take part in the lie, not to support deceit. Let the lie come into the world, even dominate the world, but not through me.[14]

Notes

1. See Leslek Kolakowski, 'The idolatry of politics', *The New Republic*, 16 June 1986, p. 31.
2. Kolakowski, *Main currents*, p. 465.

3. See Andrei Siniavskiy, 'The joke inside the joke', *Partisan Review*, no. 3, 1986, p. 360.

4. See Leonid Plyusch, 'Forwards together or down together' in Il Manifesto (ed.), *Power and opposition*, p. 44.

5. See Alain Besançon, *The rise of the gulag*, p. 287.

6. See Roy Medvedev, *All Stalin's men*, pp. 62–3.

7. See Josef Škvorecký, 'The big insult', *Crosscurrents*, p. 125.

8. Ibid., p. 135.

9. See Igor Shafarevich, 'Socialism in our past and future' in Alexander Solzhenitsyn (ed.), *From under the rubble* (London: Collins & Harvill Press, 1975), p. 66.

10. See Miroslav Kusý, 'Chartism and "real socialism"' in Vaclac Havel (ed.), *The power of the powerless*, p. 164.

11. 'Is "Glasnost" a game of mirrors?', (an article prepared by a group of prominent Soviet exiled intellectuals), *New York Times*, 22 March 1987.

12. See Karl R. Popper, *The open society and its enemies*, vol. II — 'The high tide of prophecy: Hegel, Marx, and the aftermath' — (Princeton: Princeton University Press, 1971), p. 198.

13. Ibid., p. 211.

14. See Alexander Solzhenitsyn, *One word of truth* (London: Bodley Head, 1972), quoted by Alain Besançon, *The rise of the gulag*, p. 288.

Index

Aczél, György 54
Aczél, Tamás 149
Adorno, Theodor W. 33, 69, 89
Afanasiev, Viktor 71
Afghanistan 180
Akhmatova, Anna 31 – 2, 43 – 4,
    94, 205, 207
Akselrod, Pavel 26, 82
Aksyonov, Vassiliy 223
Albania 138
Alexandrov, Georgiy 48
alienation 15, 24
Althusser, Louis 10, 69, 86
Andropov, Yuriy 71, 188 – 9
apparatchiks 132, 189 – 90
Aragon, Louis 21, 57
Arendt, Hannah 1, 3, 5, 33, 86,
    88 – 9, 148, 164
Aron, Raymond 3, 69, 85
Ash, Timothy Garton 164, 175

Bahro, Rudolf 154
Baibakov, Nikolay 194
Baklanov, Grigoriy 205
Bakunin, Mikhail 3, 28
Baranczak, Stanislaw 87
Beloff, Nora 103
Bence, György 146
Benda, Julien 221
Benjamin, Walter 3, 7, 33
Beria, Lavrentiy 62 – 3
Berlin uprising 147
Berman, Jakub 111
Besançon, Alain 69
Bialer, Seweryn 51
Bibó, István 149
Bilak, Vasil 202
Bloch, Ernst 13, 33, 53, 84, 85,
    87, 151
Böll, Heinrich 160
Bondarev, Yuriy 206
Borkenau, Franz 35
Bourdieu, Pierre 138
Brecht, Bertolt 57

Brezhnev, Leonid 61 – 2, 71, 93,
    167 – 8, 185, 190, 199, 203
Brzezinski, Zbigniew 14
Bucharest School 53
Budapest School 10, 15, 72,
    124, 128, 136 – 7, 140 – 1,
    143 – 4, 154 – 5
Bukharin, Nikolay 11, 25, 37,
    62, 64, 81, 124, 194, 208
Bukovsky, Vladimir 177, 223
Bulganin, Nikolay 77
bureaucracy/bureaucrats 28, 43,
    54, 77, 143 – 4, 170,
    173 – 4, 203 – 6, 217 – 18
    French 36
    ideology 223
    Soviet 94
    Yugoslav 103 – 4
Burnham, James 35

Camus, Albert 21, 73, 143
Canetti, Elias 175
Carrère d'Encausse, Hélène 93,
    168
Cassirer, Ernst 176
Castoriadis, Cornelius 3, 35, 63,
    69, 126, 204
Catholic Church 97
Ceausescu, Nicolae 97, 114, 217
Chakovskiy, Aleksandr 194
Chambers, Whittaker 36
Charter 77, 140
Chebrikov, Viktor 189, 198
Chernyshevskiy, Nikolay 82
Chervonenko, Stepan 194
Chisinevschi, Iosif 110
Cold War 43
Comintern 22 – 3, 26 – 7, 31,
    44, 150
Committee for Workers' Self
    Defence (KOR) 140
Conquest, Robert 24
Copenhagen World Peace
    Congress 169

Croce, Benedetto 3
Cuba 139
Czechoslovakia 43, 55, 85, 92,
    108, 128, 132–3, 147, 195,
    197, 202, 217, 219
  Prague Spring 132–3, 147,
    195, 197
  revisionism 85

Debray, Régis 164–5
Demichev, Pyotr 189
Deutscher, Isaac 8, 27, 79, 116,
    141
Dimitrov, Georgi 150
dissidents 127, 153, 156, 161–2,
    164–8, 172, 174–5,
    177–8, 180
Djilas, Aleksa 104
Djilas, Milovan 5, 80, 91, 99,
    100
Donáth, Ferenc 149
Doriot, Jacques 28
Dostoyevskiy, Fyodor 82

East Europe 42–3, 47, 51,
    54–7, 74, 79, 98, 201
  communist parties 43
  human rights 127, 217, 219
  intellectuals 74
  sociology 128
East Germany 53, 108, 217
Eastman, Max 35
Ehrenburg, Ilya 57, 94
Eluard, Paul 21
Engels, Friedrich 16, 34, 53, 66
Eörsi, István 83
Eurocommunism 118

Farkas, Mihály 111, 122
Fedosseyev, Pyotr 32, 194
Fehér, Ferenc 5, 50, 57, 123,
    137, 145, 148–50, 152,
    160, 162–4, 177
Fejtö, François 119
Feuchtwanger, Lion 150
Fischer, Ernst 64, 150–1, 216
Fischer, Ruth 80
Frankfurt School 69
Fuchs, Jürgen 162

Garaudy, Roger 64
Gëro, Ernö 111, 122
Gheorghiu-Dej, Gheorghe 47,
    114
Gide, André 35
Gimes, Miklós 149
glasnost 70–1, 127, 187, 203,
    223
Glucksmann, André 17
Goebbels, Joseph 46, 49
Goldmann, Lucien 98
Goma, Paul 5
Gomulka, Wladyslaw 77, 91, 98
Gorbachev, Mikhail 6, 70–1,
    127, 168–9, 183–210
Gottwald, Klement 47
Gouldner, Alvin 14, 86
Gramsci, Anotonio 3, 14, 35,
    68, 87, 150, 156
Granin, Daniil 205
Grass, Günter 160, 165
Grishin, Viktor 189
Gromyko, Andrey 194
Grossman, Vassiliy 31
Gusti, Dimitrie 53

Hager, Kurt 54
Haraszti, Miklós 5, 6, 172
Harich, Wolfgang 84
Havel, Václav 5, 139, 165–6,
    168–9, 171–3, 175–7,
    180, 183
Hay, Gyula 160, 165
Hegel/Hegelianism 5, 93,
    115–16, 119, 137
  Marxism 13–14
Heidegger, Martin 1
Heller, Agnes 5, 123, 137,
    148–50, 152, 160, 162–4,
    177
Heller, Mikhail 68
Hendrich, Jiří 54
Herbert, Zbigniew 176
Himmler, Heinrich 13, 67
Hitler, Adolf 27, 35
Honecker, Erich 195
Hook, Sidney 3, 35, 73
Horkheimer, Max 14, 33, 69,
    74, 89
Hoxha, Enver 66, 80

Hungary 53, 83, 85, 88, 92,
   114, 119, 122–3, 128, 134,
   147–8, 203, 217, 219, 224
   1956 revolution 88, 119, 123,
      128, 134, 147–8
   ideology 114, 122
   revisionism 85
   Stalinism 122
   de-Stalinisation in 203, 217,
      219, 224

Ideology 11, 14, 17, 18, 21,
   31–2, 34, 57, 67–9, 71,
   114–15, 132, 138, 219–20,
   222–3
   Leninism 67
   Soviet 18, 31–2, 57, 69, 71
   Stalinist 21
Intellectuals 9, 11–12, 27, 34,
   45, 56–7, 64, 74, 83–5,
   87, 93–4, 96–8, 101–2,
   116, 118–19, 127–8, 130,
   133, 140, 160, 167–8, 177
   communist 12, 118
   critical 130, 167–8
   Czechoslovak 133
   East Europe 74
   Hungarian 119
   leftist 57
   Leninist 11
   marginal 127–8
   Marxist 9
   Polish 87, 96
   revisionist 93, 130
   Romanian 96–7
   Soviet 11, 45
   West German 160, 177
   Yugoslav 101–2
internationalism 18, 23
Istrati, Panait 35
Italy
   communist party 201

Jaspers, Karl 3

Kádár, János/Kadarism 123,
   136, 140, 149, 153, 195
Kafka, Franz 55, 61, 175
Kaganovich, Lazar 62, 77, 124

Kamenev, Lev 25–6, 62
Kanapa, Jean 54
Kant, Immanuel 15
Kardelj, Edvard 99, 101
Kelly, Petra 161
Khrushchev, Nikita/
   Khrushchevism 20, 54,
   61–4, 77–8, 80, 83, 95,
   117–18, 122, 124–5, 153,
   167, 186, 194, 197
   secret speech 54, 78, 122
Kirov, Sergey 37
Kiš, Danilo 5
Kis, János 143, 146
Koestler, Arthur 9, 21–2, 27,
   35–6, 64, 73, 176
Kohout, Pavel 176
Kolakowski, Leszek 12, 18, 34,
   37, 49, 70, 72–3, 81, 87–9
   92, 95, 97, 115, 123, 126–7,
   129, 134–6, 140, 146, 216
Komocsin, Zoltán 54
Konrád, George 127–8, 142–3,
   145, 153–6, 175–6
Konstantinov, Fyodor 32
Kopácsi, Sándor 152
Kopecky, Václav 55
Kopelev, Lev 5, 37, 42
Korsch, Karl 3, 16, 33, 87, 136
Kosik, Karel 72, 146
Kostov, Traicho 91
Kott, Jan 48
Krasso, György 152
Kraus, Karl 175
Kravchenko, Viktor 36
Kristol, Irving 155
Kulakov, Fyodor 188
Kun, Béla 111
Kunayev, Dinmukhamed 185
Kundera, Milan 5, 144, 176,
   179
Kunze, Reiner 160
Kuron, Jacek 5, 146
Kuznetsov, Eduard 223
Kuznetsov, Vassiliy 194

Lasky, Melvin 73
Lassalle, Ferdinand 3
Lefebvre, Henri 3, 72
Lefort, Claude 3, 35, 69, 126

Index

Lenin, V. I./Leninism 1–4, 6, 9, 11, 16, 18, 22, 25–6, 28–30, 34, 37, 42, 49, 50, 56, 62–9, 70, 79–83, 85–6, 99, 123, 192, 216
  ideology 67
  Marxist 6, 42, 49, 56, 65–6, 70, 103
  partiinost 18
  Stalinist 11
Lenz, Siegfried 160
Leonhard, Wolfgang 66
Lepeshinskaya, Olga 50
Levi, Paul 80
Lévy, Bernard-Henri 46
Lichtheim, George 3
Liehm, Antonin 114, 133
Ligachev, Yegor 197–8, 206, 208–9, 220
Losonczy, Géza 149
Lowenthal, Richard 121
Lukács, Georg 1, 3, 13, 18, 21, 28, 42, 45, 53, 67–8, 84–7, 111, 122–3, 149–50, 216
  History and class consciousness 18, 67, 150
Luxemburg, Rosa 25, 87
Lyssenko, Trofim 52
Lyubimov, Yuriy 223

MacDonald, Dwight 35
Makarenko, Anton 53
Maksimović, Ivan 104
Malenkov, Georgiy 62–3, 77, 124, 197
Maléter, Pál 149
Malraux, André 19
Mandelstam, Nadezhda 31
Mann, Thomas 3, 67
Mannheim, Karl 36
Mao Zedong 80, 118
Marković, Mihailo 15, 72
Márkus, György 145–6
Martov, Yuliy 26, 82
Marty, André 28
Marx, Karl/Marxism 4, 9, 16, 20, 22–3, 26, 29, 33–4, 47, 63, 69–71, 81, 85, 93, 99, 101, 105, 145–6
  critical Marxism 145–6, 216
  ethical relativism 22
  intellectuals 9
  internationalism 23
  propaganda 34
  Soviet 66, 70
  Western 34, 70–1
  Yugoslav 99, 101, 105
Maximov, Vladimir 223
Medvedev, Roy 187
Mehring, Franz 87
Mensheviks 82
Merleau-Ponty, Maurice 3, 21, 73
Michnik, Adam 5, 95–7, 108, 125, 127–8, 131–2, 146, 156, 166, 176
Mikoyan, Anastas 62, 122
Milosević, Nikola 105
Milosz, Czeslaw 19, 56, 116, 176
Minogue, Kenneth 30
Misharin, Aleksandr 200
Mitin, Mark 32
Mlynář, Zdeněk 201–2
Modzelewski, Karol 146
Molotov, Vyacheslav 62, 77, 80, 124, 183
Morin, Edgar 69
Münzenberg, Willy 28
Muralov, Nikolay 150

Nagy, Imre 110–11, 123, 149–53
Nazism 1, 27, 34–5
Nechaiev, Sergey 28
Neizvestnyi, Ernst 223
Nekrich, Aleksandr 68
Neruda, Pablo 21, 57
Neumann, Heinz 28
Nietzsche, Friedrich 1, 3, 46
NKVD 111
nomenklatura 2, 15, 56, 61, 66, 124, 138, 171, 185–7, 190–4, 207, 217
North Korea 138–9

Okudzhava, Bulat 205
Ortega y Gasset 172
Orwell, George 11, 26, 80, 119

pacifists 160–5, 168–71, 174, 178, 180–1
  East German 170
  Hungarian 171
  Soviet Bloc 162, 169–70, 174
  Western 161–5, 168, 171, 178, 180–1
Pajetta, Giancarlo 54
Papaioannou, Kostas 2
Pasternak, Boris 94–8, 205
Patolichev, Nikolay 62
Patrascanu, Lucretiu 92, 98
Pauker, Anna 66
Paustovskiy, Konstantin 94
perestroyka 71
Pervukhin, Mikhail 62
Petöfi Circle 122, 217
Philips, William 35
Pijade, Moša 99
Pipes, Richard 82
Plekhanov, Georgiy 26, 82
pluralism 10–11
Podhoretz, Norman 155
Poland 8, 43, 53, 83, 92, 96, 98, 108, 115, 122, 132, 175, 217, 219, 224
  communist party 98
  de-Stalinisation 203
  ideology 114
  intellectuals 87, 96
  revisionism 85, 125, 128, 217
Ponomariov, Boris 32, 54, 194
Popper, Karl 7, 72, 176
Pospelov, Pyotr 32, 54
Pravda 50, 70–1, 92, 187, 192–3, 197
propaganda 220
Proudhon, Pierre, J. 3
Pyatakov, Yuriy 64, 124, 150–1

Radek, Karl 62, 124, 150
Rahv, Philip 21, 35
Rajk, Laszlo 98
Rákosi, Mátyás/Rakosism 47, 83, 111, 122, 150
Rashidov, Sharaf 191
Rautu, Leonte 54, 110, 111, 114
Révai, József 43, 45, 55, 111
Revel, Jean-François 165

revisionism/revisionists 12, 70, 79, 83–6, 92–3, 95, 102, 116, 121, 125–6, 128–30, 132, 135, 216
  Czech 85
  Hungarian 85
  Polish 85, 125, 217
  Yugoslav 85, 102
Rigby, T. H. 115
Romania 53–5, 96–8, 108–10, 114, 128, 138–9, 175, 217
  communist party 98, 109
  culture 55
  ideology 114
  intellectuals 96–7
  sociology 128
  Stalinism 98, 109
Rousseau, Jean-Jacques 25
Rozenthal, Mikhail 32
Rupnik, Jacques 178
Ryzhkov, Nikolay 189, 194, 198

Sartre, Jean-Paul 17, 21
Savinkov, Boris 28
Schapiro, Leonard 196
Schneider, Peter 160
Seifert, Jaroslav 154
Semyonov, Yulian 206
Serge, Victor 35
Shafarevich, Igor 221
Shcherbitskiy, Vladimir 191
Shepilov, Dmitriy 62
Shevardnadze, Eduard 191, 198
Silone, Ignazio 27–8, 35
Simonov, Konstantin 63, 94
Siniavskiy, Andrey 5
  Daniel Affair 217
Škvorecký, Josef 172, 221
Slánský, Rudolf 98, 110–11
Slonimski, Antoni 48
Socialism 97, 105, 218
Socialist International 162
Solidarity 88, 129, 140, 147
Solzhenitsyn, Aleksandr 5, 52, 69, 82, 121
Sorel, Georges 3, 35, 81
Souvarine, Boris 27–8, 80
Soviet-type regimes 68, 70, 72, 114, 116, 127, 130, 132, 134, 136, 138, 141–2,

144–6, 154, 163, 165–6, 177, 220, 222
ideology 68, 132, 222
intellectuals 130
literature 154
propaganda 220
social sciences 70
societies 72
Soviet Union/USSR (Russia) 4, 11, 16, 18, 22–3, 25, 31, 34–5, 44–5, 51, 54, 80, 92–3, 150, 161, 163, 165, 169, 175, 184, 195–7, 201, 203, 210, 217
bureaucracy 94
communist party 10, 15, 22–3, 26–7, 31, 44, 51, 65, 67, 77, 118, 150
central committee 15, 22, 44, 65
general secretary 11, 18, 51, 67
nineteenth congress 51
twentieth congress 77
twenty-second congress 118
culture 44, 46, 49, 52–3, 54
expansionism by 168, 180
ideology 57, 71
intellectuals 45
Marxism 66, 70
occupation of Afghanistan 45
politburo 16, 150, 188
propaganda 220
science 50–4
social sciences 11
writers 205–7
Sperber, Manes 27, 35, 80, 176
Stalin, Joseph/Stalinism 1–3, 8–14, 16–27, 29–37, 42–58, 61–5, 68–9, 72–4, 77–86, 91–2, 94–5, 99–100, 102–3, 106, 109, 111, 116–19, 121, 122–4, 126, 130, 133, 134–5, 138, 167, 184, 190, 199, 203, 208
apparatchicks 24
bureaucracy 18
cult of 123, 130
culture under 50, 52–4

de-Stalinisation 54, 77, 134, 190
de-Stalinisation in Hungary 122, 203
de-Stalinisation in Poland 203
ideology 21
Marxism-Leninism 11
Neo-Stalinism 187, 196, 198, 207
purges 14, 21–3, 150
Short course 10–11, 17–18, 45
Starewicz, Artur 54
Stojanović, Svetozar 72, 103
Suslov, Mikhail 32, 54–5, 62, 122, 124, 188, 200
Svitak, Ivan 5
Szabó, Ervin 81
Szelenyi, Iván 127–8, 154
Szilágyi, József 149
Szirmai, István 54

Terracini, Umberto 117
Thälmann, Ernst 28, 80
Thompson, E. P. 164
Thorez, Maurice 65–6, 80
Thorez-Vermeersch, Jeanette 66
Tikhonov, Nikolay 189, 194
Tito, Josip Broz/Titoism 62, 78, 99–104, 106, 111, 150
Togliatti, Palmiro 117–18, 150
Yalta memorandum 118
totalitarianism 10, 15, 21, 47, 68, 109–10, 141–2, 148, 167
Trilling, Diana 35
Trilling, Lionel 35
Triolet, Elsa 57
Trotsky, Lev/Trotskyism 11, 14, 26, 37, 62, 77, 80–1, 98, 124
Tucker, Robert C. 79
Tudoran, Dorin 5, 97
Tukhachevskiy, Mikhail 37

Ukraine 13
famine 13
Ulam, Adam 9, 79
Ulbricht, Walter 47, 53, 150
United States 44, 160, 165, 169, 180

Urban, George 12
Ustinov, Dmitriy 55
Usubaliyev, Turdakun 191

Vaculik, Ludvik 144
Vajda, Mihály 146
Voroshilov, Kliment 62, 77
Voznesenskiy, Andrey 205, 207
Vosnesenskiy, Nikolay 37
Vyshinskiy, Andrey 150

Walser, Martin 160
Wazyk, Adam 74
Weber, Max 3
Weil, Boris 4
Werblan, Andrzej 54
Wierzbicki, Piotr 131–2
Wilson, Edmund 35
Wittfogel, Karl 35
Wolf, Hannah 54
Wolfe, Bertram 118–19
World War II 34

Yagoda, Genrikh 37

Yakovlev, Aleksandr 189,
    197–8
Yeltsin, Boris 189–90, 197–8
Yevtushenko, Yevgeniy 205
Yezhov, Nikolay 37
Yudin, Pavel 32
Yugoslavia 43, 99–106, 129,
    224
  bureaucracy 104
  intellectuals 101–2
  Marxism 99, 101, 105
  revisionism 85, 102

Zalygin, Sergey 205
Zaslavsky, Viktor 56
Zaykov, Lev 198, 209
Zhdanov, Andrey/Zhdanovism
    42–50, 55, 114, 185
Zinoviev, Aleksandr 5, 12–13,
    26, 46, 58, 62, 79, 184, 223
Zinoviev, Grigoriy 16
Zoschenko, Mikhail 43–4